IMAGINARY BOUNDARIES OF JUSTICE

Oñati International Series in Law and Society

A SERIES PUBLISHED FOR THE OÑATI INSTITUTE
FOR THE SOCIOLOGY OF LAW

Titles in this Series

Social Dynamics of Crime and Control: New Theories for a World in Transition
edited by Susanne Karstedt and Kai Bussmann

Criminal Policy in Transition
edited by Andrew Rutherford and Penny Green

Making Law for Families
edited by Mavis Maclean

Poverty and the Law
edited by Peter Robson and Asbjørn Kjønstad

Adapting Legal Cultures
edited by Johannes Feest and David Nelken

Rethinking Law, Society and Governance: Foucault's Bequest
edited by Gary Wickham and George Pavlich

Rules and Networks
edited by Richard Appelbaum, Bill Felstiner and Volkmar Gessner

Women in the World's Legal Professions
edited by Ulrike Schultz and Gisela Shaw

Healing the Wounds
edited by Marie-Claire Foblets and Trutz von Trotha

Imaginary Boundaries of Justice

Social and Legal Justice across Disciplines

Edited by

RONNIE LIPPENS

HART PUBLISHING

OXFORD AND PORTLAND OREGON

2004

Hart Publishing
Oxford and Portland, Oregon

Published in North America (US and Canada)
by Hart Publishing
c/o International Specialized Book Services
5804 NE Hassalo Street
Portland, Oregon
97213-3644
USA

Hart Publishing is a specialist legal publisher based in Oxford, England.
To order further copies of this book or to request a list of other
publications please write to:

Hart Publishing, Salter's Boatyard,
Folly Bridge, Abingdon Road, Oxford, OX1 4LB
email: mail@hartpub.co.uk
Telephone: +44 (0)1865 245533 Fax: +44 (0)1865 794882

WEB SITE http//:www.hartpub.co.uk

British Library Cataloguing in Publication Data
Data Available

ISBN 1-84113-474-0 (cloth)
ISBN 1-84113-475-9 (paper)

Typeset by Olympus Infotech Pvt, India, in Sabon 10/12 pt
Printed and bound in Great Britain by
Lightning Source UK Ltd

Contents

The Contributors

Simon HALLSWORTH is Senior Lecturer in Criminology (London Metropolitan University, UK). In his recent work Simon has examined punitive changes in contemporary society and the local politics and practices of crime control. He is currently completing a research project examining street crime in Lambeth, and is supporting community safety providers in the area in the development of their crime reduction strategy.
email : hallswor@lgu.ac.uk

Richard JONES is Lecturer in Criminology (Edinburgh University, UK). Richard's research interests are in theoretical criminology, the sociology of punishment, and cybercrime. He is currently researching the role of new technologies in crime control and criminal justice, and on political ideologies and punishment.
email : richard.jones@ed.ac.uk

Ronnie LIPPENS is Reader in Criminology (Keele University, UK). Ronnie teaches Criminology, and Crime and Social Justice. He has published on critical criminology, social justice, utopianism, and organisational ethics. His current research interests include the place of the Imaginary in the production and reproduction of 'visions' of social justice.
email: r.lippens@crim.keele.ac.uk

Claudius MESSNER is Assistant Professor of Philosophy of Law (Lecce University, Italy). Claudius teaches Sociology of Law and Juvenile Justice. He has published in different languages on criminial justice issues, systems theory, and the semantics of subjectivity. Drawing upon hermeneutics and phenomenology, his research interests focus on the articulation of a social theory of law and legal phenomena.
email : claudius.messner@ateneo.unile.it

Rolland MUNRO is Professor of Organisation Theory (Keele University, UK). Rolland is Director of the Centre for Social Theory and Technology at Keele University. His numerous publications include *Ideas of Difference* and *Consumption of Mass* (both Sociological Review Monographs) and cover a wide range of topics including culture, identity and organisation.
email : mna32@keele.ac.uk

Andreas PHILIPPOPOULOS-MIHALOPOULOS is Senior Lecturer in Law (University of Westminster, UK). Andreas teaches European Union Law, Land Law and Law of the Environment. His research interests are typically transdisciplinary with a special focus on aspects of critical theory. He attempts to approach and interpret law from various perspectives such as geography, psychoanalysis, art theory, biology, autopoiesis, phenomenology, feminism, linguistics, sociology, and so on. He recently gave a series of lectures in Yugoslavia on the Democratic Reconstruction of the Balkans. He has published articles in the areas of autopoiesis, phenomenology and environmental law.
email : andreasphilip@yahoo.com

Claire VALIER is Lecturer in Law (University of London, UK). Claire is a graduate of Queens College, Cambridge, where she was a Munro Scholar. She works on the philosophy of crime and the criminal law. In particular, she is currently looking at the normative bases of criminal liability and punishment. She has written two books, a textbook on *Theories of Crime and Punishment* (Longman, 2002) and a monograph on *Crime and Punishment in Contemporary Culture* (Routledge, 2003). She is presently finishing *Memorial Laws: The Remembrance of the Dead and the Demand for Justice* (Cavendish/Glasshouse, forthcoming).
email : ceav_home@hotmail.com

Louis E WOLCHER is Professor of Law (University of Washington, USA). Holding degrees from both Stanford University and Harvard Law School, Louis has written extensively in various fields of philosophy, including philosophy of language and philosophy of law. One of his essays, 'Time's Language', was recently awarded Second Prize by the final jury of the Millennial International Essay Competition — a philosophical prize competition that was co-sponsored by the City of Weimar, Germany, and the European cultural magazine *Lettre International*, and that drew 2,500 entries from around the world. He has also given and published numerous lectures abroad, including at the European Court of Human Rights in Strasbourg, France, at the Institute of Political Science in Tashkent, Uzbekistan, and at the University of Ljubljana Faculty of Law in Ljubljana, Slovenia (as a Fulbright Award recipient).
email : wolcher@u.washington.edu

1

Introduction: Imaginary. Boundary. Justice.

RONNIE LIPPENS

THE VISCOSITY OF IMAGES

SOCIAL JUSTICE. THAT'S the topic of this book. But can we still speak it, write it? We are often said to have ended up in an age in which it has become abundantly clear that words cannot provide us anymore with the comfort of stability which once they seemed to be able to offer. Indeed, in the wake of deconstruction, when the sound or the sight of words is turning evermore into an experience of instability, into a relentless vertigo (Kirby, 1996: 96) that seems to reflect the spatial disorientations of lives without the clear and distinct boundaries of yesteryear, words tend to float in and through the volatile circuitries of re-signification. Try talking *social justice* in an age like that. However, one might think, if words have left their moorings, and are now adrift somewhere in spaces of undecidability, then maybe this is not the case with images. Maybe images are more stable than words. Maybe images, or imagery more generally, have a certain viscosity about them, something bodily tactile, something sensory that prevents them from evaporating into mere, disembodied volatility. This 'maybe' is what this book is about.

Now it could very well be argued that images and imagery are as prone to dissipation and evaporation in what Baudrillard, a few years ago (Baudrillard, 1996), called the 'perfect crime' of a world that has left reality altogether for a viral circuitry of simulation and illusion, and that therefore has refused us the tools or even the clues to get to grips with this perfect crime. Images, in Baudrillard's world of perfect crimes, make up this reality (as Claire Valier in her contribution to this volume aptly critiques): the disembodied sparks of simulation in a frenzied network of illusions, mere flashes of light that preclude any notion or practice of social justice. So maybe Baudrillard is not much of a guide when it comes to establishing some level of viscosity in images and imagery. Maybe not.

But then he *does* acknowledge, with regards to photography, the 'silence of the image, which requires (or should require !) no commentary', as if the image knows how to get through to us effortlessly, armed only with 'the silence of the object', this stable silence that 'photography wrests from the thunderous context of the real world' (1996: 86). 'The reflex miracle of the photographic act', Baudrillard goes on, 'has nothing to do with writing'. Although the 'seductive power' of writing is 'far superior' (thus allowing for wandering, volatile, drifting, and *floating* resignifications), 'photography's power to stupefy is far greater than that of writing'. The photographic image arrests, it comes with 'instantaneity', with a sensory, almost tactile 'manifestness' of 'a shadow, a light, a texture' (1996: 87). Stupefaction, the stability of silence, at least the immobility of silence, is what, to a certain extent, results when the image hits the retina. The image, the viscous image, sticks. Images stick. Now it may very well be the case that images, like *dissipative structures* (to borrow a phrase from complexity theory), emerge, no, better still, *merge* out of the frenetic chaotics that reign within Baudrillard's networks of viral illusion, only to dissipate in those networks back again. As Gilles Deleuze claimed, 'what counts in the image is not its meagre content, but the energy — mad and ready to explode — that it has harnessed, which is why images never last long' (Deleuze, 1997: 160). But at least for a short while, they arrest us into some sort of stability (stupefaction at the very least), however short-lived. If, in the wake of deconstruction, we now seem to realise that we have arrived in an undecidable, viral age of *blurring boundaries,* and *floating signifiers* that leave us with no fixed references, clues, or tools to speak or write social justice anymore, then perhaps it pays to focus on the arresting, stabilising viscosity of images of social justice. It might be worthwhile to *think through images of social justice*. What, in other words, is the imaginary of social justice? Let us break down this rather general question into a number of smaller, specific ones. How do images of social justice emerge? How do *visions* of social justice emerge? How do they take shape? How do they change? What is the role and place of the Imaginary in the production or reproduction of images of justice? What are its boundaries? What are its effects? How, in other words, does the Imaginary produce boundaries of social justice, imaginary boundaries of social justice? How do things merge in images or visions of social justice? How do images of social justice mobilise actors? How do imaginary boundaries *emerge* or disappear in those images (and actors)? What, in other words, are the dimensions of the stickiness of the imaginary — the imaginary of social justice in particular — and how do they provide the space for visions of social justice to arrest, to stabilise, and, possibly, to mobilise us into assemblages, however fragile, of social justice, and how do these assemblages in turn produce, however contingently, images of social justice that may, or may not, arrest us, stabilise us, or mobilise us energetically (as Deleuze would have it) ?

IMAGE, THE SENSES, AND VISION

Images and vision. We have arrived in the realm of the eye it seems. Focussing on the eye however has its drawbacks and its limitations, let us be clear about that. The eye offers only one road to social justice and some have argued that this road is utterly flawed. Feminists like Luce Irigaray (1985) for example, or writers of the postcolonial such as David Lloyd (1996) have often criticised the Platonic and Kantian assumptions underlying all endeavours that rest on the visual as the sensory space of justice *par excellence*. The overwhelming emphasis on vision in Plato's myth of the cave, for example, betrays a deeply masculine desire of mastery (says Irigaray), with the disembodied light of truth and knowledge outside the cave beckoning, shining high above the darkness of fetters and ignorant, sweaty enslavement. But this masculine preoccupation with the eye and the distance and separation which it creates and which it depends on, Irigaray continues, seems to discard, and unrightfully so, the importance of proximity, embodiedness, and tactility in the production of knowledge, in the production of community, and in the multitude of touchy, exploratory connections that, in Irigaray's world, replace the abstract, detached, impersonal and pretentious light of truth and justice. All these qualities, ie proximity, embodiedness, and tactility, as well as the opportunities of community and justice which they offer, are abounding inside Plato's dark cave. Blinded by his obsession with the shining white light outside however, Plato takes no notice.

But more criticism lies ahead. Criticising Kant's 'deduction of the universality of the aesthetic judgment' in *The Critique of Judgement*, David Lloyd tries to demonstrate how the emergence of 'taste as a kind of *sensus communis*' was always accompanied by a particular form of 'cultivation of the senses' that proceeds 'from the pleasure derived from the existence of the object that is characteristic of literal 'taste' to the contemplative relation to the object, which is the capacity of sight' (1996: 251–2). The movement, in Kant's view, from 'the charms of sense' to 'universal communicability', according to Lloyd, presupposes and is accompanied by the emergence of a 'public sphere', the locus of civilisation, where the eyes of indifferent, disinterested, allegedly universal Subjects, occupying a place of 'pure exchangeability', reproduce particularity and difference as vehicles for subordination (1996: 256). This mechanism of detached, indifferent, 'civilised' subordination in and through the constitution of a highly visual (and highly visible) 'public culture' of 'universal communicability', claims Lloyd, was never more apparent than during colonisation, when 'whiteness', the universal absence of particular colour, reigned supreme in colonial 'public culture'. 'Whiteness' was the colour of the 'subject that sees, or, more properly, the Subject that judges' (1996: 259), or the Subject 'devoid of' particular 'properties' (1996: 261), fully and interchangeably part of a public space that is visibly constituted in contrast with coloured particularities. Whiteness seemed to have been the non-colour of seeing Subjects that controlled a public space from a gazing, judging distance. With the eye having been complicit in such a history (let us call it the *injustice* of colonialism) one is not likely to privilege vision in any endeavour of *social justice.*

Indeed, both Irigaray and Lloyd do point at the limitations and historical complicities of the eye. But this is precisely our point. Irigaray's or Lloyd's reservations should not prevent us form analysing how vision, images, imagery, or, more broadly, the imaginary have played a role, and continue to do so (at an increasing pace, if one is to believe Baudrillard), in processes of social ordering (see on this eg Hetherington, 1997) and in the more or less intentional production of spaces of alleged social justice. Kantian or Habermasian 'public spheres' of en*light*ened, civilised, detached 'universal communicability', for example, are certainly amongst such spaces. But there are other spaces where the eye has a prominent place. Michel Maffesoli (1996) has been at pains to demonstrate how, in our apparently volatile and whimsical 'neo-tribal' age, emerging tribal socialities and what Maffesoli calls tribal 'puissance', tend to find expression in the often Dionysian, highly emotional consumption and/or sharing of consumer space. Images figure predominantly in neo-tribal spaces of consumption. This return to emotion and the imaginary may indeed be a sign of our times. In an age when stable boundaries are said (as well as experienced) to have grown porous, when previously assumed essences and fixities have broken into each other, writes Maffesoli, 'the imaginary is increasingly granted a role in structuring society' (1996: 118). Here the eye and vision, amongst other senses, function as the most important medium through which neo-tribal communities, however ad hoc, however Dionysian, emerge, form, and dissipate. See and be seen. With this we have left Kant's 'public sphere', his enlightened, universal communicability, and Plato's shining light of disembodied truth, behind us.

But there's more. One wonders, contra Irigaray and Lloyd, whether the eye and the image have not always been crucial in the constitution of both *communitas* and *societas*. In her seminal book, *Partial Connections* (1991), Marilyn Strathern, an anthropologist who has since been associated with actor network theory or ANT (but we'll get back to that later), describes what she saw in the foothills and jungles of New Guinea when she did fieldwork amongst some of the tribes there. In some of these tribes, the men often adorn themselves with all kinds of features which they produce out of forest materials. They always appear with a number of prosthetic devices or *extensions* attached to their body, such as feathers that are placed behind the head, making it appear to be bigger. Let us imagine here this society of men, each of them equipped with a number of extensions, regularly gathers for talks, thus reproducing connections between them, practising, as it were, their particular tribal knowledges and socialities in and through these regular assemblages of what Deleuze, in his *Foucault* (1988), terms *visibles* (their adornments, their extensions) and *articulables* (the talk). Let us explore this a little further. The men listen to each other, they argue, but most of all, they look at each other, they see fellow members equipped with extensions, knowing them to be members of the same tribe, knowing them to share the same knowledges, by sight. Now, there are no rules as to the shape or nature of the extensions that are allowed. Indeed, it often happens that some of the extensions worn by the tribesmen are lost, or get damaged one way or another. When that happens to him, a tribesman will of course go into the neighbouring jungle in search for a similar extension. The new extension, however, is not always similar to the previous one. There is a degree of freedom here for the tribesman to exploit. Often tribesmen come back from the forest wearing different extensions, after which a brief period of negotiation ensues, mostly ending with the reproduction, in practice, of tribal knowledges that, although similar to previous ones, will now have changed somewhat as well. The extensions, in turn, seem to be the visibles that connect individual tribesmen to the others, to tribal life and knowledge. Protruding from the tribesman's body, they reach into the village; they negotiate village life and village knowledge; they may radiate force as well as knowledge into the village; they may *affect* village life and village knowledge. But the village, as well as the space beyond, simultaneously may be finding ways into the tribesman's body, slipping inside, as it were, through the extensions that were gathered there. In all this highly visible circulation of visible extensions, the eye and the image are of crucial importance. They are crucially important towards the visible construction, maintenance, adjustment, and break-up of both communal *puissance* (what Rolland Munro in his contribution might call the more or less pre-reflexive ethos of 'just us') and localised justice (Rolland Munro's notion of formalised, frozen 'just ice'). *Seen* this way, both the ethos of *communitas* and the justice of *societas* are, to a considerable extent, the result of what circulates *visibly* between tribal members, or between just and civilised members of societies.

SPECIFICITY OF THE IMAGE

This leaves us with another issue to deal with. What is the specificity of vision? What is the specificity of the eye and the image? In other words, if indeed we need to focus on the eye and the image, or on the space of the Imaginary more broadly, when we try to grapple with programmes, indeed *visions* of social justice, will we then bring something really specific, something irreducible, to the analysis of social justice? Roland Barthes, for example, seemed to have been in two minds on this issue. On the one hand Barthes has, on various occasions, been at pains to read images as mere texts. In one of his essays, 'Rhetoric of the Image' (1977: 32–51), published originally in 1964, Barthes, 'without wishing to infer too quickly from the image to semiology in general', nevertheless tends to treat images as 'iconic discourse', as texts where 'discontinuous connotators are connected, actualised, 'spoken' through the syntagm of ' (...) 'iconic denotation' (1977: 51). But then, in 1970, Barthes moves away from this mere semiological position. In a close analysis of a number of stills from an Eisenstein film, *Ivan the Terrible*, Barthes suddenly realises that images, unlike mere textual material, carry something particular, something peculiar indeed, ie 'third meaning' (Barthes, 1977: 52–68). One could analyse images on a purely denotational-informational-communicational level, or one could analyse them on a connotational-symbolic level (see for example Richard Jones's and Simon Hallsworth's contributions on the *filmic* of justice). However, there is, says Barthes, something like a third level, where 'obtuse meaning', 'the third meaning', a 'supplement that my intellection cannot succeed in absorbing' (1977: 54) hits us in the face, in the eye to be more precise. And this is (Maffesoli would probably agree) an emotional, sensory event ('the obtuse meaning carries a certain emotion') that largely escapes the strictures and possibilities provided by 'the language-system', the whole event being 'outside (articulated) language' (1977: 59). This unspeakable 'third meaning' is not outside 'interlocution' however, indeed 'thanks to what, in the image, is purely image (which is in fact very little), we do without language yet never cease to understand one another' (1977: 60–1). This 'third meaning', claims Barthes, is where the really filmic begins. It 'begins where language and metalanguage end' (1977: 64). Later still, Barthes (1984) introduced another notion, ie that of the *punctum*. There is something in images that captures the eye. This little something, which may be quite inconspicuous at first, wounds the viewer, and through this wound the hidden world behind the image moves into the viewer's life. It may also *move* the viewer in turn. Through this *punctum*, this little wound, the viewer may be moved. He or she may understand, and may be moved to intervene in some way -to *socially* intervene. This punctum in the image, this wound in the eye, thus functions as a passageway through which boundaries between the self and the outside, albeit momentarily, dissolve, crumble away, or grow porous. This porosity in turn then offers opportunities for communal or societal investment, possibly communal or societal movement. This punctum, in other words, will then function as the visible, as the vehicle of (at least the onset of) communal ethos or social justice. The pictures of sons and husbands who 'disappeared', carried and displayed by the *speechless* Mothers in the Plaza de Mayo, and the scene of the Mothers carrying these pictures, worked as such a punctum (Gordon, 1997). Through this wound the world behind the images, this silent world of ghosts, moved and slipped into viewers' lives. Viewers suddenly *saw*. Suddenly, they were moved. And suddenly they moved. Before words, before politics and even before justice.

Note that Lacanian psychoanalysis never needed convincing on this point. The eye, says Lacan, is that which is able to distinguish, to draw lines, to keep things apart/together, to see movement, to see immobility, to see direction and flow. It is the eye, says Lacan, that has 'the power to separate' (Lacan, 1998: 115) or, in other words, to produce distance (here, by the way, is one of the reasons why Luce Irigaray, a student of Lacanian psychoanalysis, was never one of his staunch admirers). Indeed, we may agree here, it is the eye that has the power to separate desirable flows from undesirable ones. It is the eye that sees where to go, and where not to go at all. It is the eye that determines what line should be drawn and which should be crossed. It is the eye that *imagines* how things are on the other side, how things might turn out to be for the better, if only directions could be taken, *these* directions (not *those*), if only desire could flow from here to there (and not elsewhere), if only the hope that burns in sensuous hearts would be allowed or able to dwell in *these* spaces *here*, and steer clear of *those*, over *there*. If only life could take *this* shape, and not *that*. It is the eye that sees, that imagines, that makes images, that uses images, that shows and finds them, and that makes directions out of them, in-between them. Visuality, in short, is arguably the realm where desire flows most conspicuously, from *heres* to *theres*, along lines and curves, *on* or *off* tracks. Eyes imagine difference and identity, here and there, us and them. It is desire that flows there, in those imaginations, and, one might argue, it is those imaginations that in turn flow on the desire that flows in them. This, indeed, is the Imaginary, where visuality is both the line-drawing, curve-bending sensory realm where desire flows from *heres* towards *theres*, as well as the realm where desire itself finds its way by drawing lines and bending curves. As Slavoj Zizek, the foremost Lacanian in contemporary cultural studies, has aptly demonstrated in his Hollywood-inspired introduction to Lacan, *Looking Awry* (Zizek, 1991), images are the locations, indeed the vehicles, on or through which desire flows. First there are images. Then there is desire. Desire is drawn into the lines and spaces that are opened up by images. The desire for *communitas*, for example, or the desire for *social justice*, would not even emerge if there would be no images. Quite literally:

> the gaze marks the point in the object (in the picture) from which the subject viewing it is already gazed at, ie it is the object that is gazing at me (1991: 125).

It's the object, the image, that stirs us into the movement of desire, claims Zizek, who, in his book, focuses on

> the famous Hitchcockian tracking shot as a formal procedure whose aim is to produce a 'blot', a point from which the image itself looks at the spectator, the point of the 'gaze of the Other' (1991: ix).

This, by the way, is also the topic of Richard Jones's contribution to the volume at hand. Stronger still (please recall Lacan's essay on the 'Mirror Stage'): without images, there would be no self, no I, no subject, no desire for *communitas*, there would be no tribal *puissance*, there would be no social justice. Note in passing the echo of Barthes's notion of the *punctum* in Zizek's quotations. Note also that we're not that far away from tribesmen collecting extensions (objects in the forest that gaze at them) in New Guinea, and viewing them as *visibles* while they negotiate tribal *puissance* and local justice in front of village huts.

But this is just Lacanian psychoanalysis. Others see it differently. Gilles Deleuze, for example, often had 'doubts about the imaginary' (Deleuze, 1995: 62–67), although he would agree with Lacan that life as such basically is a matter of lines. Listen to Deleuze, in his book on *Foucault*:

> Just as statements are *curves* before they are phrases and propositions, so scenes [*seens*] are *lines* of flight before they become contours and colours (1988: 80–81; insert and italics are mine).

But rather than taking images and the visual as his starting point, Deleuze starts from desire. His is a world of flows of desire. Those flows of desire, like geological flows, coagulate with various materials (*visibles* and *articulables*, for example), and produce sediments or 'crystals' that may, or may not, 'assemble' into 'desiring machines'. These in turn do nothing but cut into flows of desire, assembling or producing yet more 'desiring machines' and more flow. Deleuze's vitalist world is at the same time also a deeply machinic world, and one could argue that in Deleuze's cyborg world of desire and *becoming*, the boundary between the vital and the machinic has collapsed. So have the boundaries between what Lacan would distinguish as the Imaginary, the Symbolic, or the Real, or the boundaries between, say, 'me' and 'non-me': 'moi et non-moi, extérieur et intérieur ne veulent plus rien dire' (Deleuze and Guattari, 1972: 7). There's only vitalist, desiring, machinic production, or 'assemblage'. Emotional *communitas*, or the justice of reasoned *societas*, appear in and as assemblages. They're the result of desiring machines cutting through flows of desire. Rhizomatic, enigmatic flows of desire, for that matter. What counts for Deleuze is not so much the images or vision as such, but rather the productive, machinic but very desiring process by which they are assembled, or through which they function. Indeed, as we've already cited, 'the energy — mad and ready to explode — that it has harnessed' (Deleuze, 1997: 160). As such there is, according to Deleuze, nothing specific about vision or about images. But they are important nevertheless. What matters is that students of and aspirers for communal ethos or societal justice try to reach the immanence of life, that is, try to reach the 'plane of immanence' that is made of pure and basic forms ('events', Deleuze sometimes calls them) that are produced by desire and that in turn provide the *machinerie* for desire to flow. There's no point, says Deleuze, in using the term 'imaginary' to describe what's going on on this plane of immanence. There, all sorts of material and boundaries just 'rub shoulders' with anything else. Images rub shoulder with text and desire, and so on. Moreover, 'visibilities' themselves are not just 'visibilities', they 'are not defined by sight, but are complexes of actions and passions, actions and reactions, multisensorial complexes, which emerge in the light of day' (Deleuze, 1988: 59). In a way, this plane of immanence resembles what Cornelius Castoriadis once called the 'magma' of the imaginary,

> the basis for articulating what does matter and what does not, the origin of the surplus of being of the objects of practical, affective and intellectual investment (1987: 145).

Deleuze however *has* been at pains to analyse images, particularly cinema. Confronted with visual material, with film in particular, Deleuze's interest is to work out how this material produces particular immanent 'events', in this case 'crystal-images', crystallised and sedimented assemblages on the plane of immanence, mere 'circuits of exchanges' (1995: 66), that, however, also express particular immanent 'percepts' and 'affects'. 'Percepts', he goes on,

> aren't perceptions, they're packets of sensations and relations that live on independently of whoever experiences them. Affects aren't feelings, they're becomings that spill over whoever lives through them (thereby becoming someone else) (Deleuze, 1995: 137).

The creative *productions of and by desire* is what Deleuze is interested in. In the *Movement-Image* (1986) and the *Time-Image* (1989) for example, Deleuze explored how a number of films produced/used particular 'crystal-images' that both expressed and allowed (viewers) to become particular, immanent affects and percepts. In the *Movement-Image*, for example, Deleuze saw systems of images that express and allow (viewers) to become rationalised, systemised wholes, while the *Time-Image* expresses and allows (viewers) to become fragments, unpredictable and irrational movement.

Now, where Lacanian psychoanalysis would tend to focus on the images themselves in order to work out how, 'looking at us', as objects that always already seem to be given, they as it were kick-start desire, and subsequently provide a somewhat external stage, or a theatre of mirrors at least, where desire plays out, Deleuze is much more interested in desire itself, in how it produces crystallised assemblages (images) and then utilises them in yet more assemblages. Some of these assemblages could then be communal collectives that are imbued in what Munro would call a 'just us' ethos, or else systems whose *imaginary boundaries of 'just ice'* are formalised, civilised, icy-white *societas*. One way of combining the exploration of the imaginary as a stage or a warehouse of images and the exploration of images as the crystallised assemblages of productive desire is to be found in Bruno Latour's (1990b) notion of objects that are 'drawn together'. Images, as objects that are 'drawn together', circulate between actor-networks, where they productively produce or assemble, indeed *draw together* social collectives (whether of the 'just us' or 'just ice' kind; whether they be tribal villagers in New Guinea, or mothers on the Plaza de Mayo) who in turn produce, assemble or *draw together* objects that again, in turn, will circulate and *draw together*. The imaginary boundaries of the objects are as irregular, jagged, porous, or smooth as those of the collectives through and by which they were drawn together. And the same could be said about the collectives, about their 'just us' or their 'just ice': their boundaries take after those of the images through and by which they were drawn together. It is to actor network theory that we will now turn.

ANT'S VISION

Boundary

Somewhere (Latour, 1990a: 138) it was asked whether it is there, somewhere 'au milieu de cette *ligne*' (italics added), between on the one hand the world of objects and the world of subjects on the other, that scientific practice takes place. The question, however, might have been: 'whether any line has a centre, or indeed, whether there is a line there, somewhere in-between, at all'. There isn't, Latour tells us on various occasions (eg Latour, 1991). The line is a network of hybrids of matter, motivations, desire, logics, strings of words, strategies that combine and disperse. In this network, combinations of actors make difference. Now, according to Latour, the founder if you wish of actor network theory, pretty much anything can be an actor. Anything that makes (a) difference is an actor: a rock, a microbe, someone called Pasteur, someone else wearing a white dustcoat, a cow slithering on mucky farm grounds, an image of a slithering cow (on the Channel 4 news, possibly), a string of words scribbled on a sheet of paper, anything really. Actors, already hybrids themselves, in Latour's actor-network, produce other hybrids: an airplane, a textbook, a company, a laboratory, an image, a theory, an empirical fact, an utopian vision, a model of justice, a sense of community, anything really that makes difference, anything that possibly could make a difference, and that, as a hybrid network itself, can make networks more or less coherent or consistent, make them behave as if a line encircles them, setting them apart from the rest, making them different. No, we've never been modern, says Latour. Not then, and not now.

Lines, according to Latour, so it seems, are networks. Networks of hybridity. Really. Hybrid networks of actors; networks, that is, of hybrid actors who, in hybrid combinations, make (a) difference. Many lines appear in this network. Lines around hybrids (let's call them *lines type 1*), for example, that allow hybrids, actors possibly, to get noticed, and, possibly, to get mobilised, or to get assembled into a bigger hybrid that just might make a (bigger) difference. Those lines tend to be the result of actors producing themselves as well as the hybrids (an adornment, a theory, a book, a painting, an authority, etc) by which they make themselves (up), when they use them as 'extensions' (Strathern 1991) which they attach to themselves (or adorn themselves with), and which, possibly, they may be able to use to mobilise others in order to share the difference. But then there's also the lines that disrupt (let's call those *lines type 2*), the lines that cut through actors and the difference(s) they make. These are the lines that split up hybrid actors as well as their hybrid products. On these lines, the bits and pieces scatter through the network of networks, only to re-assemble, or to hybridise, elsewhere. But maybe those lines are the same as the former ones. Maybe both are just the differences that the network generates in and through the assemblages and dispersals (Cooper, 2001) that make it up.

Scientific practice, says Latour (1990b), is a question of 'drawing things together'. Quite literally: various materials (microbes, strategies, ambition, enzymes, strings of words, images, resources, and so on) are being *drawn* together (in the sense of being expressed or represented) into what Latour calls 'immutable mobiles' — those are often two-dimensional hybrids such as textbooks, articles, images, graphs, and so on. These hybrids are 'immutable', in the sense that they seem to express a certain stability (one could say that a line *type 1* will have encircled them), but they are highly mobile in the sense that they tend to be circulated (a 'centre of calculation' may make sure that this happens) through the network of actors (the actor-network), as an extension, Strathern might say, for other actors to pick up and, possibly, to join in the production of the difference/knowledge. However, immutable mobiles — hybrid assemblages, hybrid extensions — are never completely immutable. Once assembled, once 'drawn together', they will, as an encircled consistency, continue to circulate across the network. But simultaneously, lines *type* 2 will start cutting across the immutable mobile and scatter its fragments throughout the network. Both, the encircled consistency, as well as the fragments, will become part of the network and will thus end up as parts of yet other hybrid assemblages or as yet other extensions in or through which actors make (a) difference, assembling or dispersing. Drawn together ... indeed: drawn *together*.

Latour's immutable mobiles, in a way, are what appears when actors draw together things from the network. That which is drawn together, hybrid combinations, when used as extensions in order to mobilise other actors into an equally hybrid collective actor whose parts/actors start to draw things together, collectively, one could argue, is a piece of technology. Its hybridity is what gives hybrid collectives a certain coherence and consistency (lines type 1 emerging); it's also what makes hybrid collectives splinter and scatter across the network (lines type 2 emerging). So we need to talk about technology here: an airplane, a painting, More's *Utopia*, Machiavelli's *Il Principe*, a vision of justice, Rawls's theory, the chapters in this book: all of them are made of disparate materials from the network that have been drawn together; all can and probably will be used as extensions; all can and probably will end up as part of an attempt to draw together collectives; all can and will probably end up being fragmented, the fragments scattering across the network, to be used in ever so many other bouts of drawing things together. Force and power are in them (indeed, they have been *drawn* together). Force and power give them a certain coherence and consistency. Force and power will tear them apart.

Technology, a vision of justice for example, one could argue, is the result of force and speed. The force that was needed to draw things together, and the speed with which actors are able to assemble things (including actors) that were previously unconnected. Technology is therefore capable of speeding things, particular things, up. True. But technology also slows down. Once drawn together, the restlessness of the network, with its manifold possibilities, comes to a particular halt. Well, not quite, it's still there, somehow, somewhere, inside the thing that has been drawn together (I've called this restlessness: lines type 2). But there is a way of looking at technology as slowed down force and speed, as machines for slowing down possibilities as well. Technology is both speed and slowness embodied. Let's take the airplane. In an intriguing paper drawn together by John Law and Annemarie Mol (2002), who follow Chunglin Kwa, this complex piece of technology — a hybrid combination of pockets of ambition, desire, rage, fear, metal, strategies, mathematical equations, tubes and fuel, all *drawn together* — is looked at in at least two ways. The first looks at the airplane's complexity in a 'romantic' way. Here one sees emerging 'homogenisation and abstraction', that which shows itself as coherence and consistency within an encircling line (a line type 1, as I called it). The airplane, as we look at its explicities, its seemingly seamless skin of steel, is one, is whole, and its essence can be represented in some immutable mobile (a cost/size/lethality equation, for example) that is drawn together in order to mobilise, indeed, to draw together. Force of slowness. This is how one could see technology as embodied slowness. But then there are other ways of seeing. Seeing 'baroque complexity', say Law and Mol, needs 'an *imagination* that looks down rather than up' (emphasis added). Here one sees 'specificity' and the 'material heterogeneity' of the parts, and the gaps in-between them, that have been drawn together. Here one sees the non-coherent, here one *imagines* the implicit, the lines (type 2) that snake through it, that pierce through the airplane's skin, connecting onto a multitude of imagined and non-imagined locations in the network. Breakfast tea. The fluctuating price of crude oil. The plant shut-down. Foreign affairs. The tricky bolt. The rivalry at the office. The G force limit. Blood pressures. Here and over there. The multitude of desires, everywhere we can imagine them, and everywhere we *don't*. Force of speed. Here one looks at technology as the embodiment of speed — the very speed that made it up; the very restless speed that is just waiting to drag the airplane or any of its parts towards ever so many places in the network, where they are destined to be adopted-betrayed (Law, 1996) in ever so many bouts of drawing things together.

The airplane is both. And this is just the airplane. But what about village life in New Guinea? Let us go back to the village in Marilyn Strathern's New Guinea. Make a mental image. Picture yourself hovering in the air above the village. You will see a number of huts built in an open space in the jungle forest. Tribal members are walking on and off. And you will see a number of men, all equipped with *particular* extensions, gathered together, looking and talking. Although individual extensions and adornments will be particular you will nevertheless have the impression that the group of men are exactly that, a group. You will see it in their eyes, you will hear it when they speak. What is keeping them together? Is it the same thing that keeps them apart as well, ie that which allows them to appear before others as particular assemblages of extensions? And is this, that which allows them to keep apart (lines type 2), is it also the force that brings them together, sharing and reproducing tribal *puissance* and knowledge? Let us resume hovering. Please hover a little higher now. You should be able to see the village in the forest now. Now try and look for the village boundary. Where does the village stop, and where does the forest begin. Does the village stop where the trees begin? You see, the trees do form a line around the village huts. The shape of the village is more or less circular. So is this line of trees, clearly visible, like a blackish-inky line (a line type 1) drawn on a white sheet of paper — is this line the village boundary? Perhaps it is. But look a little closer now. You will see that this line is often interrupted by a number of paths that snake themselves from the huts into the forest. Some of these paths are regularly used by the villagers and are clearly visible. Others are sneaky little paths and barely visible. But they are there. Villagers use them to go into the forest for a variety of purposes of course. The men sometimes use them to collect adornments and cyborg extensions. The village, in a way, extends itself into the forest through these paths. So where's the village boundary now? Is it somewhere in this mesh, this assemblage of lines, some clear and regular, some sneaky and irregular, that penetrates deep into the forest, into that other mesh of lines and assemblages? Is it this space where villagers negotiate the jungle, and that stretches on and across a multitude of lines and gaps? Is it this assemblage of lines through which the forest in turn finds ways into the village, for example as visibles and articulables that will appear as cyborg extensions during the practice of tribal life and tribal knowledge? Let's rephrase that: is this assemblage of lines and assemblages through which it (ie the forest) emerges *as* the practice of tribal life and tribal knowledge, is this assemblage of lines the village boundary? The ambiguous and irregular openness with which cyborgs have assembled visibles/extensions and therefore also themselves, and which is very much alive in the negotiations through which they *draw together* their communal ethos and their societal justice, seems to be also alive in the rhizomatic, sneaky irregularities of the village boundary.

And this is just this village. But what about the boundaries of this or that particular *Utopia*? What is keeping it apart/together? What about *Il Principe*? What about Rawls? What about this or that painting by Jean Fouquet, or by a Flemish master, as mentioned in Ronnie Lippens's contribution? What about that culture? What about Timothy McVeigh's justice in Claire Valier's contribution? Office culture, as dealt with by Rolland Munro in his contribution? Your metaphysical system, any system, any system theorist's system for that matter (see on this Andreas Philippopoulos's and Claudius Messner's contributions)? This town? That environmental policy document? This Hollywood film, why not *Pale Rider*, as dealt with by Simon Hallsworth in his contribution? What about this policy? That vision of social justice? Your force — your force of slowness, your force of speed? What about the chapters in this book that deal with these issues? In Latour's network, things drawn together are *both*. They are both imaginary boundaries.

Justice

Now let us change tack. But only just a little. Robert Cooper (2001), in a paper on collection and dispersion of mass, is interested in Walter Benjamin's writings on passers-by emerging from the mass of crowds. But first, Cooper defines collection and dispersion. Collection, he says, 'is the cultivation and selection of material elements from primal mass in order to construct visible and thinkable worlds' (Cooper, 2001: 19). From 'an imperceptible background', like an emerging passer-by, there it appears: that which is being collected, that which shows itself to be a figure, or an object, and that is destined to disappear into the background again, like any passer-by eventually would. However, 'the act of collection is (...) always shadowed by an act of dispersion' (2001: 19). Mass, like Latour's network, seems to be both — baroque and romantic. Mass, Cooper tells us, is 'plastic', like desire: 'infinite, boundless, unlocatable mobility', the place where one might be able to find what Rolland Munro (1996) termed 'motility' — undecidable possibility, something waiting, promise and the potentiality for ... making (a) difference. Figures collect/disperse in it (we sense them, we see them, like we see passers-by emerging from and disappearing in crowds), and this constant movement of collection/dispersal is the mass of the world we live in — a mass, and a world, as one might see it, of imaginary boundaries.

Benjamin's figure emerging from and disappearing back into the crowd. There seems to be force involved when the figure *cuts itself* loose from the background mass. There also seems to be force involved when we direct our eyes towards the figure — *cutting the figure* (to adopt/betray one of Munro's phrases here). The figure apparently emerges (and then disappears back again) in the line (Latour's line) between the subject and the object, the line that itself is nothing but the network of actors that draw things together so as to make (a) difference. The figure emerges on the line — the network — that spans and touches both the force of the background and the force of the gazing eye. The question now emerges what happens when one particular difference holds out, or, put differently, when one figure stabilises (a) difference, when the gaze is locked onto the contours of a stable object, when a force spreads, becomes viscous, dominates, when forces stop making (a) difference. What happens if gazes are stuck on a particular figure? What happens if the figure remains, and when the background fades away? What will happen if the romantic gaze dominates? Or what if there's no figures emerging at all? What happens if the baroque wins out? Suppose there's only collection? Or only dispersal? What happens if 'motility', although ever-present, ever-promising, is held (somewhere) at bay? It is here that the need for angels is felt.

In his chapter, Louis Wolcher mentions Walter Benjamin's *Angel of History*. The Angel regularly featured during the discussions we (ie the contributors to this volume) had during a seminar. In his *Theses on the Philosophy of History,* Benjamin (1968) wrote down some meditations on a 1922 painting by Paul Klee, *Angelus Novus*. It is worthwhile to quote the passage in full (it's actually Benjamin's ninth thesis):

> A Klee painting named 'Angelus Novus' shows an angel looking as though he is about to move away from something he is fixedly contemplating. His eyes are staring, his mouth is open, his wings are spread. This is how one pictures the angel of history. His face is turned towards the past. Where we perceive a chain of events, he sees one single catastrophe which keeps piling wreckage and hurls it in front of his feet. The angel would like to stay, awaken the dead, and make whole what has been smashed. But a storm is blowing in from Paradise; it has got caught in his wings with such a violence that the angel can no longer close them. The storm irresistibly propels him into the future to which his back is turned, while the pile of debris before grows skyward. This storm is what we call progress.

Let us now focus a while on this vision of justice — a vision of justice as witnessing (see Wolcher's chapter on this) — which Benjamin drew together, in 1940, when he was fleeing Nazism. Let us focus. Let us use it as an extension. Let ourselves be mobilised by this piece of technology. We will allow it to splinter and disperse later. Why did Benjamin choose Klee's angel in this passage, why did he choose an angel at all? Maybe it's because angels are not of this world. They don't fix themselves on futures. They turn their back to Future. They don't see differences or hierarchies. They are not in the habit of making (a) difference. But, on the other hand, angels are not completely out of this world either. Indeed, angels do have senses at their disposal. They can, for example, see things. They can witness. Indeed, Klee's angel *sees* history. He does not see it as a progressive succession of nicely bordered justices. But he *does* see something: an amorphous pile of wreckage, 'one single event'. That's the difference angels make, that's what they are able to draw together: non-difference. Maybe angels are in that space which Latour wrote about: 'au milieu de cette ligne', in the middle of the line between subjects and objects, in the interstices of what happens in the network, somewhere in-between background mass, figures cutting, and gazes cutting figures. Somewhere between countless bouts of *drawing things together*, in this interstitial zone where all things drawn together, and all who are drawing things together, are seen to be just that: force producing undifferentiated differences, indeed, just force, just wreckage. From this non-specified place, not completely out of this world, but not in it either, angels apparently have the ability to not see difference as difference; they can only witness the whole of a history of undifferentiated differences, but they can't see anything in particular. Just undifferentiated wreckage. An angel's space is somewhere in that imaginary boundary, *au milieu de cette ligne*, from where all boundaries are seen-imagined to be imaginary. That's the non-difference, that angels make. But this non-difference, flowing from the inability, or the refusal to make (a) difference, is of course (a) difference itself. And, judging from Benjamin's ninth thesis, angels themselves seem to realise this very well: eyes staring, mouth open, yes, but speechless. They can't speak out — to speak out, to draw things together, to use force, to mobilise force, to cut figures, all of this would need them to leave their interstitial home, only to end up contributing to the piles of wreckage which, having left their imaginary boundary, they would be unable to see-imagine *as* wreckage pure and simple. Fixed on figures, 'clinging' to visions of justice (Wolcher, 2002), dragged along by extensions such as the 'guiding images' of Utopian 'homeland' Ernst Bloch wrote about (1986: 931), which they would have been drawing together, speaking or painting or writing, they would have lost their ability to not see-imagine boundaries. They would have become romantic (using Law's, Kwa's and Mol's words). Or baroque. But nothing in-between.

'Order' is not universalisable, and any attempt at universalisation of any *particular* 'order' will just end up multiplying 'disorder', Bauman concluded a few years ago (Bauman, 1993: 209ff). That which mortals have drawn together is not universalisable. Any attempt to do so is futile and *bound* to heap wreckage upon wreckage. That which shines as coherence and consistency in visions of justice is not universalisable. That which 'guides' in the figures we cut, that which 'guides' when we cut ourselves a figure, that which 'guides' when we disperse in the background, that which keeps drawing together (force and the 'motility' that restlessly lurks within it) is always located in the network — if not, 'it' would be unable to draw things together. But its boundaries stretch and move, collect and disperse, encircle and cut apart. One can only imagine the location of 'its' boundaries at any particular moment or place. It's those imaginary boundaries we imagine we see whenever figures appear or disperse; whenever, for example, visions of justice are drawn together or torn asunder. Humans are hardly angelic. We have to live in a world of boundaries. But we could try and imagine the imaginary of any particular boundary. In vertiginous times like ours, says Kirby, this is what is bound to happen anyway: ' the inside flies to pieces and explodes outward, the outside melts and fragments, and elements from both sides' start to 'drift freely across an indifferent boundary' (1996: 102).

Images

So let us repeat the questions that we mentioned at the beginning of this chapter. How do visions of social justice emerge? How do they take shape? How do they change? What is the role and place of the Imaginary in all this? What are the boundaries of the Imaginary? How does the Imaginary produce boundaries, imaginary boundaries? How are things drawn together in visions of justice? How do such visions mobilise actors? How do imaginary boundaries emerge or disappear in visions of social justice? What is collected in them, and what disperses through them? And, to repeat, how do images, as objects that are 'drawn together', circulate between actor-networks, where they productively produce or assemble, indeed draw together social collectives who in turn produce, assemble or draw together objects that again, in turn, will circulate and draw together. The contributors to this volume took to these questions in an interdisciplinary way.

In chapter 2, Louis Wolcher, from a reading of Levinas, shows how images of social justice, as soon as they function as *grounds* for action, tend to blind us from suffering *as* suffering. With Benjamin's Angel of History, Wolcher proposes to 'let go' of images of justice as grounds. Wolcher thinks the avoidance of suffering as such — an avoidance which, according to Wolcher, chimes with an ability not 'to cling' to the prison-houses of any of our particular imaginary visions of justice. Wolcher's imaginary boundaries of justice, in a way, are to be found in a gentle refusal to produce, or *draw together,* and circulate particular images, and, as such, in a refusal to *draw together* particular social forms and particular modes of life.

Coming from organisational theory and organisational studies, Rolland Munro, in chapter 3, develops the idea that justice is 'outside the group'. Groups and organisations tend to be spaces where (talk of) justice is deferred by either an ethos of 'just us' or formalised, frozen 'just ice', and is left hanging 'between bidding and evaluation'. The possibility of justice, according to Munro, opens up in interstitial moments of 'motility', in splits and ruptures, when boundaries get reshuffled or when, one could say, opportunities for bouts of *drawing together* emerge.

In chapter 4, Andreas Philippopoulos-Mihalopoulos rethinks general systems theory and legal autopoietics. He explores the permeability of system boundaries, or, if you wish, the imaginary boundaries of systems, indeed the imaginary boundaries of systems theory. There he finds a space of possibility that allows him to rethink systemic justice as memory, ie as the remembrance of 'the process of forgetting' of 'waste' that lies at the heart of all autopoietic, coded productions of justice. Philippopoulos, in this chapter, attempts nothing short of a rethink of a closed *discipline* (legal autopoietics) by thinking through the issue of the imaginary boundaries of its objects.

Chapter 5, by Claire Valier, imagines the implosion of imaginary boundaries in ironic/iconic modernity. Analysing images of iconic victimhood and terror, Valier shows how attempts to reach the heart of Law's imaginary, the justice of 'closure', are torn apart ever-anew from the interstitial space of irony. Valier's contribution invites us to explore the moves and boundary-crossings that go on 'on the edge of irony' of contemporary media culture. This is an edge where the production and circulation of images and collectives *drawn together* is bound to end up in ironic instability.

Richard Jones, in chapter 6, argues how in the spectacle of what some would call post-disciplinary societies, the visual allows for subjectivities to swap places. Analysing the taking of and inter-changing of subject positions in two films, *Heath*, and *Three Colours: Red*, Jones shows how in contemporary visual spaces subjects explore, and come to 'know' their and others' imaginary boundaries by *taking each others place*. The imaginary production of subjectivities, according to Jones's Lacanian-Zizekian inspired reading, occurs through the Other.

Chapter 7, by Simon Hallsworth, shows how the imagery in two Clint Eastwood westerns, High Plains Drifter' (1973) and 'Pale Rider' (1975), prefigures a gendered penal politics that was to form the base, in the United States, for what authors like Nils Christie have come to describe as a penal Gulag. Like criminal justice administrators and practitioners after him, Eastwood's lone avenger does away with lawless masculinity (the underclass), bringing effeminised masculinity (a *welfarised* state) back to order, restoring the imaginary boundaries of law and order in the process.

Ronnie Lippens, in chapter 8, demonstrates how cultures inevitably produce hybrid images of justice. Revisiting Huizinga's classic on Burgundian culture, and contemplating a number of fifteenth century paintings, Lippens shows how the visual often is the sphere where emergent 'newness' (hybridity that makes (a) difference) often expresses as well as becomes the imaginary boundaries of historical change first, well before symbolic articulations are *drawn together*.

In the final chapter, Claudius Messner, observing *world society* from Luhmann's (eg Luhmann, 2000) systems theoretical framework, reads the contemporary imaginary of 'victimhood' as a bounded though flexible 'script' that allows for an 'increase of operative complexity by reducing the structural complexity' which a globalising world of insecurities and risks is producing.

Let me now end on another note. I'm very grateful to all participants at the May 2002 seminar on Imaginary Boundaries of Justice, held at the Onati Institute for the Sociology of Law. Special thanks go to Claire Valier. Some of the discussions the both of us had during previous joint projects will have left conspicuous traces in this introductory chapter. All flaws and errors, of course, are entirely mine.

REFERENCES

Barthes, Roland 1977. *Image, Music, Text.* Translated by Stephen Heath. London: Fontana Press.

Barthes, Roland 1984. *Camera Lucida.* London: Flamengo.

Baudrillard, Jean 1996. *The Perfect Crime.* Translated by Chris Turner. London: Verso.

Bauman, Zygmunt 1993. *Postmodern Ethics.* Oxford: Blackwell.

Benjamin, Walter 1968. Theses on the Philosophy of History. In *Illuminations: Essays and Reflections.* Edited by Hannah Arendt and Translated by Harry Zohn. New York: Schocken.

Bloch, Ernst 1986. *The Principle of Hope.* Translated by Neville Plaice, Stephen Plaice, and Paul Knight. Cambridge: MIT Press

Castoriadis, Cornelis 1987. *The Imaginary Institution of Society.* Cambridge: Polity.

Cooper, Robert 2001. Interpreting Mass: collection/dispersion. In *The Consumption of Mass*, edited by Nick Lee and Rolland Munro. Oxford: Blackwell.

Deleuze, Gilles 1986. *The Movement-Image.* Translated by Hugh Tomlinson and Barbara Habberjam. Minneapolis: University of Minnesota Press.

Deleuze, Gilles 1989. *The Time-Image.* Translated by Hugh Tomlinson and Robert Galeta. Minneapolis: University of Minnesota Press.

Deleuze, Gilles 1988. *Foucault.* Translated by Sean Hand. London: Athlone.

Deleuze, Gilles 1995. *Negotiations.* Translated by Martin Joughin. New York: Columbia University Press.

Deleuze, Gilles 1997. *Essays Critical and Clinical.* Translated by Daniel W Smith and Michael A Greco. Minneapolis: University of Minnesota Press.

Deleuze, Gilles and Felix Guattari 1972. *Anti-Oedipe.* Paris: Les Editions de Minuit.

Gordon, Avery 1997. The Other Door; Its Floods of Tears with Consolation. In *Ghostly matters. Haunting and the Sociological Imagination.* Minneapolis: University of Minnesota Press.

Hetherington, Kevin 1997. *The Badlands of Modernity. Heterotopia and Social Ordering.* London: Routledge.

Irigaray, Luce 1985. Plato's Hystera. In *Speculum of the Other Woman.* Translated Gillian C Gill. Ithaca: Cornell University Press.

Kirby, Kathleen M, 1996. *Indifferent Boundaries.* New York: Guilford Press.

Lacan, Jacques, 1977. The Mirror Stage as Formative of the Function of the I as Revealed in Psychoanalytic Experience. In *Ecrits. A Selection.* London: Tavistock.

Lacan, Jacques 1998. *The Four Fundamental Concepts of Psycho-Analysis.* London: Vintage.

Latour, Bruno 1990a. Sommes Nous Modernes? Non, Amodernes ! In *La Pensée Métisse.* Paris: Presses Universitaires de France.

Latour, Bruno 1990b. Drawing Things Together. In *Representation in Scientific Practice*, edited by Michael Lynch and Steve Woolgar. Cambridge: MIT Press.

Latour, Bruno 1991. *Nous n'avons Jamais été Modernes.* Paris: La Découverte.

Law, John 1996. Traduction/Trahison. Notes on ANT. Published by the Department of Sociology, Lancaster University, at www.lancaster.ac.uk/sociology/ slaw2.html.

Law, John and Annemarie Mol 2002. And if We were Small and Non-Coherent? Method, Complexity and the Baroque. Published by the Centre for Science Studies and the Department of Sociology, Lancaster University, at www.comp.lancs.ac.uk/sociology/soc096jl.html.

Lloyd, David 1996. Race under Representation. In *Culture/Contexture: Explorations in Anthropology and Literary Studies,* edited by E Valentine Daniel and Jeffrey Peck. Berkeley: University of California Press.

Luhmann, Niklas 2000. *The Reality of the Mass Media.* Translated by Kathleen Cross. Oxford: Blackwell.

Maffesoli, Michel 1996. *The Time of the Tribes.* Translated by Don Smith. London: Sage.

Munro, Rolland 1996. The Consumption View of Self: Extension, Exchange and Identity. In *Consumption Matters*, edited by Alan Warde, K Hethington and S Edgell. Oxford: Blackwell.

Strathern, Marilyn 1991. *Partial Connections.* Lanham: Rowman and Littlefield.

Wolcher, Louis 2002. The Third Mountain: A Meditation on Chaos and Order. *International Journal for the Semiotics of Law* 15: 25–52.

Žižek, Slavoj 1991. *Looking Awry. An Introduction to Jacques Lacan through Popular Culture.* Cambridge: MIT Press.

2

Thought's Prison: An Image of Images

By Louis E Wolcher[*]

ABSTRACT: The idea of the 'image of social justice' is paradoxical. On the one hand, having some image of a better future is felt to be a necessary condition and ground of progress towards the goal of universal justice. On the other hand, once it is imagined the image replaces human freedom and responsibility with a materialised conception that reigns over people during the period of progress towards its realisation. This paper is a critical meditation on the interpretation of images of social justice that portrays the latter as entities whose value consists in their potential to ground beneficial transformations in social arrangements. It draws out the paradox created by this vision of the way our imagination works, and confronts reason with an alternative image of images — one that offers emancipation through *letting-go* of all yearning for and clinging to the comfort of self-justification.

INTRODUCTION: JUSTICE AND SUFFERING

THIS CHAPTER EXAMINES the widely-held belief that our pictures of a better world can and should become the *ground* of their realisation. A ground is both an origin and a destination: it is that from which an action is launched and that to which it returns by way of goal, meaning, and justification. A cause is different. Causation is merely the relation of one element preceding another element in a temporal sequence in such a way that we think the second element probably (Hume 1961, 346–48) or necessarily (Schopenhauer 1974, 56) 'followed' from the first. A ground, however, underlies the entire sequence of cause and effect as that which gives the

[*] Professor of Law, University of Washington School of Law, William H Gates Hall, Box 353020, Seattle, WA, 98195, USA. E-mail address: wolcher@u.washington.edu.

sequence the value and the meaning that it has for those who are involved in it. Causes lie behind the caused in the shadows of the past, and therefore do not come with the caused when it arrives. Grounds lie under, and therefore together with, the grounded in the sunlight of the present.[1]

In sociology, methodological individualism reduces grounds to motives, and then imputes behaviours to motives that it finds and then projects onto the actors whose conduct it wants to explain. From this point of view there is no essential difference between the causes and the grounds of an actor's behaviour. Sociologists observe in order to *impute*: even if their explanations strive to become what Weber (1978, 11) calls 'adequate on the level of meaning,' this only means that sociologists try to capture a 'typical complex of meaning' in order to make their causal explanations of an actor's behaviour coherent and comprehensible. For example, the concept of ideology in sociology is an explanatory tool and not a judgment of value: it is used to explain why people do what they do, but it does not also play the role of justifying their behavior. This is why sociology calls itself a 'science.' Nevertheless, sociologists *qua* actors know that the metaphysical and ethical distinction between cause and ground will not go away, for they often explain *why* (in the sense of ground, not cause) they practice, and even ought to practice, sociology the way they do.[2]

A particularly powerful conception of the way grounding works in the domain of social justice — an important image of images — portrays human beings and their images as co-creators of the social world. In this interpretation, which ultimately goes back to Kant and Hegel, our dissatisfaction with existing social arrangements stimulates us to imagine a better world. Sometimes our idea of a better world takes the form of what Hegel (1975, 130) calls a 'pictorial conception,' full of concrete content, and sometimes it emerges as a lofty but compelling 'notion' that we fancy to be 'free from all sensuous admixture.' In both cases, however, there comes a point when our imaginings take on a life of their own: they become both the motive for and the ground of change. As motive they induce us to perform actions aimed at realising them. As ground they are what we offer as the 'meaning' of our efforts, and what we come back to once the image becomes reality: our dream of *X* becomes *X* on the basis of *X*. Our actions move towards the imagined state of social justice in the way that the work

[1] It should be noted that the causal nexus itself is a ground, not a cause. In this idea the separate identities of cause and effect are suspended in the unity of reciprocal action (Hegel 1975, 217–18). Reciprocity forms the infinite and meaningless repetition of causes and effects into a self-contained relationship that is perspicuous and meaningful. To say that the causal nexus 'causes' something to happen is therefore nonsensical: it is the very expression of the meaning of causation in general, and as such it grounds the practice of imputation in a special way (219).

[2] Max Weber's famous essay *Science as a Vocation* (1958, 129–56) is an excellent example of a sociologist attempting to establish the value (as ground, not cause) of value-free inquiry in the social sciences.

of builders moves towards the completion of the building that their architect imagines. This image of images construes freedom as the decision to construct, and then follow or reject, the image of social justice. It construes necessity as the relation between the image and the project of those who have chosen to follow it. The idea is that human beings freely decide to become the objects of their object, and that this is what it means to be principled and just.

Although I do not claim that this image of images is false, I do say that this way of thinking about images of social justice constructs a kind of prison for the human spirit. Yearning for relief from unjust conditions is a form of suffering, and it often triggers a release of energy aimed at overcoming the given. In expending itself, this energy always feels the need to justify what it does on the *basis* of something else. This something else is the image of social justice, which is taken as a kind of warrant for the pursuit of the Holy Grail of justice. In the quest for this Holy Grail, sacrifice and suffering occurring in the course of the quest are either overlooked or else interpreted as necessary byproducts of progress. The ubiquitous phenomenon of suffering *as such* — suffering, that is, without reduction or qualification on account of the justifications that may be offered to excuse it — is hardly ever confronted squarely and unblinkingly.

If, as Spinoza (1955, 135) says, all existing beings strive to continue in being (*conatus essendi*), then it must also be acknowledged that their striving frequently comes at great cost to themselves and to others. The Latin roots of the word 'suffering' are *sub* (under) and *ferre* (to bear). To be borne under by what weighs upon one in the course of existence is to suffer. In this sense, 'suffering as such' names the sedimented and ever-sedimenting accumulation of *each and every* concrete moment of suffering, however justified and whatever its causes and conditions may be. Here may be found little sufferings and big ones, suffering that is someone's fault and suffering delivered out of the blue by an impersonal fate, the agonies of the oppressed as well as the mortifications of oppressors called to judgment, the torments of the unjust and unethical as well as those of the righteous, the craving desire for a better world and the gnawing fear that the world may be changing for the worse. Life is suffering, according to the Buddha;[3] 'Everything disappoints,' wrote Kierkegaard (1993, 62) in his diary: 'Hope, the hoped for does not come, or the hoped for comes — and disappoints.' Although these ideas interpret suffering as an ontological determination of life, one need not go that far in order to catch sight of its ubiquity as a human affect. Physical pain is but one of the modes that bear down upon us in suffering; the list of nouns that identify the others is impressively long,[4] and a

[3] This is the first of the Buddha's 'Four Noble Truths' (Van de Weyer 2000, 1–7).

[4] Here is a partial list, in no particular order: grief, despair, anguish, fear, anxiety, regret, revulsion, bitterness, envy, hatred, jealousy, longing, disappointment, boredom, agitation,

phenomenology of all these modes of suffering that did justice to each of their many ways of appearing would fill the shelves of a good-sized library.

Suffering as such is therefore ubiquitous — indeed, it is one of the commonest commonplaces on earth. Nevertheless, these days one hardly ever hears, let alone heeds, Schopenhauer's (1969, 315) so-called 'pessimistic' message about all would-be cures for suffering: 'The ceaseless efforts to banish suffering achieve nothing more than a change in its form.' One meaning of this statement is that the satisfaction of desire for relief from a particular mode of suffering is merely a *negative* good: it is not itself 'happiness.' Indeed, this kind of satisfaction is completely consistent with being unhappy on account of other discrete sufferings, and even with the more diffuse feeling that existence itself has become a burden. A deeper meaning of Schopenhauer's saying is that *all* desires are a form of suffering, arising as they do from the feeling of want. Experience teaches that once we get what we want it almost never manages to satisfy us for very long. New desires are always bubbling up, and hence the satisfaction of any particular desire gives us but a momentary respite from the existential condition of suffering as such. As far as our opinions of social arrangements go, this suggests that today's social justice can easily metamorphose into tomorrow's social injustice, and vice versa.

Still another interpretation of Schopenhauer's remark — one that is directly relevant to the theme of this chapter — touches upon the intimate relationship between justice and suffering. It alleges that the very most that justice can do is reallocate suffering, and that justice can never attend to suffering as such. This is true for two reasons. First, justice employs means, including law, that disturb only certain narrow aspects of the given social world. Justice does not and cannot declare war on suffering as such without becoming a self-defeating tyranny. And second, the means used to effectuate justice *disturb* the status quo: not only do they discomfit those 'wrongdoers' who suffer justly, they also oppress all the 'innocents' who have come to care about or depend upon the punished wrongdoers. Here is revealed an uncomfortable truth: the just suffering of individuals can have negative as well as positive social ramifications — a point that most liberal theories of justice tend to overlook. The pain that comes from watching your justly convicted son or daughter get incarcerated or executed can feel all the worse if you do not believe that an injustice is being done that eventually will be rectified. This observation uncovers the paradox that injustice, however much it affronts, can also give its sufferers a kind of comfort. The paradox, which explains the oddly ambiguous phenomenon of martyrdom, shows *just* suffering in a light that makes it seem all the more terrible: for it is in the nature of truly

embarrassment, shock, guilt, hunger, thirst, resentment, compassion (suffering for another's suffering), loneliness, panic, shame, helplessness, and greed.

just suffering to exclude the succor of a possibly better justice-to-come. (Redemption is another matter, of course, and its relation to justice will be addressed at a subsequent point.) However right and necessary it may be, therefore, just suffering is still a kind of suffering. Indeed, it would appear to be axiomatic that some people must *always* suffer if justice is to be done. This is a circumstance that might and perhaps ought to give us pause, especially if we contemplate how many questionable things have been labeled 'wrong' in the course of history, and how much blood has been shed under various contradictory (and often odious) banners of 'justice.'

These observations seem pessimistic only if one thinks (as Schopenhauer himself did) that the truth of suffering as such implies something negative about the *value* of the world.[5] The *truth* of universal suffering is obscured or denied by most interpretations of social justice, but this truth does not have to *lead* anywhere in particular unless we let it. This chapter will not offer a plan for eliminating or reducing suffering, if only because the very idea of a 'plan' is one of the things that it wants to put into question. One might well ask, then, what good can come from noticing suffering as such. If, as Levinas (1998, 100) claims, the suffering of others is 'useless,' then the truth of universal suffering is probably even more useless. It is quite literally 'good for nothing,' in the sense of lacking any connection to an end that has been ratified in advance as valuable. But the criterion of utility to a pre-existing frame of reference blocks all access to thinking about the criterion of utility itself. It also prevents us from noticing the ways in which the useful *hurts,* and the useless (sometimes) *helps.* While the absence of any provable utility undoubtedly puts the truth of universal suffering out of fashion in the relentlessly pragmatic age in which we live, the aim of this contribution is to break open a space where, at long last, reason can allow the mind to bear witness to this nonetheless mighty truth.

THE IMAGE OF JUSTICE (*Δίκη*) AND INJUSTICE (*Αδικία*)

The Greek word ἀδικία appears in the earliest fragment of Western philosophy that we have, attributed to Anaximander.[6] A-ἀδικία is the privative

[5] As Franz Rosenzweig (1985, 8) says, 'Schopenhauer was the first of the great thinkers to inquire, not into the essence but into the value of the world.' Schopenhauer's evaluation was notoriously negative, and his solution — to devalue and renounce the will and willing — became a major point of contention for Nietzsche in developing his philosophy of will-to-power (Nietzsche 1968, 52).

[6] The English translation of Nietzsche's German translation of the fragment reads as follows: 'Whence things have their origin, there they must also pass away according to necessity; for they must pay penalty and be judged for their injustice [A-δικ?α], according to the ordinance of time.' (Heidegger 1975,13). Kenneth Atchity (1996, 73) gives a pithier (albeit more insipid) translation: '[To that they return when they are destroyed] of necessity; for ... they suffer punishment and give satisfaction to one another for injustice.'

form of δίκη, and thus is used to indicate that δίκη is absent. In today's world, δίκη is usually translated as 'justice,' ἀδικία as 'injustice.' But as Heidegger (1975, 41–3) says, these terms signified to the ancient Greeks well beyond the realm of the narrowly juridical: they were also used to denote order and disorder in general. From a Greek point of view, wherever there is ἀδικία all is not right in the world — things are 'out of joint' (Heidegger 1975, 41). Conversely, if there is δίκη then jointedness prevails — things fit together as they should. Both δίκη and ἀδικία are silent, and hence ambiguous, on the origin of the order and disorder to which they refer. Aristotle's characterisation of the one as a virtue and the other as a vice (1984, 1781–97) does provide a useful interpretation, however, since it locates their site, if not their origin,[7] in human beings. Αδικία, for example, can emerge when we compare the disjointed present with the (presumptively) well-jointed order of the past, as in Aristotle's notion of a corrective justice that aims to restore everything to the state of affairs that used to prevail (1984, 1786–87). In this sense the idea of justice is a conservative if not reactionary force. Alternatively, ἀδικία can come from our comparing the present with a state of affairs that has never yet prevailed, as in Aristotle's notion of a distributive justice that holds the existing distribution of entitlements to account by comparing it with the way the world would look if entitlements were distributed according to the criterion of merit (1984, 1785–86). In this sense the idea of justice is a progressive if not revolutionary force.

The word 'image' ultimately comes from the Latin root *imitari*, meaning to imitate. It we think of images as imitations of something else, then what is the 'something else' that the image of social justice imitates? It follows from what has been said already about δίκη that an *image* of social justice, in the Greek sense, would simply mirror what exists if everything fits together exactly as it should in the society of which it is the image. Indeed, it probably would not be right to call such an image an image of social *justice* in the first place. At best it would serve as a description and an encomium, saying something like this: 'Look at this society! See how perfect it is?' Only where social *in*justice prevails do images of social justice show themselves as contrasting with the way things are. Contrary to what is implied by the grammatical form of the word, injustice (like wrong in general) is really the original and postive, and justice the derivative and negative. As Schopenhauer (1969, 339) puts it, 'there would be no talk of *right* if there were no wrong.' The image of social justice in a context of injustice is not itself ἀδικία — it is not the *image* that

[7] Aristotle took issue with the famous thesis of Protagoras that 'the human is the measure of all things, of beings that they are, of non-beings that they are not,' at least to the extent that it posits that the reality of beings is a mere artifact of human perception (Heidegger 1995, 171–74). For Aristotle (and for Protagoras too, according to Heidegger) beings must already be 'empowered' (δυνατόν) beforehand to *be* perceived if perceiving and becoming manifest is to occur at all.

is out of joint with the way things are. The image of social justice in an unjust world is rather the very measure and meaning (and hence the ground) of the given world's being ἀδικία. The image reproaches existing social arrangements by virtue of its very existence in relation to those arrangements. It also invites a project of transformation aimed at realising the image that it projects of a just social world. In short, the image of social justice in an unjust world offers itself as a motive for action. In this capacity it says: 'Look at me, and then look at the way the world is. Can't you see that you need to *change* things so they look more like me?'

At first the image of social justice in an unjust world shows itself as a motive, a limit, and a boundary. If a determination is a *limit* that allows a thing to be itself, *as* itself, then the flip side of a limit may be called a *boundary* that prevents the thing from dissolving into its environment, thereby losing its self-identity. Moreover, the limit and boundary of a thing also limit other things in the environment around it: the determination of *X* brings out *Y* in its determination of being not-*X*. Being limited — being what it is — the image of social justice seems to yield a motive: it becomes the cause of human actions that are aimed at transforming the given. As a determined thing, the image of social justice also limits injustice by standing opposed to it as its other. Without the limitation provided by the image of its other, the given state of affairs could not emerge *as* 'unjust.' Lacking any contrast, it would tend by the law of social inertia to hold itself together as 'just the way things are' — neither just nor unjust. In Hegelian (1975, 166–9) terms, such a society would be a mere indifferent self-relation, and would not yet possess the kind of identity that is also different from its other. The image of social justice changes all this by confronting the existing world with an image of what it is not. But not only does the image of social justice limit its other, the existing world, it is also itself reciprocally limited by its own others: namely, whatever is and whatever else may be. It is just *this* possibility that is opposed to the given in the image of social justice, and thus it and it alone becomes the standard for measuring progress towards justice.

In this last respect the image of social justice is fundamentally different from the image of social *in*justice. The latter always exhausts itself by holding up a mirror to an unjust world. The ἀδικία depicted in the image of social injustice is the real world bounded by an implicit 'not' — it is what should not be — but the real world is not additionally put into relation with anything *else* in particular. Such an image — Picasso's painting *Guernica*,[8] for example — may indeed become a motive for action, but it

[8] Pablo Picasso, *Guernica* (1937). Oil on canvas, 11'6"×25'8", currently located in the Museo Nacional Centro de Arte Reina Sofía, Madrid. The painting was inspired by the terror-bombing of Guernica, the ancient capital of the Basques, during the Spanish Civil War (Janson and Janson 2001, 792).

yields no clue for how to *re*construct the world once the injustice that it depicts is swept away. Like Walter Benjamin's (1978, 291) conception of the revolutionary general strike, the image of social injustice is a 'pure means' that seeks no end beyond the destruction of unjust conditions. The one who successfully depicts social injustice has managed to tap into the more-or-less inchoate sense of his readers or viewers that 'this is not right.' The image of social injustice thus limits and motivates, but it does not lead people beyond an upsurge of energy to negate the given. The image of social justice likewise limits the existing world as unjust and motivates its destruction, but unlike its negative counterpart it additionally attempts to limit and bound the future by offering to replace what is by what might be. In doing this it gives meaning to the *transition* between the present and the future: it can be cited as the self-evidently valuable reason why people are doing what they are doing to effectuate it.

Now it has been observed again and again since antiquity that the many conceptions of justice and injustice in the world are not just different, they also frequently contradict one another. What is more, each group of people tends to believe that its conception of justice is universal, and thus fits Aristotle's (1984, 1790) definition of 'natural justice': 'that which everywhere has the same force and does not exist by people's thinking this or that.' Commenting from a distance on this well-known tendency in human beings, Pascal (1941, 101) wryly adds that '[t]hree degrees of latitude reverse all jurisprudence; a meridian decides the truth.' One need not go as far as Pascal does, however, in order to perceive and acknowledge that the *images* of social justice that people make are often radically out of joint with one another. By way of example, consider these two different images of the justice that is said to be owed to one people by other peoples:

> I have a dream that one day on the red hills of Georgia, the sons of former slaves and the sons of former slave-owners will be able to sit down at the table of brotherhood. I have a dream that one day, even the state of Mississippi, a state sweltering with the heat of injustice, sweltering with the heat of oppression, will be transformed into an oasis of freedom and justice. I have a dream that my four little children will one day live in a nation where they will not be judged by the color of their skin but by the content of their character. I have a dream today! I have a dream that one day, down in Alabama, with its vicious racists, with its governor having his lips dripping with the words of interposition and nullification, one day, right there in Alabama, little black boys and black girls will be able to join hands with little white boys and white girls as sisters and brothers. I have a dream today! (in Garrow 1988, 283–84).

> If, in the world of our present parliamentary corruption, [the Nazi Party] becomes more and more aware of the profoundest essence of its struggle, feels itself to be the purest embodiment of the value of race and personality and conducts itself accordingly, it will with almost mathematical certainty some

> day emerge victorious from its struggle. Just as Germany must inevitably win her rightful position on this earth if she is led and organised according to the same principles. A state which in this age of racial poisoning dedicates itself to the care of its best racial elements must some day become lord of the earth (Hitler 1943, 688).

Martin Luther King's image of integration and harmony among historically divided peoples stands in the starkest sort of opposition to Hitler's image of social segregation and strife. Nevertheless, and although it almost sticks in the throat to say it, both of these images have something important in common: each depicts what its author claims to be social justice. In the sense already noted, each image of social justice reproaches the given world by standing opposed to it as its other, each offers itself as a motive for change, and each provides a sketch of the end-point towards which change can be directed. What is more, both images *did* motivate and ground change towards their respective ends. Social arrangements in America are different in 2002 than they were in 1963, when King delivered his influential 'I Have a Dream' speech. Social arrangements in 1939 Germany were different than they were in 1924, when Hitler wrote his equally influential book *Mein Kampf*. And in both cases the images of social justice that were projected by these otherwise utterly dissimilar men played a significant role in the transformation — as motive and ground.

THE 'ROLE' OF THE IMAGE AS THE GROUND OF ACTION: THE PRINCIPLE OF REASON

'A significant role': What does this mean? The hypothesis that launched all of the papers presented in this book is as follows: '*Visions* of social justice, one might argue, emerge within and, in turn, produce *imaginary* boundaries.' The most important question evoked by this hypothesis seems to be this: How do visions of social justice emerge and sustain themselves? This way of putting the relation between humans and their imaginings invites a kind of answer that, together with the question, projects a particularly powerful image of images. In this image of images Leibniz's *principium rationis* (1934, 8–9) holds sway: 'no fact can be real or existing and no proposition can be true unless there is a sufficient reason, why it should be thus and not otherwise.'

Leibniz was the first to make a formal statement of what has in fact been a fundamental principle of Western thought since antiquity. At the level of ontology, the Latin form of the Principle of Reason is *nihil est sine ratione* ('nothing is without reason'): this represents the law that nothing *is*, in the sense of being an existing being, unless there is a sufficient reason why it is. But the word 'reason' in this usage is ambiguous. Although Leibniz himself did not clarify the ambiguity, his immediate intellectual heir Christian Wolff became the first Western philosopher to distinguish reason as *cause* from reason as *ground*. Wolff saw that the first kind of reason pertains to the kindred realms of cause and effect in nature (*principium fiendi*) and motive and action in human affairs (*principium cognoscendi*); whereas the second kind of reason touches what things are in their essence (*principium essendi*)(Schopenhauer 1974, 24–27). In its first form the Principle of Reason is the law of causation, which has served as a regulative principle for scientific inquiry since at least the Age of Enlightenment. Any critique of existing social arrangements that attends to the 'conditions' of their present production and their possible future transformation is a science in this sense: it is beholden to the causal form of the Principle of Reason. In the form of *ground*, on the other hand, a 'reason' becomes the Origin of the world (God) in theology, and the being of beings in ontology. Each of these disciplines construes its subject-matter in terms of what it takes to be an *ultimate* ground. But the concept of reason-as-ground is also an essential component of the mundane and everyday concept of normativity in ethics and law. Thus the image of social justice represented as a *cause* is a different kind of 'reason' (in the sense of the Principle of Reason) than the image of social justice represented as a *ground*. The first merely explains action in the way that sunshine explains the growth of plants. The other justifies and gives meaning to action in the way that the norms of law and morality justify and give meaning to their application.

At the level of language and logic, Leibniz transformed the Principle of Reason into what he called the *principium reddendae rationis*: the 'principle of rendering reasons' (Heidegger 1996, 22–23). Under this conception of the way humans relate to truth, men and women become the beings who render reasons for their assertions: for every truth it claims, the faculty of reason must be prepared to render a reason. It is in thinking about our practice of rendering reasons for our *own* behavior that we first perceive the difference between cause and ground. Whether we say that the relation of cause and effect is necessary (like Schopenhauer), or merely an observed regularity in repeatable sequences of like events (like Hume), we do not usually speak of our own reasons for acting in either manner. No one knows *all* the causes of their actions, down to the last detail, but it is only in exceptional cases that we find ourselves unable to answer the everyday question 'Why did you do that?' To put the matter in Wittgenstein's (1958, 106e) terms, the language-games we play with the word 'cause' are different from those we play with the words 'reason' and 'ground': The list of a thing's causes is in principle infinite — it is as long as we have time and energy to make it — but the chain of reasons that we give for our actions always has an end beyond which we will not go no matter how much time and energy we have. That end is the ground of our action.

Indeed, if we thought that ethical reasons were always causes, then the concept of ethical responsibility would be an oxymoron — an extreme position that is actually made explicit in the philosophy of Schopenhauer. For Schopenhauer (1999, 27) motivation is simply 'causality that passes through cognition,' and the only point of law and ethics is to confront an otherwise greedy will with counter-motives (the prospect of guilt and punishment) to the ever-present motive of individual aggrandisement. On this view the feeling we have of making an 'elective decision' about how we treat other people is an illusion: our decision-making is merely 'the scene of a conflict of motives' (Schopenhauer 1969, 301), and only one of these motives can and will emerge victorious as the cause of our action. Schopenhauer's modern intellectual heirs are thinkers like Richard Dawkins and Jack Balkin, who claim that 'memes' (forms of information) compete with one another as units of evolution within humans conceived as their biological 'hosts' (Balkin 1998, 62). However, one need not take sides for or against Schopenhauer and the meme-ologists on this point in order to notice that we use the word 'cause' differently than the way we use the word 'ground.' We say that our prediction of the future based on the past is sometimes wrong because we are dealing with imperfect information. But we never say that we are in doubt about whether the norm or principle that we have decided to act upon is the reason why we are going to act. Once we have decided on a course of action 'based on principle' (as we are wont to say), we do not *then* stand back in bewilderment and ask, like a sociologist might ask about us, 'I wonder what I am going to do next?'

According to the Principle of Reason, therefore, the possibility of an image of social justice can be secured only by a cause that leads to it or a ground that founds it, either 'empirically' (in the case of a cause) or 'logically' (in the case of a ground). Leibniz's law is a powerful image of the way images must be expressed in the court of reason: namely, always in the form of an 'account' that puts a logically limited and bounded image in touch with its logically limited and bounded cause or ground. Sociology and psychology give *causal* accounts of images of social justice; metaphysics and ethics *ground* them in determinations such as the 'freedom' of the universal thinking subject (Hegel 1975, 39). Moreover, the image of social justice itself, once it is caused or founded, is taken up by the Principle of Reason as the cause and ground of its future lines of development, as if it were in the nature of images to determine in advance what can or will be done with them. This image of images subordinates human beings to their own abstract visions of social justice, in much the same way as the man in Kafka's parable 'Before the Law' (1937, 267–69) is portrayed as waiting his whole life for justice before the door of a Law that was always meant for him and him alone. Humans — the ones who do and must give meaning to their world — become lackeys to the very meanings that they themselves have created. Instead of man revolving about himself as his 'own true sun,' as Marx (1964, v) puts it, images become the 'illusory sun about which man revolves so long as he does not revolve around himself.'[9]

Thus are images of social justice *legalised*: they are legislated by, and then raised above, those who did the imagining as the latter's law for determining progress. Enter the great Kant. From his point of view there is nothing untoward in the legalisation of images, for this philosopher makes self-legislation into the very meaning of a freely chosen responsibility (Kant 1996, 162). For Kant, 'being principled' and 'acting on principle' mean willing a norm that then determines what one 'ought' to do. Willing on the basis of a norm then becomes the very definition of goodness (Kant 1993). Seen in this light, 'being doctrinaire' and 'acting dogmatically' are interpreted as merely defective modes of acting on principle — defective not because they produce bad results, but because the dogmatist failed to construct a sufficiently subtle maxim for acting. This image of images turns the project of social justice into the execution of a *plan* that is oriented to a chosen image of social justice in the way that a means is oriented to its end. Violence in the name of progress is sanctified in advance by the image, as are all 'necessary' sacrifices and sufferings. Even deeds as extreme as Benjamin's 'revolutionary killing of the oppressor' (1978, 298) can be interpreted as inevitable costs of progress, at least so long as one can say in good faith that the oppressor was not used in his execution 'merely' a means. The dialectically linked notions of freedom and responsibility — a freedom that chooses the law to which it is then responsible — are worn as blinkers that keep progressive forces on track, undistracted by the spectacle of suffering that accompanies all historical yearning and struggle as its intended or unintended consequence.

'What the eye doesn't see the heart doesn't grieve over' (Wittgenstein 1983, 205): this homely saying makes the quintessentially logical point that what we do not notice counts as nothing to us. And what we do not notice is not *just* linked to the images that pre-orient the projects of the living, as merely causal accounts of historical 'events' tend to claim. It is not *just* the case that we are what Heidegger (1962, 321) calls 'thrown' into existence in a world that preceded us and that pre-frames our possibilities for acting. There remains the problem of the *unity* of the ground to consider. For only if the image of social justice is, in some important sense, *itself* can it hope to play the role of ground.

THE UNITY OF THE IMAGE OF SOCIAL JUSTICE: KANT AND HEGEL

There is much more to the story of images of social justice than is captured by conceiving of them as loosely defined (but 'obviously' self-identical)

[9]Marx says that religion is man's illusory sun. I have generalised and radicalised his point in a way that he doubtless would not like, however, since Marx too makes use of images of social

objects that confront subjects with possibilities for acting. This way of putting it portrays the relation between subject and object as external — as if we were billiard balls always sent on our way by other billiard balls. The unity of the image for those who act upon it as a ground remains mysterious without an account of how people are able to make it their own *as* just the image that it is. If, in a Kantian tradition that is with us still in countless ways, men and women are said to 'represent' images of social justice, then it must be remembered that they do so in two different senses. The German word *Vorstellung*, in its philosophical sense, is used to indicate that the subject pictures an object to itself in the form of a mental representation (a *Vorstellung* — literally, 'placing before'). The word 'object' (*Gegenstand*, in German, translated literally as 'standing against') names that which stands over against the subject as its other within the phenomenal realm of a consciousness that places objects before itself. This phenomenal realm includes both immediate sense data and mediate images (memories and fantasies) that all somehow get organised as unities through or by the faculty of understanding according to its inventory of concepts. Concepts plus contents thus become co-equal conditions of the possibility of experience, which is defined as the unity of what presents itself to consciousness in the form of an 'object.' Hence Kant (1998, 193–4) will write this often-quoted sentence: 'Thoughts without content are empty, intuitions without concepts are blind.' On this view the ground of just behavior — the image of justice — acquires its unity solely in, and by virtue of, the subject. One of the primary effects of Kant's 'Copernican Revolution' in philosophy is thus to interpret humanity (not God, not Nature), in the form of the *subject*, as the ultimate ground of its own conceptions of justice.

In Roman and medieval philosophy the word *subjectum* (literally, 'thrown under') meant anything that lies-in-front, open to all: it included trees, books, animals, people — in short, tangible beings of all sorts. The word *objectum* (literally, 'thrown before'), was reserved for human representations. The 'unreal' representation of a unicorn, for example, was a kind of *objectum*. To the Romans and the Scholastics, therefore, the *real* was subjective, and the merely ideal was objective — just the reverse of common usage today (Heidegger 2001, 117–18). The reversal was first effected by Descartes, and brought to full maturity by Kant. It consists in positing the human being as the *only* real *subjectum*, and reducing all of the other beings that surround us to the status of mere *objects* that stand before the subject. The primal world of the ancients, untroubled by the distinction between subject and object, was thus reduced by Descartes and especially Kant to the 'objective' world: the world became that which is grounded in what-stands-under *all* objects, namely, the (human) subject. The *certainty* of

justice. One of the most famous, of course, is the image that by revolting against the status quo '[t]he proletarians have nothing to lose but their chains' (Marx and Engels 1998, 77).

the Cartesian subject became both the criterion of truth and the foundation of modern science and technology. What Žižek (1999, 1) calls 'the spectre of the Cartesian subject' continues to haunt post-modernity in the form of the very world-view that it so powerfully projects and 'successfully' carries into effect. Doesn't nature lie (almost) defeated at our feet, a (mostly) dominated and (nearly) understood aggregation of matter and force to be put at the disposal of human beings? Doesn't common sense, at least in the West, generally count the intensification of our domination of nature and the perfection of our scientific understanding to be the self-evident criteria of success and progress?

If, on this view, mental representations deliver an objective world on the basis of the subject's subjectivity, when the time comes for the subject to communicate with other subjects it must represent what it knows by means of a different kind of 'representation.' The German word for this kind of representation is *Darstellung* (literally, 'placing there'). A *Darstellung* is a sensible 'external' representation, in words or pictures, of the objective phenomenal world. If the image of social justice in this sense is sometimes called a 'text,' then this text remains to be read and 'internalised' by the subject in the form of a *Vorstellung* — an image of the image, if you will. In the Kantian tradition 'truth,' in its most profound sense, is not the mere correctness of a *Darstellung*. It is not a mere relation between a proposition and what the proposition is about. Truth is rather *adaequatio intellectus et rei* ('correspondence of mind and thing'): we know a thing thoroughly when our mental picture (*Vorstellung*) of it is grounded securely in all that it has to offer to us as a possible object of consciousness. The certainty of the self-certain subject concerning this offering becomes the *fundamentum absolutum et inconcussum* — the one absolute and unshakable ground. The meaning (and hence ground) of this secure grounding — this 'correspondence' between mind and world — is then secured by what Leibniz called a *harmonia praestabilita*: a 'pre-established harmony' between matter and spirit, body and soul, and the physical and the moral, whereby each member of these dualisms is synchronised relative to its other by God or Nature (Schopenhauer 1974, 139). And lest we hip and sophisticated postmoderns imagine that this way of thinking is hopelessly old-fashioned, it should be remembered that the impulse to say that there is a correspondence between thought and reality that is *grounded* in something profound lies deep in us, and exerts an extremely strong grip on our intelligence.[10]

[10] Consider, for example, the young Wittgenstein's (1974, 9) assertion that 'What a picture [*Bild*] must have in common with reality, in order to be able to depict it — correctly or incorrectly — the way it does, is its pictorial form.' Here correspondence is grounded in a 'pictorial form' that is 'displayed' but cannot be 'depicted,' and which Wittgenstein says 'reaches right out' to reality. Wittgenstein later repudiated (1958, 12e & 48e) his earlier 'picture theory' of language, and gave up on the project of trying to understand language as if it had a unified 'essence' that philosophy could find and describe.

From a Kantian point of view, therefore, an image of social justice is full of content only because the categories of unity, possibility, and causation — all of which reside within the subject — delimit it in advance. Its parts cohere as the image that it is, and, with its unity thus secured, it is then capable of becoming the certain ground of its realisation. Kant's categories of the understanding, taken together with the receptivity of the senses and the faculties of pure intuition of space and time, *are* subjectivity, on this view. From the perspective of this way of interpreting subjectivity, it is neither a surprise nor a disappointment that men and women are destined to become the objects of their objects. Kant modernises Parmenides' famous equation of thinking and being[11] just in time for two centuries of obsession with the idea of progress. If, as Kant contends, being an active subject is the same as doing what you think, then after Kant the only a priori limit on what can be done is what can be thought.

Nowhere is this subordination of doing to thinking more evident than in Kant's interpretation of ethics. As is well-known, Kant makes duty the ground of ethical behaviour: the ethical subject is always *beholden* to something other than its own willing. That something is the subjective maxim of action that the subject is supposed to construct in accordance with the Categorical Imperative.[12] Ethical action is preceded by a kind of *halt*, as if the subject were constantly forced to say, to himself and others: 'Pardon me for a minute or two, while I construct the general principle of my next bit of behaviour.' Although Kant admits that the actual maxim that the subject constructs can be right or wrong, he nonetheless presupposes that once a maxim is constructed it can, in principle, lead automatically and without further ado to an act of willing that attempts to make its command a reality.

Of course, Kant knows that willed *actions* can and often do go astray, producing unintended and unfortunate consequences. But the relation of the maxim and the act of will that precedes our voluntary bodily actions is hard-wired for Kant: there is and can be no gap between maxim and willing-on-the-basis-of-maxim. The maxim 'Do X' must signify and hence undergird the project of 'doing X,' for otherwise no one could ever act 'on' principle, or be judged as immoral for having failed to act on it. At best the ethical subject would be caused by the image of a principle floating in its head to act in a way that has no a *priori* and necessary connection to the principle (Schopenhauer's thesis). The practice of ethics and justice would then come down to predicting what people are likely to do when they apprehend a certain image. There would be no more talk about what people 'ought' to do, except as a rhetorical strategy in the service of the speaker's

[11] A portion of Parmenides' (1984, 71) fragment number eight reads, in translation: 'The same thing is for thinking and [is] that there is thought.'

[12] 'Act only on a maxim by which you can will that it, at the same time, should become a general law' (Kant 1993, 187).

interests. Repelled by such a bleak prospect, Kant interprets the ethical maxim as a mental representation of a rule that can in principle determine the willing of action aimed at effectuating it. The maxim, just like an image of social justice, is thus projected as the ground (not the cause!) of its own instantiation. Subjects need only attempt to will into existence what the image portrays as right and just.

'To do what we think is just': this deceptively simple phrase, so plain and clear to common sense, obscures the main difficulty with the Kantian conception of how images work. The well-known Achilles' heel of the Kantian system is the alleged unity of the image in general — its being just *this* image having a stable content. In the *Critique* of *Pure Reason* Kant attributes the unity of mental images to a 'synthesis' performed by a faculty he calls 'the imagination' (1998, 211). The faculty of imagination is supposed to be what gives us intuitions even without the 'presence' of the object — it spans time and therefore injects temporality (which is supposed to belong only to the faculty of intuition) into the faculty of understanding. And on what basis does Kant know that there is such a thing as the faculty of imagination? He does not claim to have located a *material* faculty of imagination (a little nodule) lurking somewhere in the human brain. He does not even claim to have discovered it as an image by introspection. No: the faculty of imagination is supposed to be what unifies and gives us images in the first place, and this means that it cannot itself be an image. For what is prior can never be determined by what depends on the prior without falling into tautology. The embarrassing truth is that Kant *invented* the faculty of imagination in order to account for our having images that he took to be unities. If the Principle of Reason requires the unity of images to have a 'reason,' and if you cannot say that you have actually observed an entity within the human body or mind that makes images possible, then you have got to hypostatise an entity, like the faculty of imagination, that 'must' be there as the ground of images. Only by this rather fanciful means does Kant's transcendental deduction of the categories acquire its ground — a point that Nietzsche used to great effect in writing his cruel burlesque of the Kantian system.[13]

In the first edition of the *Critique*, Kant characterised the imagination as a 'blind though indispensable function of the soul.' He deleted this rather mystical phrase from the second edition, however, substituting a description of the imagination that demotes it to the undetermined status of a

[13] As Nietzsche (1954, 391) puts it, the central question in the *Critique* — 'How are synthetic judgments *a priori* possible?' — receives an essentially question-begging answer from Kant: 'They are possible by means of a means (faculty).' Nietzsche (1954, 392) took Kant's answer to be a silly tautology, and he compared it to words that Molière puts in the mouth of a doctor in one of his farces. The doctor, having been asked how opium induces sleep, replies: 'By means of a means ..., namely the *virtus dormativa* [the power of making sleepy].' This comparison convinced Nietzsche that the Kantian system belongs less in philosophy than in the 'realm of comedy.'

'function of the understanding' (1984, 211 n.a). This change shows, as Heidegger (1997, 191) says, 'how fundamentally uncertain Kant was, not only with regard to the power of imagination but also with respect to the basic relation between intuition and thinking.' For the alleged 'synthesis' that pushes the manifold of intuitions into conceptual unities, as well as the one that unifies the pure concepts of understanding in the first instance, *takes time to accomplish*. Reflecting judgment, which passes from the objects of perception to the concept, and subsuming judgment, which passes the other way, are no longer secured by a power of judgment that has been enabled by the categories before it enters time. Instead, the unity of the categories themselves must await the work of the faculty of imagination *in* time. This implies that reason is not a pure, isolated, and 'logical' faculty after all. Reason does not first apprehend or consist of timeless truths that only *then* get applied in time. On the contrary, the time-relatedness of the categories and concepts, which are pushed together as unities by an imagination that requires time to act, always precedes them as a condition of their possibility (Heidegger 1997, 193). It would seem that Kant put the cart of subjectivity before the horse of history. His alleged transcendental subject is always already an immanent historical subject — a thesis that will be made explicit by Hegel.

If the unity of images in general is a hostage to history, then the unity of the image of social justice is doubly time-bound. The propositional or pictorial 'representation' (*Darstellung*) of an image of social justice — like those of King and Hitler quoted earlier, for example — presents itself to the consciousness of each subject that perceives it as the concrete-here-and-*now* of a stream of sense impressions that (as yet) lack unity of form. The manifold of the sensible image (*Darstellung*) of social justice still awaits the moment in which the pluralities that it loosely contains are transformed by abstraction from what the senses perceive into what the understanding knows as the unified image (*Vorstellung*) that it is. These days the name that is sometimes given to this process of transformation of plurality into unity is 'interpretation'. Having to undergo just *this* particular time-bound act of interpretation is the first historical moment of the image of social justice. Recall the moment that you read the earlier passages from King and Hitler, and try to remember exactly what you thought (then) that they meant: this phenomenological exercise ought to show you that your reading *was*, but no longer *is*, in all its immediacy.

Thus, the second historical moment for the image of social justice comes once a particular interpretation slips into the past. This 'second moment' is in fact the possibility of multiple time-bound acts of interpretation, whereby the image of social justice is exposed to still more contingency. Always on the verge of breaking up into a multiplicity of possible or actual interpretations, it loses all claim to *absolute* self-identity. Deconstruction, a much-maligned concept in certain quarters, is at bottom simply a reminder and demonstration of how the identity of an image is always a function of work in time. Once human work is seen to be prior to the identity of the image, it follows that different works can and do yield different identities. The 'same' image is also always a 'different image,' because *this* work of interpretation is not *that* work of interpretation. At best the law of identity permits the two works of interpretation to by judged 'alike' by means of still another time-bound act of interpretation. And lest it appear that at least each individual subject must carry around a unified image of social justice in its head, it must be said that the temporal dispersal of unity does not exempt even that one from the flux of history. The subject's interpretation of the world changes, in other words. It follows that having an image of social justice to begin with, and thereafter attempting to accomplish it, mark the nodal points of a passage that ruptures the image's claim to absolute self-identity. If unity is always the work of time, then these two nodes lack any sort of *necessary* connection that would make 'the' abstract image into 'the' criterion of its accomplishment. 'To think *X* and to accomplish *X*': this way of putting people's relations to their images represents *X* as an abstract and unmediated unity. It fails to account tor the *passage* between thinking and doing: a passage that sunders *X* as idea from *X* as accomplishment. The passage that makes *X* into not-*X* is what Hegel (1975, 128) calls 'Becoming.' Borrowing the metaphor of fire from Heraclitus, the original philosopher of becoming,[14] Hegel (1975, 69) describes the historical subject as 'the crucible and the fire which consumes the loose plurality of sense and reduces it to unity.'

Hegel's (1975, 168) solution to the problem of unity is to posit the subject-knowing-the-object as a 'pure self-contained unity' *in* time: a dialectical unity wherein the concrete and the abstract are constantly being synthesised at ever-higher levels of truth. Hegel privileges *process* as unity and promises *progress* as its inevitable outcome, thus transforming metaphysics into philosophy of history. The task of the mind, as Arendt (1968, 6) puts it, is brought back to earth. Before Hegel, thought was always speculating about the transcendent and the abstract — Plato's Ideas and Kant's conditions of the possibility of experience, for example. After Hegel, however, thought's only legitimate task becomes the attempt to understand *what has happened*. From an Hegelian point of view, the image of social justice is merely one moment in the dialectic of history, always destined to be overcome by its own negation and synthesis into what it has not (yet) become. Hegel's slogan 'The truth is in the whole' (Balbus 1977, 587) means, in this context, that the true unity of the image of social justice is not a bounded abstraction — it is not the empty unity of a mere interpretation. Rather,

[14]Fragment number thirty of Heraclitus (1987, 25) reads, in translation: 'The ordered world, the same for all, no god or man made, but it always was, is, and will be, an everlasting fire, being kindled in measures and being put out in measures.'

its true unity is forged in the ongoing march of history: the image of social justice is (in its truth) as it is instantiated. If image plus the ongoing realisation-of-the-image together form the relevant unity, this means that the abstract image of social justice as it is encountered in the here and now by the subject is merely a 'flash' that yields what Benjamin (1999, 492) calls 'dialectics at a standstill.' This abstraction is nothing in itself, for 'things, as they immediately are, have no truth' (Hegel 1975, 164). Instead, Hegel (1975, 135) makes following-and-thus-instantiating-the-law into the reality of a freedom that always remains a mere abstraction unless and until it lays down the law for itself. The unity of acting-on-what-you-think-is-right is thus projected as the concrete and real synthesis of the two abstractions 'freedom' and 'responsibility.'[15] On this view, the image of social justice is what it becomes, and the inevitability of its becoming Absolute Idea is simply the 'axiomatic convergence' (Hegel 1975, xxvi) of what is with what ought to be.

THE IMAGE OF SOCIAL JUSTICE AND THE JUSTIFICATION OF SUFFERING

The 'ground,' for Hegel (1975, 175), is therefore the unity of identity and difference — a unity that is not itself an abstract identity but rather is conceived as the concrete mediation of identity and difference. If the truth of being and nothingness is the unity of becoming (128), then mediation is the sweaty *passage* that transforms being-and-becoming into essence (162). The Hegelian alchemy of the dialectic explicitly transforms the Principle of Reason into the 'assertion that things should essentially be viewed as mediated' (176). No longer does the image of social justice ground its realisation as something that stands apart from the activity of realising it. Its being and its becoming (its not-yet-in-being) are the same. The ground is the grounded — they have, as Hegel (176) puts it, 'one and the same content,' as they gradually become the future.

No longer will time be ignored by philosophy — Hegel made sure of that. But Nietzsche's critique of Hegel's dialectical image of images introduces more than a little doubt about the *value* of that image. For Nietzsche (1968, 147), Hegel's 'self-revealing and self-realising ideal' projects yet another kind of Western belief in otherworldliness, analogous to Platonism and Christianity. The latter two movements devalued *this* messy world of becoming and suffering in favor of a purer 'other world' of Ideas (Plato) or heaven (Christianity). Hegel does at least *try* to stay focused on the world of sweat, blood, and tears, unlike Platonism and Christianity. But as

[15] 'In short, man is most independent when he knows himself to be determined by the absolute idea throughout' (Hegel 1975, 220).

Nietzsche observes, Hegel manages to overcome the moral God and the notion of abstract essences only to substitute the idea of the *future* in their place. This is because Hegel's dialectical ideal manifests itself in becoming. It is never presently achieved, but is always deferred in favour of process and progress. Given that progress towards realisation of the ideal is an essential tenet of Hegel's, Nietzsche (1968, 147) acutely remarks that his system directs 'faith . . . into the *future* when, in accordance with its noble requirements, it can worship' (Nietzsche 1968, 147). This deflection of attention into the future assures that criticism is never directed at the Idea itself, but only at the obstacles that stand in the way of its achievement.[16]

How comforting the Hegelian system is for certain people who yearn to transform social arrangements! For now they are able to interpret history as the gradual working our of an Idea — indeed, probably the very idea that they themselves hold dear. What is necessary is also right: is this quintessentially Hegelian thought not dangerously akin to Goering's infamous declaration, '*Recht ist das, was uns gefält*' ('The right is whatever pleases us')(Rhees 1965, 25)? As Nietzsche (1968, 60) puts it, 'Hegel seeks reason everywhere — before reason one may submit and acquiesce.' How convenient this is for those who would explain the costs of transformation in terms of what their reason tells them is necessary for the unfolding of the human spirit! Here 'costs' refers both to the new suffering of those who are transformed against their will, and to the continuing suffering of those whose plights are left untouched by the onward and upward march of history-as-Idea. What I have called suffering *as such* plays no role in Hegel's philosophy because it bears no relation to the realm of ground and grounded — indeed, it is completely invisible from the perspective of the ground. History becomes a story that is told by and for the ones whose Idea has survived — the ones whom fate has crowned with victory.

If Kant would have us believe in a realm of abstract and universal moral values, each a unity that is binding on reason, then Hegel offers us belief in progress: 'a demonstrable development, a becoming visible of the moral realm' (Nietzsche 1968, 223). Whether the image of social justice is projected as a *value* or as an *element of progress*, either way an alleged unity is supposed to explain and justify — to provide a ground for — what we do to ourselves and to others during the project of making social justice a reality. In Western thought the notion that *grounding* as such — grounding without regard for 'progress' — constitutes the ultimate justification for how we comport ourselves will reach its apex in the philosophy of Heidegger. Indeed, Heidegger (1996, 113) will, in the end, say of being and

[16] One can perceive this tendency in Hegelian thought most clearly, of course, in Marx's (1986, 187–8) idea of historical change through social praxis: it is said to be grounded in the historical inevitability of progress towards a social formation where all antagonism among classes will disappear. Social praxis is therefore justified and comforted by the inevitability of a Glorious Future.

ground that they are 'the same.' His interpretation of human freedom as the origin of the Principle of Reason — 'freedom is the ground of ground' (Heidegger 1998, 132–34) — makes what we do with our possibilities into an inevitable giving-and-taking of grounds. If freedom itself is an 'abyss of ground' (Heidegger 1998, 134), then enacting the *meaning* of being becomes the task of freedom, on this view. Authenticity conceived as an 'impassioned freedom towards death' (Heidegger 1962, 311) thus is offered as the ungrounded ground of a life of passionate (from the Latin *passio*, for 'suffering') doing. The *Dasein* that is as it *does* is so absorbed in care (*Sorge* — Heidegger 1962, 225–74) for itself that the suffering that lies within it and all around it is either overlooked or else absorbed into the noble and grand project of living out the meaning of being. Heidegger thus transforms suffering, like a bit of bitterness called for in a recipe, into a mere element in the glorious unity of being.

Meanwhile: children starve, and convicts await execution; the right to acquire property enables many, and those who own nothing *but* this abstract right live miserably from hand to mouth; formal opportunity is denied to some, and real opportunity lies beyond the reach of most; the pleasures of life are reduced to the pleasure of conspicuous consumption in affluent societies, and the pleasures of life are subordinated to frenzied efforts to satisfy basic material needs in most of the Third World; more attention is directed towards the international protection of human rights in the public sphere, and little attention goes to the socially harmful exercise of rights in the private sphere; the Internet allows everyone to shop on-line for dog food, and it makes many of its users into solitary and unhappy prisoners of their computer cubicles; well-to-do people in the West get Viagra and hair-replacement therapy (not to mention AIDs medications), and tens of millions are dying of AIDs in Africa for want of any medicine at all. If there were an angel of history with his face turned towards the past, as Benjamin (1968, 257) imagines him, then he would see what we do not: 'Where we perceive a chain of events, he sees one single catastrophe which keeps piling wreckage upon wreckage and hurls it in front of his feet.' While *we* may believe that a 'storm of progress' keeps blowing this angel into the future, *he* cannot see the future. All he sees is that 'the pile of debris before him grows skyward' (Benjamin 1968, 258). This pile of debris is none other than suffering as such, which refuses to depart the world despite being ignored for so very long by so very many great thinkers.

In his important essay *Useless Suffering*, the phenomenologist Emmanuel Levinas (1998, 91–101) characterises the concrete suffering that is ignored by all 'systems' of social justice in terms of a passivity that *undergoes* rather than achieves. No longer seen as the attainment of an active consciousness, this suffering becomes the very submission or irrelevance of that consciousness. Even sensibility is already a 'reception' that is eager to transmit its 'data' to an active and thematising consciousness, whereas suffering as such is 'more profoundly passive than the receptivity of our senses' (Levinas 1998, 92). Suffering is a helpless opening to pain and the burden of being, a 'pure undergoing' that rends rather than knits the humanity of the sufferer. We may complain to and take comfort from others, but we always suffer alone. Suffering as such is thus the tragedy of the *ego*'s impotence to achieve more than merely momentary relief from the cycle of craving and satisfaction — a cycle that lets desire be satisfied only to have it promptly re-launched in the form of a different desire. Suffering as such appears phenomenally as a solitude locked within itself, afflicted and beset before and despite all projects. The suffering of boredom is perhaps its purest form, bearing witness to the unfortunate truth that it is even possible to suffer on account of not suffering anything in particular. Hence Levinas (1998, 93) will conclude that 'the least one can say about suffering is that, in its own phenomenality, it is useless: "for nothing".'

If the moment of suffering as such is for nothing, however, Levinas also rightly notices that this moment almost always undergoes a dramatic metamorphosis in consciousness. We proceed to rationalise suffering's brutal phenomenality by making it useful for something, perhaps as the sign of merit and a hoped-for reward. The appeal of the eternal rest that awaits sufferers in heaven, and the earthly compensation of wisdom that comes to those who suffer and survive, allow consciousness to transform suffering into a necessary means to a desirable end for the suffering individual. Even the criminal, when punished, can comport himself gloriously, as a 'free man,' if only he is able to recognise that his punishment 'is not foreign constraint to which he is subjected, but the manifestation of his own act' (Hegel 1975, 220). Reason also gives suffering a use-value in constructing its political teleologies, as Levinas (1998, 95) so acutely describes:

> It is said to be necessary to the teleology of community life, when social discontent awakens a useful attention to the health of the collective body. Perhaps there is a social utility in the suffering necessary for the pedagogic function of Power in education, discipline, and repression. Is not fear of punishment the beginning of wisdom? Do people not have the idea that suffering, undergone as punishment, regenerates the enemies of society and humankind?

'It's all for the best — just you wait and see': Is this not one of the many slogans we employ to transform violence into therapy, law into justice, and power into progress?

Yet for all of its obvious utility, there remains something darkly suspicious about the rational practice of justifying suffering, especially the suffering of others. Somehow the alleged historical necessity of the Hegelian synthesis of being and becoming into the unity of Absolute Idea never *completely* succeeds in assuaging the consciences of those who feel that they must break eggs in order to make the omelette of progress. 'There is [an] anxiety of responsibility that is incumbent on everyone in the death or suffering of the other,' Levinas (1996, 164) says, and it leaves the ethical person 'troubled at the prospect of committing violence — albeit necessary for the logical unfolding of history.' If, as Benjamin (1978, 286) contends, the death penalty shows law's violent nature more transparently than anything else law does, thereby revealing something 'rotten in law,' then Levinas (1998, 95) too will find a 'strange failure of justice' amidst the oppression of the weak by the strong that is lurking 'behind the rational administration of pain in the penalties meted out by human courts.' When Levinas (1998, 95) says that suffering shows itself, in its phenomenality, as meaningless and malignant beneath all 'the reasonable forms espoused by the social 'uses' of suffering,' he initiates a claim on anyone who would justify the infliction of suffering on the basis of a mere image of social justice. This claim leaps over all reason, and the possibility of ethical casuistry that it contains, to reach the vast ocean of suffering in its entirety. This claim is, at a bare minimum, to *bear witness* to the truth of universal suffering.

FROM JUSTIFICATION TO REDEMPTION

Bearing witness to suffering without *doing* something about it is difficult — it is perhaps the most difficult task of all. In Western thought the truth of universal suffering, though only very rarely perceived and made into a theme, places the punished and those who punish on the same level, and puts justifications on the same level as cruel masks. Schopenhauer (1969, 369) claims that the person 'who, for the sake of orthodoxy, commits the heretic to the flames, is just as much as a murderer as the bandit who earns a reward by killing.' For those who are able to comprehend the truth of suffering as such, it is but a small step to the larger insight that there exists a level at which the person who condemns the bandit to his death for the sake of law and justice is not essentially different than the one he condemns. The point is not that the law 'Thou shalt not kill' is a universal injunction. *The point is that no human judgment of the deed can be derived, either before or after the deed, from the norm taken as a ground.* As Benjamin (1978, 298) puts it (in characteristically theological terms):

> This commandment precedes the deed, just as God was 'preventing' the deed. But just as it may not be fear of punishment that enforces obedience, the injunction becomes inapplicable, incommensurable once the deed is accomplished. No judgment of the deed can be derived from the commandment. And so neither the divine judgment, nor the grounds for this judgment, can be known in advance. Those who base a condemnation of all violent killing on the commandment are therefore mistaken. It exists not as a criterion of judgment, but as a guideline for the actions of persons or communities who have to wrestle with it in solitude and, in exceptional cases, to take on themselves the responsibility for ignoring it.

Here at last is an interpretation of a so-called ground of action that deprives it of all capacity to justify those who take it as a ground. Although the command 'Thou shalt not kill' remains in existence as a textual 'guideline' for those who accept it, it sheds absolutely no light on the question of the justice of any particular killing. It enjoins all killing as such, but it also denies human judgment *about* the deed the comfort of ground. Benjamin's interpretation shows that the religious fanatic who uses or defends violence in order to vindicate God's commands does not *follow* His law, for this attitude heretically presupposes that the fanatic knows what only God is supposed to know: the content of divine judgment.

For those who possess what Benjamin (1978, 286) calls 'a finer sensibility,' the suffering of others always seems ordered, in the end, by an inscrutable fate, and human justifications for that suffering always appear in the form of mere window-dressing. Deprived of the comfort of justification either before or after the deed, yet needing *something* to comfort it, such a sensibility takes refuge in the idea of future redemption. The redemption that comes from forgiveness, however beneficial and desirable it may be, is always dependent on a victim's act of forgiveness, and therefore is insufficiently general. Strictly speaking, the redemption bestowed by a victim's forgiveness occupies the temporal horizon of a present that may or may not arrive: for victims do not always forgive those who wrong them. On the contrary, they usually hunger after justice and revenge. In the phrase 'May God (or History) forgive me for what I must do in the name of justice,' thought catches sight of the possibility of another kind of redemption.

This is a redemption-to-come from a source whose judgments are, as Benjamin (1978, 300) says, 'not visible to men.' In this idea lies a kind of solution that is purely and simply a ground: redemption lies under the aspect of an *insoluble problem* as its ultimate meaning, allowing us to make peace with what we do. It is therefore a ground without consequences for anyone other than the lonely one who bears witness to the tragedy of suffering as such. In a word, the idea of redemption comforts. Its appeal can be seen in the idea of the redemptive power of art, and love of fate (*amor fati*), which act as palliatives for the otherwise horrific prospect of the eternal recurrence of the same (Nietzsche 1968, 536) — in the idea of a divine violence that strikes and expiates without warning or proof of origin (Benjamin 1978, 300) — in the idea of self-effacement and a denial of the will that stills craving, and that stands alone as world-redeeming (Schopenhauer 1969, 362) — in the idea of justice and necessary violence subordinated to, and redeemed by, the ethical relation between the *I* and its Other (Levinas 1998, 229) — and in the idea that the sense and value of the world must lie outside the world (Wittgenstein 1974, 71–72). All of these philosophical fairy tales bear witness to the truth of universal suffering, but they do not purport to cure it. They offer it the hope of redemption, not justification.

Although justification and the kind of redemption just mentioned are both kinds of grounds, their manner of grounding is radically different. Justification lays down the law, redemption transcends it. Justification lies within history, redemption lies outside history as its ultimate meaning. The time of justification is the past — it props up the present. The time of redemption is the future — it promises that the sum of our presents, once passed, will count for something. The organ and faculty of justification are the brain and its reason: justification thinks and blames. The organ and faculty of redemption are the heart and its hope: redemption loves and excuses. The virtues of justification are justice and righteousness. The virtues of redemption are compassion and atonement. The possibility of justice grounds the project of distinguishing between the just and the unjust. The possibility of redemption grounds the result. The *δίκη* of justice is ordering. The *δίκη* of redemption is the restoration of harmony after the violence of human ordering has been accomplished.[17] Images justify existence. The unimaginable redeems the guilt of existence. People justify. God (or His replacement) redeems.

The loftiest peak of Western thought about the nature of justice is reached when a thinker thinks the possibility of redemption for what happens when humans do justice to one another. For that peak lies far above the relation between justice and injustice, and thus cannot appeal to justice as its ultimate value. From this perspective the image of social justice always bears the seed of guilt within it on account of what it is capable of doing and leaving undone. Living life with a constant presentiment of guilt is suffering. The possibility of redemption makes peace with this kind of suffering by deflecting our attention from the here-and-now to a 'beyond' that lies beyond the end of our works and days. If justification is what humans are constantly doing by way of implementing their projects, then redemption makes sense of their need to do it. When thought thinks redemption it is thinking the final ground in the domain of human relations — the ground of all mere grounds of social justice.

BEYOND JUSTIFICATION AND REDEMPTION

It should be clear by now that the critique of images of social justice taken as ideologies is far less radical than the critique of those images taken as grounds. The standpoint of ideological critique is always external, in the sense that the ideological image is projected, in one way or another, as the

[17] In my view, this is the deepest meaning of Anaximander's famous fragment, which reads: 'Whence things have their origin, there they must also pass away according to necessity; for they must pay penalty and be judged for their injustice [ἀδικία], according to the ordinance of time.' (Heidegger 1975, 13).

cause of what it causes — namely, the behavior of those in its grip. To criticise grounds requires an internal point of view: for the ground is what gives meaning to *our* behavior. The ground as origin and destination shows itself phenomenologically in the form of *self*-justification. Criticism of the very concept of grounds is therefore the same as criticising self-justification.

Traditional Western thought is used to criticising *particular* self-justifications, especially when they are offered by others. It is far less well-practiced in criticising the idea of justification itself, and it hardly ever criticises the thinker's *own* need for self-justification. Certain non-Western traditions, however, have plenty of practice in piercing to the root of our craving for grounds to support what we think and do. Without meaning to convert this chapter into a treatise on Zen Buddhism, permit me to offer one example from that particular tradition. The example is drawn from *Transmission of Light* (Cleary 2001, 3–225), a major classic of Japanese Zen that is attributed to Keizan, a fourteenth century master. The text (Cleary 2001, 115) relates an interview that was conducted by the Indian master Vashashita with Punjamitra, the man who would become his successor. The first question the master asks, together with its answer, are of the greatest interest to us here:

> When Punjamitra was a prince, the Buddhist master Vashashita asked him, 'Why do you want to leave home?' Punyamitra said, 'If I do leave home, it is not for anything else.'

Punyamitra shows a complete indifference to the comfort of grounds in his remarkable response to the master's question. This is why Vashashita, we are told, permitted him to leave home and become a mendicant. Punyamitra's answer shows that he has *let go* of justification. He *feels no need* for the succour of redemption. If he leaves home, he will just leave home. Period. The text concludes: 'So you shouldn't fear home life, and shouldn't be proud of leaving home. Just stop seeking outwardly; turn to yourself to understand' (Cleary 2001, 117). Ground and no-ground are just words, on this view, and all you need to do to discover this is look inside yourself. This 'all you need to do' names no small accomplishment, however. It represents a difficult *journey* whose end-point is formally the same as its beginning (Wolcher 2002). Hence it will always remain incomprehensible, not to mention a waste of time, to those whose busy journeys are enchained to the idea of progress towards pre-determined goals. But one feels entitled to ask: when, if ever, has a busy journey to a pre-determined end ever brought a traveler anywhere but back to himself? When, if ever, has it brought him peace?

'Nihilism' is the epithet that some people use when confronted with a way of being that so brazenly lets go of the gnawing need for self-justification. They worry that such a way of being, by eschewing the comfort of grounds, threatens to spin dangerously out of control. They forget that grounds cover-up as well as support, and that what grounds always cover up is the visibility of suffering as such. To bear witness to suffering as such is not the first step in a program — it is not itself a ground. It is the groundless contemplation of the intimate connection between justification and pain. And if that contemplation brings with it a revolution in being human, this will not be 'because' of anything. The Principle of Reason is, without a doubt, indispensable to daily life and to the life of reason. We could not get along without the question 'Why?' and our various practices of answering it. Social life, not to mention academic life, has grown dependent on the idea of grounding. This chapter does not set its face against the practice of rendering reasons — *please* do not read it as going 'too far against accounts and accounting for things.' Neither does it eschew planned efforts to reduce or eliminate suffering, and even to inflict suffering on those who would hurt or destroy us. If it is against anything, it is against the practice of *puffing up*, and then *hiding behind*, the mere reasons that reason clings to.

Even granting all of the utility and even necessity that pertains to the Principle of Reason, I say that it has become a prison-house of the human spirit. If thinking belongs to the idea of justice, and feeling belongs to idea of redemption, then both thinking and feeling belong to what I will call the original mind. The original mind is not a subject, ego, or will; nor does it ground anything in particular. It is neither being nor becoming. The Principle of Reason prevents the original mind from achieving its last and most important insight: namely, that it is possible to live life without the craving need to be constantly comforted on account of what we do. While the prospect of such a life may seem unattractive (or worse) to those who long for their images of social justice to be *more* than just elements in the ceaseless flow of causes and effects, it will be liberating for those who are able to bear witness to universal suffering in the spirit of universal compassion.

REFERENCES

Arendt, Hannah 1968. *Between Past and Future*. New York: Penguin Books.

Aristotle 1984. The Nicomachean Ethics. In *The Complete Works of Aristotle (Volume II)*, edited by J Barnes. Princeton: Princeton University Press.

Atchity, Kenneth ed 1996. *The Classical Greek Reader*. New York: Henry Holt.

Balbus, Isaac 1977. Commodity Form and Legal Form: An Essay on the 'Relative Autonomy' of the Law. *Law and Society Review 11*; 571–87.

Balkin, JM 1998. *Cultural Software: A Theory of Ideology*. New Haven: Yale University Press.

Benjamin, Walter 1999. *The Arcades Project*. Translated by H Eiland and K McLaughlin. Cambridge: Belknap Press.

Benjamin, Walter 1978. *Reflections*. Translated by E Jephcott. New York: Schocken Books.

Benjamin, Walter 1968. *Illuminations*. Translated by H Zohn. New York: Schocken Books.
Cleary, Thomas 2001. Transmission of the Light. In *Classics of Buddhism and Zen (Volume 4)*. Boston: Shambhala.
Garrow, David 1988. *Bearing the Cross*. New York: Vintage Books.
Hegel, GWF 1975. *Hegel's Logic*. Translated by W Wallace. Oxford: Oxford University Press.
Heidegger, Martin 2001. *Zollikon Seminars*. Translated by F Mayr and R Askay. Evanston: Northwestern University Press.
Heidegger, Martin 1998. *Pathmarks*. Edited by W McNeill. Cambridge: Cambridge University Press.
Heidegger, Martin 1997. *Phenomenological Interpretation of Kant's* Critique of Pure Reason. Translated by P Emad and K Maly. Bloomington: Indiana University Press.
Heidegger, Martin 1996. *The Principle of Reason*. Translated by R Lilly. Bloomington: Indiana University Press.
Heidegger, Martin 1995. *Aristotle's* Metaphysics Φ 1–3: *On the Essence and Actuality of Force*. Translated by W Brogan and P Warnek. Bloomington: Indiana University Press.
Heidegger, Martin 1975. The Anaximander Fragment. In *Early Greek Thinking*, translated by D Krell and F Capuzzi. New York: Harper & Row.
Heidegger, Martin 1962. *Being and Time*. Translated by J Macquarrie and E Robinson. New York: Harper Collins.
Heraclitus 1987. *Fragments*. Translated by TM Robinson. Toronto: University of Toronto Press.
Hitler, Adolf 1943. *Mein Kampf*. Translated by R Manheim. Boston: Houghton Mifflin.
Hume, David 1961. An Enquiry Concerning Human Understanding. In *The Empiricists*, edited by R Taylor. New York: Dolphin Books.
Janson, HW, and A Janson 2001. *History of Art* (6th Edn). Upper Saddle River, NJ: Prentice Hall.
Kafka, Franz 1937. *The Trial*. Translated by W Muir and E Muir. New York: Modern Library.
Kant, Immanuel 1998. *Critique of Pure Reason*. Translated and edited by P Guyer and A Wood. Cambridge: Cambridge University Press.
Kant, Immanuel 1996. *Practical Philosophy*. Translated and edited by M Gregor. Cambridge: Cambridge University Press.
Kant, Immanuel 1993. *The Philosophy of Kant*. Translated by C Friedrich and J Meredith. New York: Modern Library.
Kierkegaard, Søren 1993. *The Diary of Søren Kirkegaard*. Edited by P Rohde. New York: Carol Publishing.
Leibniz, Gottfried Wilhelm 1934. *Leibniz: Philosophical Writings*. Translated by M Morris. London: JM Dent & Sons.
Levinas, Emmanuel 1998. *On Thinking-of-the-Other: Entre Nous*. Translated by M Smith and B Harshav. New York: Columbia University Press.
Levinas, Emmanuel 1996. *Basic Philosophical Writings*. Edited by A Peperzak, S Critchley, and R Bernasconi. Bloomington: Indiana University Press.
Marx, Karl and Frederick Engels 1998. *The Communist Manifesto*. London: Verso.

Marx, Karl 1986. Preface to *A Critique of Political Economy*. In *Karl Marx: A Reader*, edited by J Elster. Cambridge: Cambridge University Press.
Marx, Karl 1964. *Early Writings*. Translated and edited by TB Bottomore. New York: McGraw-Hill.
Nietzsche, Friedrich 1968. *The Will to Power*. Translated by W Kaufmann and RJ Hollingdale New York: Vintage Books.
Nietzsche, Friedrich 1954. Beyond Good and Evil. In *The Philosophy of Nietzsche*, translated by H Zimmern. New York: Modern Library.
Parmenides of Elea 1984. *Fragments*. Translated by D Gallop. Toronto: University of Toronto Press.
Pascal, Blaise 1941. *Pensées and the Provincial Letters*. Translated by WF Trotter and T M'Crie. New York: Modern Library.
Rhees, Rush 1965. Some Developments on Wittgenstein's View of Ethics. *Philosophical Review* 74; 17–26.
Rosenzweig, Franz 1985. *The Star of Redemption*. Translated by W Hallo. Notre Dame: University of Notre Dame Press.
Schopenhauer, Arthur 1999. *Prize Essay on the Freedom of the Will*. Translated by EFJ Payne. Cambridge: Cambridge University Press.
Schopenhauer, Arthur 1974. *On the Fourfold Root of the Principle of Sufficient Reason*. Translated by EFJ Payne. La Salle, IL: Open Court.
Schopenhauer, Arthur 1969. *The World as Will and Representation (Volume I)*. Translated by EFJ Payne. New York: Dover Publications.
Spinoza, Benedict de 1955. *Ethics*. Translated by W White. New York: Hafner Publishing.
Van de Weyer, Robert, ed. 2000. *366 Readings from Buddhism*. Cleveland: Pilgrim Press.
Weber, Max 1978. *Economy and Society (Volume I)*. Edited by G Roth and C Wittich. Berkeley: University of California Press.
Weber, Max 1958. *From Max Weber: Essays in Sociology*. Translated and edited by HH Gerth and CW Mills. New York: Oxford University Press.
Wittgenstein, Ludwig 1983. *Remarks on the Foundations of Mathematics*. Translated by GEM Anscombe. Cambridge: MIT Press.
Wittgenstein, Ludwig 1974. *Tractatus Logico-Philosophicus*. Translated by DF Pears and BF McGuinness. Atlantic Highlands, NJ: Humanities Press International.
Wittgenstein, Ludwig 1954. *Philosophical Investigations*. Translated by GEM Anscombe. New York: Macmillan.
Wolcher, Louis 2002. The Third Mountain: A Meditation on Chaos and Order. *International Journal for the Semiotics of Law* 15; 25–52.
Žižek, Slavoj 1999. *The Ticklish Subject: The Absent Centre of Political Ontology*. London: Verso.

3

Just Waiting: Endless Deferral and the Social Injustice of 'Suspending' Participants between Bidding and Evaluation

ROLLAND MUNRO

Because I could not stop for Death,
He kindly stopped for me;
The carriage held but just ourselves
And Immortality.

Emily Dickinson

THEORY 1 — THE EXCLUSION OF JUSTICE FROM THE EXPERIENCE OF GROUP

BY THE TIME we ask for justice, it is too late. We are already in ruins. When someone calls for justice, we are no longer group. To ask for justice is immediately to 'breach' our bond. What once held the group together is no longer enjoined — a sense of *being us* is over. The relation of 'we' is gone.

The eyes of the angel of history see only ruins. Pile upon Pile. Looking back, nothing is to be seen of all those fragile, momentary, bonds, the uplifts and surges of spirit. For when we are together, we have no call for justice. We come together for other things. To play, to make things happen, times for love and companionship, even to kill. Never for justice. *This is our sacrifice*. Our deferral of justice.

Just asking for justice may be sufficient to spoil our fragile sense of communality, this inward-looking mimetic and mutual regard. To stop for justice is to suggest things have gone wrong. It is to separate, to split apart. Suddenly we no longer just 'go along' to see where things lead. Someone has called a 'stop'. This is all an individual can claim: foul! So things cannot *just* go on, they have to be settled.

A need for justice is the 'invisible worm' that comes in the night and destroys our sense of sociality. Paradoxically, justice must still wait. For it is only the possibility of *injustice* that can be raised and investigated. Along with the effervescence of group, justice must be deferred, pending settlement of the putative injustice.

Commentary

Sociality is the blind spot of history, it is always invisible to Benjamin's angel; our very coming together evaporates in the first call for justice. To say what happened, to see with the eyes of the angel, is to step outside group and outside time.

As Mary Douglas captures the problem of social order, cooperation is not to be accomplished through collective agreement alone. Sacrifices are often demanded:

> Solidarity involves individuals being ready to suffer on behalf of the larger group and their expecting other individuals to do as much for them (Douglas, 1986: 1).

The critical question is of course who suffers? How is suffering distributed? Are there asymmetries of power that distribute sacrifice in ways that benefit some more than others? To answer these questions, the social has been re-engineered. The attempt is to make the social visible and transparent through the institutions of the law, the market and audit. *All in the name of justice.* This would not matter were justice actually achieved. But the opposite is the case.

For as long as it is recalcitrant to history, and it ever must be so, sociality must be *extruded* from the social by an increasing privileging of the law, the market and audit *as* technologies. Each of these purports to act as 'spokesperson' for the individual and so become the major contemporary institutions, fighting respectively for one's 'rights', one's 'freedoms' and one's 'value for money'.

THEORY 2 — THE EXCLUSION OF EVENTS FROM THE DISCUSSION ON JUSTICE

Justice appears in the beginning and it appears at the end. It has no place in the middle of things. *The middle belongs to the event.* The event, in contrast, has no origin. And can have no conclusion. The effects of events live after them.

This, or something like this, is how the Time of the Event seems to get 'organised out' of arguments about justice. In terms of Sam Weber's (1996) distinction over the place of technology — Heidegger's technics — justice is something that can 'come after' an event and it can be something we orient 'toward'. We cannot stop to let it take place in between.

Within the event, we cannot stop for justice. We bubble in what Durkheim (1912, 1995) has called the 'collective effervescence'. Justice can have no part of the hunt, the chase, the excitement of *going* after. When we get caught up in the hunt — the chase — that *is* where we are. Whatever is taking place is also 'taking' place, shaping and shifting the social materiality in the udder of its effects.

So we are *after* the spoils, not just in the sense of being aimed toward them, but more actively in the sense of 'going after' them (Weber, 1996). Since justice *comes* after, it can never have its place in our *going* after.

Can we say, then, that justice takes up what the event itself cuts out? If so, it is probable that we have a choice. Either justice is to be sorted out before things happen. Perhaps. Or justice can be sorted out afterwards. Possibly. For once time is out of the picture, then so is the event; and the way is open to field a different, and more abstract kinds of argument.

Commentary

Justice is always in suspense to the logic of the event, we wait to see what happens, to see what unfolds. *Justice takes place in the time of the stop.* Yet traditional theorising of justice appears to exclude the Time of the Event. In the paper that follows I try to reverse this effacement of time.

In the one view, then, justice needs to get in ahead of the event, say in the form of some kind of *bidding*. Among other things, earlier forms of bidding involved settling beforehand the proportions for distributing any eventual spoils. Since this kind of justice attempts to settle matters by looking ahead 'toward' the event, before we can know what happens, such bidding always involves a bet. For example, the spoils may be more or less than imagined and the numbers of participants sharing the spoils may either increase or reduce.

Alternatively, justice is seen as something to be settled only after the event. It also involves a sharing of the spoils, a dividing up of these among participants. But where no proportions have been agreed beforehand, this likely involves undertaking an *evaluation* of sorts, possibly settling shares in proportion to the relative 'deserts' of participants. This kind of justice attempts to proceed, so to speak, after the facts. Here knowledge becomes the prerequisite of justice.

It is not, however, the actual events themselves that matter to these kinds of justice, but more and more what I shall call procedural events. Because, as has been said, justice tries to get in before the event. Or after. Each to reckon what is due. Justice in the form of 'due' process works outside of events and outside of life

It is thus not justice, but the *due process* of bidding that comes under the (l)eagle eye. And when events themselves are finally brought to account, it is the *due process* of evaluation that brings in the (ac)counting fingers. Because what animates both processes today is the exchange of money.

PRELIMINARY REMARKS

My concern in this chapter is over justice as an *absence*. As having a necessary absence from group [Theory 1] and as being necessarily absent from the event [Theory 2]. In such a view, justice is ephemeral and is intimately concerned with sociality at the moment of things happening. Conversely, formal justice — the settlement of what is due to individuals as individuals — has an intimate relation with what Derrida has called the logic of presence, the centring of the individuated consciousness.

But I need to start somewhere else. Conventions of interdisciplinary debate dictate speakers offer a range of caveats and apologies for stretching across boundaries in order to talk about things that are normally outside their field of eminence. It is not my habit to follow this convention. Not only do I often find disciplinary boundaries as imaginary as the title of this conference implies, I also usually try to avoid holding myself out as an expert in any particular domain.

If I begin then with apologies and caveats for the simplicities of the above theories, and my lack of definition over what I mean by justice, I hope no-one thinks I am being too ingenuous. For in undertaking this chapter about social justice, I have become genuinely puzzled about why my long interest in organisation — which covering science, literature, technology and culture is about as wide as it gets — has left me so remedially uninformed about justice. Why should this be so? Why, I want to ask, would someone steeped in the study of organisation not also be intimately familiar with contemporary debate about justice?

This is not to suggest I find myself altogether overawed by an engagement with social theories of justice. Far from flashes of insight lighting up my foray into social justice, it is the incommensurability of the approaches that is so striking. Where recent work on organisation has eschewed the approach of universal principles, writing on social justice continues to appear abstract and normative. In what follows I make predictable swipes at the literature, finding much (eg MacIntyre, 1981; 1988) depressingly naïve about organisational and institutional matters. Such books as I have consulted on social justice also seem bizarrely prescriptive in their approach, even when cloaked in the veil of social science (eg Miller, 1999).

So justice will have to wait. Indeed, the theme of my paper is exactly this: waiting. Or rather (and more specifically) what I want to discuss is the injustice that is made possible, and intensified, by endless deferral.

Elsewhere I have explained how contemporary management is not working to speed up decision (as many writers assume), whether on justice or anything else, but is increasingly *withdrawing* from organisation (Munro, 2001). The effect is for institutions to act in ways that stretch the intervals of time between what I shall call *moments* of justice. Between the bidding and the evaluation, between the drawing up of the contract and the time of reckoning, between the setting of expectations and the settlement of accounts lies 'endless deferral'.

Taking up the theme of Theory 2, that justice in the form of due process is always a supplement that attempts to overtake events, I emphasise the potential for individual pleas of injustice to act as a 'stop'. The chapter then explores the potential for management to weaken this 'will to stop' by a process of endless deferral, extending for example the temporal intervals between these moments of justice, bidding and evaluation.

ORGANISATIONAL FOUNDATIONS

The classical presumption is that justice is like the sun. Nothing can flourish without it. Justice is to be made central and it must be built into the foundations. Only thus can society thrive. This, or something like it, is the message of *The Republic.* (Even truth, it has to be added, looks to be ancillary to this demand of Plato's, a seemingly necessary, although hardly sufficient, adjunct to the need for justice.) And it is the kind of message with which I had little difficulty when I first entered university teaching and made it a set text for my Junior Honours class.

All the more strange, then, to find myself waking up to a near vacuum over justice of the field marked off as organisation theory. If it is not too silly to offer myself as a litmus paper, my relative ignorance suggests something of a lacuna in organisation studies. Within Pugh's (1971) influential collection of readings, for example, I have to go back to Fayol (1949) to find a mention and even here the mention is curious. Under the heading of 'equity', the theme he pursues, the following remark can be found:

> Why equity and not justice? Justice is putting into execution established conventions, but conventions cannot foresee everything, they need to be interpreted or their inadequacy supplemented.

So justice will have to wait. As with Weber's stress on legitimation, questions of justice are left, at best, on the backburner.

This kind of displacement, substituting one term in preference to another, is not untypical still today. Justice is rarely treated as a topic in its own right. Although there is some discussion of theories of justice within the burgeoning field of business ethics, Parker's (2000) edited collection is a rare excursion into ethics among contemporary organisation texts. But why ethics and not justice, I want to ask?

It is as if, for most writers on organisation, there are too many other 'virtues', all of which they find more pressing than justice. Efficiency and effectiveness, of course, are the most notorious managerial preoccupations. Why are these values not seen to be subject to questions of justice? Instead, the literature is replete with references to control and authority. Values, all to often, are left as the prerogative of the founder or the leader (eg Schein, 1991).

So is thinking about justice incompatible with the study of organisation? Well, surely not. Much certainly has been written about the organisation *of* justice, a field I have only recently, and partially, become involved myself. But where exactly, one wonders, can we read about the justice of organisation? Have we just assumed organisations are just? That, as rationally organised spaces, justice inhabits them naturally?

Or do writers, for the most part, slavishly accept that institutions are spaces in which justice is *organised* out? For example, a number of organisation researchers, particularly those engaged in what we call critical management, often focus specifically on the abuse of power. As angels of history, they certainly have much to say about 'injustice', particularly when one class of employees benefits from the exploitation of the rest.

What is surprising is when the more critical authors have less to say than might be expected about justice, rather than injustice. What, for example, are the unintended consequences of organisations on the distribution of justice. How does the existence of organisations interrupt and redistribute resources? Or, more specifically, how do organisational devices, such as hierarchy, affect the visibility of deserts?

This virtual evacuation of the topic from organisation studies calls for attention. Here the question arises as to whether matters of justice are being deferred or subsumed? If justice is being deferred, then to which other disciplines does organisation theory owe its reckoning — to political theory or to sociology? Or if justice is being deferred to other kinds of institutions, which are these? And how do the precepts of organisation reconcile with these? Or if justice is being subsumed, which values are seen as more appropriate? Is discussion on justice just to be left implicit ?

JUSTICE AS DEMARCATING OFF OTHER DISCIPLINES

Justice almost seems to mark off the distinction between what is organisation and what is regarded as more properly belonging to the fields of the social or politics. In this way, a silence over justice may actually speak volumes about a kind of regicide by which organisation studies cuts itself off from its forebears in the disciplines of politics and sociology. For example,

Fayol's idea that justice is putting into execution 'established conventions' sits ambiguously between the symbolic order envisaged by Durkheim and the kind of bureaucracy that Weber had in mind.

For Durkheim, the symbolic order is built around representations of what is sacred to group. These are the aspects of life that are 'set apart and forbidden' from the profane and have a virulent energy 'always on the point of escaping the places they occupy and invading all that passes within their reach' (1912, 1995: 322). Shilling (2002) argues, for example, that this is how the sacred is able to stimulate such an intense 'collective effervescence' on those who experience its contents: the experience of the sacred strengthens individual minds and actions and individuals are revitalised by the heightening of emotion (Durkheim, 1912, 1995: 353).

By contrast, in thinking out formal aspects of organisation, Weber relied on a concept of 'formal justice'. Although he saw the 'abstract character' of this as infringing upon the ideals of 'substantive justice', he also felt it 'diminished the dependency of the individual upon the grace and power of the authorities' (1978: II 812). Paradoxically, at least to those who conflate bureaucracy with mechanistic authority, Weber saw formal justice as capable of 'opening up individual opportunities and liberating capacities' (813).

This theme of emancipation has been taken up most forcibly by Habermas. Unfortunately, Habermas (1970) all but abandons organisational perspectives in favour of his 'ideal speech conditions', an idea that leans heavily upon the ideal of a co-presence of three types of social action (instrumental, strategic and communicative) that he derives from Weber (1978). This has tended to make his emphasis on justice heavily normative and weakened its empirical application:

> As must be evident, were the stakes to be pitched like this, they might well be free of moral relativism but they would almost be entirely bereft of empirical application in a systematically distorted world, that is one in which real interests cannot be grasped. (Clegg, 1989: 94)

The point is not to ask what people would do if they knew what their 'real interests' were. The crux of the matter is to recognise, contra Connolly (1972), that we never can experience the consequences of our 'choices'. This is not only to argue, as I already have suggested, that consequences do not stop with events, but live after them. It is also to recognise, in the way Lukes (1974) has more or less stressed, that many, perhaps most, of our decisions are prefigured, or manipulated.

Most recently, this position has been taken up by Bauman (1989), who identifies administrative systems as being one of the conditions of possibility for the holocaust. In focusing on questionable assumptions about the historic specificity of persons, du Gay's (2000) defence of bureaucracy thus misses completely the force of Bauman's analysis. Bauman is focused not at all on the putative ethics of bureaucracy (in its attempts to avoid patronage and overcome corruption), but rather on the 'distance' created between decisions and their moral effects.

The extent of this manipulation is never more prevalent when it is accepted that all aspects of justice are dominated by our living in institutions. As I have supplanted Bauman's (1991) argument elsewhere (Munro, 1998), those who collect the names of the Jews can be kept in ignorance from those who have the job of putting them of the trains. So, too, neither group may know about the existence of the camps. But, regardless of any lack of knowledge of consequences, the moral force *as an employee of the institution* is still to collect the names, or put people on trains.

OPENING PANDORA'S BOX

Bauman's answer is to mark the social as immoral. Abandoning institutions as 'administrative' mechanisms, he wants instead to have recourse to the integrity of the individual in responding to what he calls, after Levinas, 'the face'. But to mark the individual as the site of justice, as Kant did, is to open Pandora's box. It is to return justice from the rivers of sociality to the swamp of emotions. (Reminding us that justice is not the only matter expulsed from organisation theories, emotions are also effaced in any rational-functionalist account).

Kant viewed emotions as an impediment to self-determining actions. As Shilling (2002) notes, his demand was for each individual to transcend their emotions and desires and comply with the universal categorical imperatives. But what he failed to see was that rationality is itself a *social* emotion. In place of the bond, there are now negotiations, differences to be observed, especially differences between those that a moment before had constituted the justice of 'just us'.

The context of injustice — for it is important to remember that it is injustice, not justice that is usually being thought — thus becomes more that of a grid, particularly the kind of grid in which individuals instantly have rights. And once within the grid of individuals, we ask a lot. Our sense of injustice becomes sharp. Respect is needed, not mutual regard; dignity must be given and granted. There are procedures and there is due process. Only the law may be appealed to. Thus the one who asks for justice must go outside group. She or he stands *as* an individual. Instead of a bond, in which self *and* Other meld, there are now ropes that bind each to her or his post.

At this point, the individual can go beyond just asking for justice. Once she or he can effectively also determine the kind of justice being meted out, we are into a new organisational territory in which all matters are at stake. Instructions can no longer be issued as orders, but must be given as a request; the tone of the request must be appropriate to the dignity of the other with no hints of condescension. Even the kind of work allocated must be commensurate with the standing of the person if a lawsuit of constructive dismissal is to be avoided.

MONEY AS SETTING THE FORMAL STRUCTURE

It is the contribution of Adam Smith to have most strongly challenged the presumption of building justice in with the foundations. As he pointed out, the prospect of the creation of greater wealth can draw people together and make them co-operate.

Here is the argument. Provided the contract I enter benefits me more than the scheme I was already in, it pays me to transfer. I would be a fool to settle for 50 per cent of £100, when in the same period I could get 10 per cent of £600. But what sort of justice would it be that forced me to go for equal shares and leave me worse off?

Seemingly, there need be no justice, merely gain. No doubt to counteract such ideas, Miller (1999) raises the distinction between justice and self-interest and suggests that in 'order to draw a line between self-interest and justice, we need a normative theory to do so'. (44). He wants: 'to show why social scientific and philosophical studies of justice are necessarily interdependent' by arguing that 'empirical studies of justice must rely upon a normative theory of justice in order to distinguish those beliefs and activities that are guided by justice from those that are not (43).

Yet this insistence on normative theory is to overlook the effects of a money economy that treats everything in terms of exchange value. As Simmel notes in his essay on the Metropolis, a 'rationally calculated economic egoism' (1971: 327) replaces an earlier reliance on gratitude and loyalty. The heady stimulation of city life is muted by our becoming blasé. An 'alienated emotion of distance, remoteness, and indifference' (Barbalet, 1998: 55) in turn effects a reduction of one's own worth and that of others.

And yet it is our 'own worth' that, perversely, seems to be becoming paramount. Everything today insists on a reckoning up in *individual* terms. Nothing counts here like money, the perfect medium of disaggregation (cf Munro, 1998). Our contribution to group, the ineffable of what we do together during the event, all this becomes 'just water under a bridge'.

INSTITUTIONS AS PLAYERS

Yet no-one should argue that ours really is a society of individuals. Individuated we may be, but this is also an effect of the kind of institutions we inhabit today. The busier we are with our individuality, it seems to me, the more likely we are to be pawns in a larger power play. It is institutions who are players, not individuals, albeit some like Jacques Derrida balloon to occupy the simulacra of individuality.

Individuals can never frame what is justice; all each can do is focus on injustice, by drawing attention to their plight *as* individuals. Lyotard's insistence on a multiplicity of justices should be seen in this light. He is not seeking to set the many against the one, having merely re-discovered the idea that a centred justice is asymmetrical in its effects. Lyotard's insight is to see just how many different sets of common rules there are; and, then, notice a struggle among these 'multiple language games' as institutions begin to merge and tumble together (Lyotard & Thebaud 1985). His is not a post-modern 'anything goes' plea for individualism; otherwise he could throw out the idea of games altogether. [But of course he cannot; since he is following Wittgenstein in the idea of language games, he is also caught in the conviction that there is no such thing as a private language].

And it is exactly the times and spaces *between* the language games that opens up the time/spaces and space/times of injustice. Between the formal rules for bidding and the informal, tacit abandonment of justice, between the time-tube of communality and the formal processes of evaluation and review, these are the spaces that are open to manipulation.

This agenda is much too large to make much inroad within the scope of a single paper and, in the closing sections, I can but hint at what might be at stake here. For this reason I shall focus on the notion of deferral in order to bring out how institutions have reintroduced the venture, or 'project', as a device within which to create a non-institutional space; a time/space that is to say in which ethos can reign and Weber's concept of 'formal justice' is suspended.

THE JUSTICE OF THE VENTURE

An oddity of the accounting historian's lore is the notion of the *venture*, typically illustrated by the voyage of a ship. Essentially a voyage in the early modern period might last only some months, but often some lasted several years or more. Thus the calculation of profit for the venture differed from the contemporary conception of 'periodic income', the profit that is estimated annually, if not quarterly.

As a one-off measurement, total profit for the venture could be ascertained only after the voyage — usually by the simple device of setting off all recorded cash disbursements, including the hire of the ship and crew, against the eventual revenue derived from the sale of the cargo. In contrast to the calculation of periodic income, entries in the ledger would be largely cash driven — with little recourse to the multiplicities of estimation involved in accrual accounting.

In such a venture there would be two moments for justice. One moment before the ship sailed, when terms for joining the venture would be settled; and again, afterwards, when the venture itself was being wound up. Either moment could itself involve a long drawn out process, but these can be kept distinct from the event of the voyage itself. Withdrawing during the actual voyage might entail extra heavy penalties, such as charges of desertion or losing any rights to the eventual spoils.

In the context of modern-day projects, such as the building of a large bridge or motorway, the convention of making annual estimates of profit can be understood as interrupting this suspension of justice. Indeed, the notion of profit (periodic income) is held to *speed up* due processes; by, say, allowing earlier distributions of income without waiting for a final reckoning. Likewise annual appraisals can be understood to anticipate deserts and thus speed up the potential for justice, without waiting for an actual post to become empty before promotion can take place.

REINTRODUCTION OF VENTURE AS PROJECT

The irruption of the project into the formal running of institutions, where previously it was kept invisible, is often presented as an attempt to devolve responsibility and so decentralise authority and empower expertise. Rather spuriously, the advent of project management is presumed to facilitate a greater degree of decentralisation of decision-making by utilising a management technology in which progress is made visible and accountable to senior managers.

In these terms, the project would seem to offer itself as a paradigm example of the attempt by management to speed up decision-making. However, the kind of speed involved here usually involves the creation of semi-autonomous entities within the institution. The advantage is that these offer themselves as sub-units within which formal justice is suspended. Those involved in the project, by common consent, begin to form a kind of group solidarity that lets them be, and act, on their own.

Thus projects lend themselves to a Janus like existence in which employees can enjoy the sense of 'going after' something in the atmosphere of a hunt or chase while senior managers continue to enjoy a sense of being 'in control' (Munro, 1999a). Project leaders gain a sense of 'governing' their province at the same time as the empire itself expands. The result is the creation of what might be called time-tubes, in which projects gather their own momentum, often tacitly making their 'own' decisions, unimpeded by the scrutiny of a centralised bureaucratic machine.

Employees sometimes report themselves as being apprehensive of being transferred into a project, particularly when they fear 'disappearing' both from the sociality and the due process of the unit they are already in. That is they are no longer 'visible' to their normal colleagues in ways that protect them from isolation and exclusion on their eventual return. In short, they can lose 'membership' of their main group.

Employees also worry about their reputation being caught up in a more general project failure. There is a *Bund* effect (cf Hetherington, 1994) in which they may be incited to work outside the safety of their expert field. The sacrifices they are expected to make are greater in terms of giving up family time, or other projects more oriented to the self, in order to help meet deadlines.

BELATED EVALUATION

A project I helped to run on strategic values in a large, prestigious organisation (Munro, 1992) illustrates several aspects of this suspension of justice. I should stress this is a retrospective view, since any frustration I experienced could be attributed at the time to the novelty of the experiment as well as to my own political shortcomings and opposition to senior management agendas such as budgeting.

The setting up of the project emerged out the research I had been conducting on one of the operating divisions for about a year. The aim was to test out, with the help of an internal researcher appointed by top management, the general impact from introducing a strategic value I had devised. In the light of earlier findings about conflicting priorities (the managers own view) and a tendency for managers to be inward-looking (my critique), the Head of Division was keen to be doing something novel and we had the support of nearly all the middle managers involved.

Researchers, along with most employees, have become ennured to the practice of change managers talking up success and playing down failure and we were careful ourselves to avoid this pitfall. However, by anybody's standards the project was a runaway success, bringing forth a huge response in suggestions from staff and resulting in a large number of significant changes to procedures and processes. Much later, after I left the organisation having forestalled the advent of budgeting for almost five years, management operationalised the strategic value approach across the whole company.

At the time, however, top management deferred giving the project their full affirmation. While the project was generally treated as successful by managers and employees, the senior executive as a body was not yet ready to announce the experiment a complete success and reservations remained in the air. In particular, several senior managers wanted proof over its effectiveness as a cost reduction process (not one of the original aims) and others pressed me to come up with a single, key measure of effectiveness (also thus missing the point of the exercise).

The point I want to make here is that this delay had consequences for the distribution of justice. Several junior and middle managers had given the project their unqualified support and enthusiasm. The delay, and uncertainty generated by senior managers, allowed these people to be overlooked in terms of recognition to say nothing of rewards. By the time senior managers were ready to commit themselves, the time to acknowledge good work has passed and several of the 'change agents' had already been moved to rather mundane posts that hardly reflected their recently demonstrated capabilities.

Perhaps, too, the delay obviated something of even greater importance. When I first turned up to conduct my research, senior managers were quite scathing about the quality of much of their middle management and, beneath a traditional patronage, probably thought of the majority of staff as little more than 'hands'. The success of the project on strategic values really put the lie to this. It suggested that what employees and middle managers alike had lacked were 'permissions' for doing things and that the strategic values project was successful largely because it galvanised a much frustrated energy and intelligence.

What the delay engineered, possibly unwittingly, was a refusal to enable a more genuine form of 'empowerment' and a return to top down management control. The fruits of the project did not spread across the company as an 'effervescence' of energy and emotion, as it had the potential to do. Instead, it was 'rolled out' as part of an increasing senior management commitment to quality and change management. The consequence has been that senior management is able to take full credit for all the fruits of the project and keep their doubts about the quality and ability of their staff and middle managers.

SLOWING DOWN JUSTICE/ GATHERING AND DISPERSAL

Theories of justice have been elaborated around a naïve understanding of institutional power. Specifically, a number of relations between time and power have been overlooked, including the motility of technologies to a connection/ disconnection by managers (Munro, 1999b). Drawing on technologies of managing, the withdrawal of managers from the scene of action in organisation is helping to stretch the intervals between moments of justice into an 'endless deferral'.

Often the contemporary exercise of power depends more on deferral than decision. Without claiming originality, I have for some time defined hierarchy as a social process in which credit is accumulated upwards and blame gets divested downwards (Munro, 1993; 1995). Whereas, more typically, hierarchy is viewed as a necessary organising and co-ordinating device in which the broad, difficult decisions are made at the top leaving others free to make the more mundane, detailed decisions below.

The point of my definition is to point to some social consequences, unintended or not, which flow from the continued existence of hierarchy. The aim is to up-set too narrow a reliance on what can be called the production view of organisation. Emphasis on the production of organisation creates a kind of myopia in which it is the 'rational' functions that serve to give focus. Typically these are the 'system' level justifications.

The problem with the production view, however, is not simply that it is overly functional in its orientation, as many sociologists have claimed. It is as much that only a limited *range* of functions are captured within the production view. A production perspective overlooks aspects taken up in what has been called the consumption view (Munro, 1996; see also Douglas & Isherwood, 1980). Interest here accumulates around how social processes become consumed once these are instituted in taken-for-granted forms.

Within the consumption view, the conception of decision-making is a chimera. For the most part, things happen and people usually go along with matters 'to see where they lead'. Although 'decision-taking' forms an important function in Euro-American organisations, this is usually staged as a ritual in which people perform illocutionary acts, such as the word 'I do' in a marriage ceremony (cf Austin, 1962).

The performative aspects of such acts are largely that of 'stock taking', a moment in which a stop can be called. In line with Turner's (1967) injunction, these ceremonial acts are largely 'affirmative'. Although transformative effects may begin to flow from such moments, it is likely that much of the institution has already 'factored in' the change well ahead of any announcement being made.

This is not to suggest that decisions, as ceremonial acts, do not constitute moments of justice. For I think it could well freshen up our thinking about structure and agency to start considering decisions exactly in these terms; not just as a cognition of events that are about to take place, but as the moment within which consequences are assumed to be frozen — as the 'just ice'. *Just-ice takes place in the time of the stop.*

Decisions are a moment of stock-taking, moments for viewing consequences. They are thus vital and senior managers here play a vital role in checking and questioning. But let us — in organisation studies at least — stop confusing due process with events and put a stop to conflating management with organising.

INJUSTICE AND THE *LESS* EXCLUDED

Looking back, it seems some of my research, if obliquely, has focused on justice. In part my concerns over the nature of justice reflect my commitment to ethnography and a disengagement from normative, universalising approaches. The close focus of my work also reflects, I think, my nose — and that of others involved in the critical movement — for *injustice*. This may be in marked contrast, as I have noted, to mainstream organisational approaches, from which justice can be said to have been all but expulsed.

Yet the concerns pressed in this chapter hardly marry either with the kinds of abstract justice extolled by contemporary political and moral theory. To end on the note of exploitation, even if nuanced by the chapter's emphasis on endless deferral, fulfils my earlier contention that organisation speaks more about injustice than justice. This said, I want to close on injustice by pressing a finer discrimination. Yes, injustice takes place within the very production of organisation, in the design of procedures and in the building up of processes. But these formal matters, as others have indicated, are usually aimed at reducing, or restricting, the realm of *in*justice.

The traditional idea is that, through the institution of *common* rules, the potential devastation of opening up a Pandora's box of emotions can be avoided. Interest in injustice focuses therefore either on the excluded, those who fail to be included as members, or on those who get excluded from the gains and are thus exploited as a class. Yet, as the example of projects indicates, this is not the only alternative. The sacrifice of each member of a pseudo-community is not only in giving up their 'rights' to an individualistic, ego-centred justice.

Between the bidding and the evaluation, there is the Time of the Event. Once the project gets started, the rush is on; and there is no stopping, or asking to get out. We are caught up together within a fold, a 'time-tube' inside which justice is suspended. It's all hands to the pump. So there is no time for dignity, no time for formalities and no time for custom. And there is no space for insisting on one's usual role or staying within the limits of one's expertise.

In the delirium of the chase or what has been called the heat of battle, the potential for injustice is built *into* the event. Everyone expects the rough with the smooth, but as long as the effervescence is high, no-one is expected to call a stop and demand justice. Those who do, the whistleblowers of the local, can expect to receive 'rough justice' from their colleagues, an expulsion from 'membership' of the group and possibly negative sanctions on friendship or collegial ties.

At their best, then, projects offer a kind of romantic, quasi-communitarian space in which 'formalities' and other kinds of justice are suspended. At their worst, a project can become a kangaroo court in which blame is forever being ascribed and credit denied. The rewards therefore are intrinsic and this may be why people are drawn in to projects, despite the fact that their organisation is open to much exploitation.

All this is relatively well known to the more critical researcher. The focus of this paper, however, is to edge towards paying more attention to the kind of injustice that occurs for the *less excluded*, for those increasingly positioned being *between* the formal and the informal. Here my perspective on projects has been somewhat unusual. Rather than stress the usual distribution of injustice, which I take to be on-going, I have focussed on the way in which evaluation is being increasingly deferred.

The new danger, if this is not melodramatic to say so, is to be suspended *between* the ethics and the ethos. By senior managers suspending the moment of evaluation into a process of endless deferral, justice can be short-changed and the benefits and profits reaped elsewhere. The fruits of the project are transported elsewhere in the shape of patents and other forms of knowledge and expertise, or in the form of new products or new processes.

CONCLUSION

This chapter has sought to open up debate on justice by drawing attention to certain, usually implicit, organisational assumptions that underpin a predilection over injustice. The argument builds on my observation of the *withdrawal* of management from organisation. Specifically, I argue hierarchy is no longer, if it ever was, an arrangement in which difficult decisions are made at the top and whereby more mundane, everyday routines are practised below.

Instead of instruction being issued in the image of a command and control model, managers rely on hierarchy being a device for accumulating credit upwards and divesting blame downwards. In such circumstances, particularly where senior managers act as spokespersons for outside interests, such as shareholders or government, it is arguable management has lost any 'superior' right to adjudicate over the 'needs' of the institution.

Indeed, it is the argument here that senior managers often no longer do attempt so to adjudicate, but instead defer and even 'suspend' moments of justice. Baldly, and one wants to say increasingly, their job seems to be as much one of *deferring* on calls for justice and so prevent the 'stop'. Where this is so, exploitation may centre less around the excluded, where most interest has centred, and more around those who are caught 'waiting'.

A question also arises is whether the process of democratisation — the individuation of liberty — has now begun to erode the ethos of institutions to their detriment. As individuals, we play along with projects because we see their potential to raise our visibility and distribute new gains. But frequently no individual actually gains, since management inevitably uses the call of sacrifice to further its own, individuated ends.

REFERENCES

Austin, J 1962. *How to Do Things with Words*. Oxford: Oxford University Press.
Barbalet, J 1998. *Emotion, Social Theory and Social Structure: a Macrosociological Approach*. Cambridge: Cambridge University Press.
Bauman, Zygmunt 1989. *Modernity and the Holocaust*. Cambridge: Polity Press.

Bauman, Zygmunt 1991. 'The Social Manipulation of Morality: Moralising Actors, Adiaphorizing Action'. *Theory, Culture & Society*, 8: 137–51.

Clegg, S 1989. *Frameworks of Power*. London: Sage.

Connolly, WE 1972. 'On "Interests" in Politics', *Politics & Society*, 2: 459–77.

Derrida, Jacques 1982. *Margins of Philosophy*, translated by A Bass. Hemel Hempstead: Harvester Press.

Douglas, Mary 1987. *How Institutions Think*. London: Routledge & Kegan Paul.

Douglas, M and Isherwood, B 1980. *The World of Goods: Towards an Anthropology of Consumption*. Harmondsworth: Penguin.

du Gay, Paul 2000. *In Praise of Bureaucracy: Weber, Organization, Ethics*. London: Sage.

Durkheim, Emile 1995. *The Elementary Forms of Religious Life*, translated by K E Fields. New York: Free Press. Originally published 1912.

Fayol, Henri 1971. 'General Principles of Management'. In *Organization Theory: Selected Readings*, edited by D S Pugh. Harmondsworth: Penguin. Originally published 1949.

Habermas, Juergen 1970. 'Toward a Theory of Communicative Competence', *Inquiry*, 13: 360–75.

Hetherington, Kevin 1994. 'The Contemporary Significance of Schmalenbach's Concept of the Bund', *The Sociological Review*, 42: 1–25.

Lukes, Steven 1974. *Power: A Radical View*. London: Macmillan.

Lyotard, J-F and Thebaud, J L 1985. *Just Gaming*, translated by W Godzich. Minneapolis: University of Minnesota Press.

MacIntyre, Alistair 1981. *After Virtue*. London: Duckworth.

MacIntyre, Alistair 1988. *Whose Justice? Which Rationality?* London: Duckworth.

Miller, D (1999) *Principles of Social Justice*. Cambridge, Mass: Harvard University Press.

Munro, Rolland 1992. 'Enabling Participative Change: The Impact of Strategic Value'. *International Studies in Management and Organization* 21: 52–65.

Munro, Rolland 1996. 'A Consumption View of Self: Extension, Exchange and Identity'. In *Consumption Matters*, edited by S Edgell, A Warde and K Hetherington, Sociological Review Monograph: 248–73. Oxford: Blackwell.

Munro, Rolland 1999. 'The Cultural Performance of Control', *Organization Studies*, Vol 20, No 4, 1999, pp. 619–39.

Parker, Martin (ed) 1998. *The Ethics of Organization*. London: Sage.

Pugh, D S 1971. *Organization Theory: Selected Readings*. Harmondsworth: Penguin.

Schein, E H 1991. *Orgnizational Culture and Leadership: A Dynamic View*. San Francisco: Jossey-Bass.

Shilling, C 2002. 'The Two Traditions in the Sociology of Emotions'. In *The Sociology of Emotions*, edited by J Barbalet. Sociological Review Monograph. Oxford: Blackwell.

Simmel, Georg 1971. 'The Metropolis'. In *Georg Simmel: On Individuality and Social Forms*, edited by D N Levine. Chicago: University of Chicago Press.

Turner, V 1967. *The Forest of Symbols: Aspects of Ndembu Ritual*. Ithaca, NY: Cornell University Press.

Weber, Max 1978. *Economy and Society, 2 volumes*. Los Angeles: University of California Press.

Weber, Samuel 1996. *Mass Mediauras*. Stanford: Stanford University Press.

4

Boundaries of Exclusions Past: The Memory of Waste

ANDREAS PHILIPPOPOULOS-MIHALOPOULOS

THE DIVISIONARY ROLE of boundaries in autopoiesis has often been seen as an indication of a positivist, exclusionary and discriminatory theory. Admittedly, there is little point in denying the decisive role that boundaries have in the theory. The system (the self) is differentiated from the environment (alter) with the help of a boundary. What lies this side of the boundary is known, accessible, comprehensible. What lies that side of the boundary is generally invisible to the system. The system recognises only what constitutes itself. While this is a basically accurate description of autopoietic identity, it remains schematic and fails to capture the intricacies of the theory. In what follows, I attempt to deal with the concept of autopoietic boundaries and their potential for contingent crossings. Keeping to the transdisciplinarity of both autopoiesis and the concept of boundaries, I engage in a discussion of geographical and juridical issues with an aim to show that autopoiesis is capable of describing its boundaries as permeable. To this effect, I am attempting an autopoietic description of the common concept of waste as it appears in the urban environment and in the legal system. Before that, an epigrammatic exposition of the general traits of autopoietic theory for familiarisation purposes will be presented. Particular emphasis throughout the discussion will be given to the temporal dimension of autopoietic structures. The reason for such a viewpoint is the subject matter of the essay, which deals with the location of waste in the past of its producer.

Locating waste in the past means that waste cannot be dealt with except as a past value. But 'dealing', which is an operation of the present, cannot occur in the past. The process of dealing with waste is always subject to the undulation of displacement and deferral. The same of course applies to the more general notion of the 'past'. The past is not present. The use of the present tense ('is') when referring to the past is a construction that attests to the constructed nature of the past itself. The past cannot 'be' in the present without being present. If the past is remembered, relived or re-enacted, it is present. If the past is forgotten, it *was* past — it no longer *is*. Its elusiveness is reinforced by its monadic nature: the past is always of a system and can never be collective — and by *system* here I mean the autopoietic formation of a system as a unit that forms its identity through differentiation from its environment.[1] If the past is collective, it is a multiple present construction, or a construction of the present, and never of the past. The past cannot be constructed as past — only as present. And that construction would, once again, be a construction of a system, which couples and co-evolves with other systemic constructions that can be found in the system's environment. The problem with the past, however, is not that it is a construction — there is nothing unique to this. The problem is that the past of a system was only the past of the particular system and no system has access to it, not even the system whose past it was, for the simple reason that a system cannot have access to its environment, only to itself. The fact that the past *is* not and can never *be* means that the system cannot access it. The system expels its past to its systemic environment and refuses to itself any accessibility to it. The expelled past may become part of other systems, but not as their past but as their present.[2] As far as the system is concerned, its past is invisible. Except for the past that *is*, namely the remembered past (which is already present). This remains part of the system and forms the memory of the system, which, in its turn, facilitates systemic cognition.

The part of the past that *is* (memory), is retained in the system in the form of self-observation: the system observes itself and forms its identity. The part of the past that *was* (forgotten), lies in the systemic environment and its relevance for the system depends entirely on whether the system will select it as relevant or not. There is little else that links the two except for the availability of the phenomenological horizon. In fact, the discarded past stands little chance of being reselected by the system because it has been expelled from the system as unnecessary, inoperative, burdensome, obsolete: in short, waste. In this context, waste goes beyond the non-selected and includes a reference to future avoidance. Waste becomes risk. Waste passes in the atemporality of the systemic environment because this is a normal operation of the system. To discard is part of the system's becoming. Not all of the already selected and used is waste — some is retained in the form of memory — but what is deemed to be waste is already out there, a cleared cache from the system's capacity.

Thus, waste will be dealt with from the point of view of memory. Waste is treated here as the rejected value of a system, but in its potential as a reselectable ('recycled') value. In that sense, waste appears both as unnecessary, rejected and therefore forgotten, and as potentially useful value that can be 'remembered' by the system once the latter has rejected it. This means that waste can be remembered only once it has been forgotten. The temporal dimension brings together the two concepts of memory and waste through an inversion of the forgotten that finds its expression in what will be later (section IV) referred to as the *memory of forgetting*.

In this essay, waste will be crossing boundaries in two ways: first, in spatial terms as the urban waste and its possibility of being recycled, thereby

[1] Maturana and Varela, 1972, 1987; Luhmann, 1995.
[2] Since systemic operations always take place in the present: Luhmann, 1995.

re-entering the urban system. Second, as law's waste, or else the non-selected part of a legal decision, which has been discarded to the systemic environment as obsolete. In both cases, the systems attempt to forget the discarded by consigning it to the environment, thereby alienating it temporally and spatially. While this is a necessary operation of the system's being, I suggest that both systems are too keen to discard the 'unusable' with a consequent loss of valuable cognitive opportunities. The boundary between the system and its environment is crossed ambidirectionally, with the result that the environment claims an operative position in the definition of the system by dint of cognition, memory, and the process of becoming. The epistemological aim of this essay is to show how autopoiesis, a seemingly divisive and exclusionary theory, contains the necessary tools for an inclusion of alter in the description of the self. However, such a description will be conducted necessarily and exclusively in the idiom of the self, for a system cannot describe anything but itself. Alter here is represented by waste. The self is the city and the law. The first has been chosen as a tangible spatial analogy to the overproduction of legal waste, in the hope that the application of the abstract concepts of autopoiesis onto the urban system prepares the reader for the consequent application of the same onto the legal system. In both cases, the past that has been excluded returns to haunt the system in a cognitively instructive way. This discussion presupposes an exposition of some basic autopoietic concepts as defined in biological autopoiesis by Maturana and Varela, and also in the social interpretation of autopoiesis by Niklas Luhmann. These concepts will be employed in an attempt to imagine a differentiated use of boundaries, one that would allow alterity to cross and re-enter and define itself according to the axis of the self.

I AUTOPOIETIC OPENNESS

Autopoiesis describes the world in terms of systems.[3] An autopoietic system has been defined by the fathers of biological autopoiesis as a system that reproduces itself, all its constituent elements, and even the processes of its reproduction.[4] The immediate consequence of such circularity is that a system recognises no *telos*. There is no inherent purpose in the system except for its own existence. An autopoietic system exists and the product of its existence is itself: in autopoiesis being is becoming,[5] whereby the tautology between the given of existence and the beyond of creation constitute the schizophrenia of the autopoietic paradox.

Although concerned with systems, autopoiesis differs from general systems theory, since here the focus is not the relation 'parts-whole' but that of a

[3] The word 'autopoiesis' — from the Greek words 'auto', which means 'self', and 'poiesis', which means 'creation' — has been coined by Maturana to describe the process of self-production which is the main characteristic of autopoietic systems.
[4] Maturana and Varela, 1987.
[5] *Ibid.*

system to its environment. An autopoietic system comes into being, constructs its unity and acquires its identity via a differentiation from its environment: everything that is not system will *perforce* be environment. The differentiation between system and environment is mainly achieved through a binary code which contains a positive and a negative value — eg, for the legal system it would be 'lawful/unlawful'.[6] The binary code ensures the insulation of the system because it functions like a switch situated on the borders of the system. The criterion is not whether the specific notion is lawful or unlawful: at this stage of 'waiting' outside the system's boundaries there can be no judgement on the lawfulness or unlawfulness of the notion in question. If, however, the question whether a concept is lawful or unlawful can be raised with reference to a particular concept, then the concept in question will belong to the legal system. The binary code is the bastion of the system's autopoiesis that safeguards the distinction between system and environment, offering at the same time the flexibility of fluctuation between the positive and the negative value. The flexibility of coding is further enhanced in two ways. Firstly, the communication between the two values is allowed in the sense that something can be easily converted from lawful to unlawful and vice versa: in principle, there is no obstacle in a concept being resemiologised as lawful when earlier has been considered unlawful.[7] Secondly, as the later Luhmann admits, the code is only one of a 'galaxy of distinctions' employed bythe the autopoietic organisation.[8] Coding is coloured by what Luhmann calls *programming*, or else the procedural tool that guides the allocation of the values lawful/unlawful in specific factual situations.[9] The combination of code and programme make the legal system 'an open-ended, ongoing concern structurally requiring itself to decide how to allocate its positive or negative value.'[10]

Differentiation is the basis of the existence of any system: it is through differentiation (from a system's environment — from other systems) that a system strengthens its *selectivity* and constructs its identity.[11] Selectivity refers to the ability of a system to reduce the possibilities that originate in its environment. Axiomatically, however, the environment is always more complex than the system, and a system's selectivity aims to reduce this complexity — namely the infinite possibilities that an environment represents.[12] Through selectivity a system deals with environmental complexity and reduces it to a manageable systemic complexity, thereby differentiating itself from its environment and, hence, acquiring its identity.

[6] Luhmann, 1989. Luhmann obliges the reader by repeating and refining the general premises of autopoiesis in nearly every book he writes, making it easy to understand the theory whether approached from sociology, law, economics and so on.
[7] Luhmann, 1989b: 36–43.
[8] Luhmann, 1993: 26.
[9] *Ibid* and Luhmann, 1998.
[10] Luhmann, 1992: 1428.
[11] Luhmann, 1982: 213.
[12] Luhmann, 1982: 70.

In autopoiesis, the schism of identity formation is exemplified in its most graphic, not only through the *sine qua non* condition of the system's *distinction* from its environment, but also because of the exercise of systemic selectivity, which, for the system is an essay in *contingency*. The reduction of complexity — a precondition for the system's identity — entails a selection that includes a distinction: when one chooses A over B to Z, one makes a binary selection. Momentarily, the non-selected side of the distinction is inertisized. It returns to the scene of selections only after the previous distinction has been fixed and a need for another distinction has arisen. The identity of the system is the offspring of the initial selection, for a system is nothing less than the 'interruption of continuity in the spectrum of the possible.'[13] An evolutionary anomaly? Even better: a happenstance or a structurally predetermined serendipity.

Through selectivity, the system reinforces its closure:[14] according to Luhmann, all social formations — just like biological entities — are closed systems. Thus, the legal system, just as the political, economic, religious systems, whose organisation is analogous to the organisation of the living cell, are closed systems with no input/output with their environment. Instead, the system develops internally through the reflexive mechanism of applying a process to itself. In the legal system, for example, a norm generates identical norms in the manner of evolutionary DNA code. By the replication of the procedure, the system continues to create norms based on its previous norms, and even creates norms on how to create norms. However, such internal evolution guaranteed by the autopoietic boundary between system and environment does not equate normative stagnation. Indeed, autopoiesis — eternally replicating Edgar Morin's oft-citedoft-cited adage 'the open rests on the closed'[15] — likes to think of closed systems as open. A system is closed in its operations but open cognitively to other systems. This openness is a necessary precondition for the system's evolution, without which the system would not be able to learn. Perhaps the most prominent manifestation of such openness is what Luhmann after Maturana and Varela calls *structural coupling*. In the introduction to *Autopoiesis and Cognition*, Beer analyses briefly how structural coupling comes about:

> [system] and environment operate as independent systems that, by triggering in each other a structural change, select in each other a structural change.[16]

[13] Luhmann, 1982: 34.5.
[14] Closure and normative isolation of the system from its environment is arguably the main thorn in Luhmann's theory, and one that has been misinterpreted as often as it has been fiercely criticised. SeClosure and normative isolation of the system from its environment is arguably the main thorn in Luhmann's theory, and one that has been misinterpreted as often as it has been fiercely criticised. See Beck, 1994; Munch, 1992; Bankowski, 1996; Weisberg, 1992; Wolfe, 1992; Lyotard, 1984; Norrie, 1993; Cotterrell, 1993; Lempert, 1988; counterarguments can be found in Luhmann, 1993; Weisberg, 1992; Teubner, 1993; King, 1993, 2001; Paterson, 1996; Murphy 1984, 1994.
[15] Morin, 1986: 203.
[16] Maturana and Varela, 1972: xix. Structural coupling has been considered the demise of autopoiesis (see Munch, 1992), largely interpreted as a reaction to the mounting pressure

Of course, nothing can happen in the system that the system cannot accommodate through its binary code. In a sense, structural change is akin to systemic fate: what is to be done will be done and nothing else could have been done considering the specific parameters, although the probabilities — what Luhmann after Husserl calls *horizon* — are infinite and always present. The development of a system takes place through recursive distinctions, and the application of distinctions onto distinctions. Take the example of a meteorological system, where at any given moment only one phenomenon occurs out of a chaotic array of probabilities, and this phenomenon holds well until the next given moment where a new need for a new selection occurs. At that point, the horizon of probabilities reappears and offers its tempting contingencies for selection and a new selection is erected on the basis of the previous selection. Exactly like a meteorological system, an autopoietic system exists and evolves (is and becomes) through continuous selections that reinforce its identity and enable it to undulate its boundaries to include more or less of the probabilities offered by its environment. Still, the horizon of probabilities remains as complex and infinite as the system's environment. Even the existence of what Maturana and Varela call *cognitive domain*, which is defined as that part of a system's horizon whose irritations the system receives and accordingly evolves cognitively,[17] cannot offer any conclusive predictability of the system's operations. The only avenue available for prediction is the one opened by the inherent predictability of *structural coupling*, as it is based on the historically established and verifiable co-evolution of two systems.

Structural coupling takes place through the operation of *observation*. In the void of an unintelligible environment, a system 'senses' the rotation of other systems by observing, not them but itself. This is the schematic difference between observation and *self-observation*: while superficially one talks about observation between systems, in autopoietic reality all observation is self-observation.[18] Observation, in its internalised form, is the only avenue of contact a system has with other systems. So, one would think that observation of a system by another system is a form of 'openness' to its environment. But no! Observation is simply another way of increasing selectivity and therefore closure: '[t]he states of the system are exclusively determined by its own operations'[19] and any allowance to environmental influences is strictly limited to what Luhmann calls *environmental perturbations*. Despite

coming from criticisms on the incomprehensibility of closure. The fact remains, however, that structural coupling is not a manoeuvre determined by need but a notion originating in the biological version of autopoiesis.

[17] Maturana and Varela, 1972; 'Cognitive domain' brings to mind Bourdieu's (1977: 95) *habitus*: 'a system of lasting and transposable dispositions which, integrating past experiences, functions at every moment as a matrix of perception, appreciations and actions and makes possible the achievement of infinitely diversified tasks.'

[18] A simplification: a system can only observe itself through self-observation and perceive the existence of other systems through its internal 'reactions' to them. See Teubner, 1993.

[19] Luhmann, 1992: 1424.

their epithet, these too are internal constructs that, as far as the system is concerned, do not derive from the environment but only appear as deviations from expectations the system has of other systems.[20] Thus, one system couples with another when a series of perturbations and a reciprocity of observation lead to the production of a commonality of structural history between the systems in question. Structural coupling presupposes and provides a *continuous* — as opposed to isolated events[21] — influx of disorder, which enables the system to learn and change while maintaining its structures, for as biological autopoiesis points out, 'the organisation of the system is conserved while it undergoes structural changes.'[22] Structural coupling, being a historically defined process, forms part of the *memory* of a system. The systemic memory is built up by the binary code, together with regular checks for internal consistency performed by the system itself, 'for memory is nothing but checking for consistency.'[23] But, again, this cognitive process does not take place through input/output with the environment but via observation.

II MEMORY

Systems learn from their environment. A system is cognitively open to its environment in that it makes its structures available for validity testing or modification. The cognitive exposure of the system is analogous to its observational proactiveness: whatever the system does, it does it to itself and through itself. As Schütz mentions, the system cannot accomplish any operation outside its boundaries, including on the cognitive level.[24] Learning follows the same reflexive principles of autopoietic reproduction which demand that the cognitive process is a process of superimposition of cognitive layers that project one another in a spiral of self-production: 'learn from experience' takes on an entirely different dimension, for even experience should be understood as the environmental perturbation that instigates in the system the production of another layer of cognitive modification or confirmation of its structures.

Biological autopoiesis states clearly that

> learning as a process consists in the transformation through experience of the behavior of an organism in a manner that is directly or indirectly subservient to the maintenance of its basic circularity.[25]

Since the basic circularity of the system (organism) is that of being and becoming, learning is inseparable from living: 'living systems are cognitive

[20] Luhmann, 1992: 1432. For an explanation of expectations, see below and Luhmann, 1985a.
[21] Luhmann, 1993: 441.
[22] Maturana and Varela, 1972: xix.
[23] King and Schütz, 1994: 140.
[24] Schütz, 2000: 134.
[25] Maturana and Varela, 1972: 37.

systems, and living as a process is a process of cognition.'[26] Referring to law, Luhmann accepts the link between normative (being) and cognitive (becoming) operations but he also differentiates them on the basis of their function. Thus,

> the norm quality serves the autopoiesis of the system, its self-continuation in difference to its environment. The cognitive quality serves the coordination of this process with the system's environment.[27]

Although complementary, the two have different functions for the system. The former provides for the cognitive openness of the system as an avenue of external reference; the latter provides for the identity constitution of the system in the form of internal cohesion by dint of external differentiation. The two interpenetrate and presuppose each other: 'self-reference implies external reference, and vice versa.'[28] Indeed, one of the most noteworthy features of autopoiesis is the indissociability between being and becoming. Any attempt to separate the production from the consumption of meaning is futile: 'the being and the doing of an autopoietic unity are inseparable.'[29] Remarkably, the two operations can be functionally different only because of their existential indivisibility.

Memory exemplifies the relation between being and becoming. It links what has happened in the past with how it is remembered in the present. Memory is the bridge between cognitive openness ('learn from experience') and operational closure ('learn from *my* experience'). Mnemonic science tells us that the operation of memory is not situated in the past but in the present: 'remembrance is always now.'[30] In so doing, it connects a systemic becoming — for becoming is not only future but also past — with a systemic being — which invariably lies in the present. What is inscribed in memory — if this metaphor is still allowed — is, on the one hand, the link between past and present by dint of the processual ability of the system to reconstruct its past behaviour in the present, and on the other, the link between the present and the future in the form of an expectation of unperturbed repetition unless something else occurs that would interrupt it. Constructivism teaches us that cognition is *computation of computation of...*, or else a never ending recursive process of computation.[31] Accordingly, memory must be the speed of computation, or else the facility with which the system reconstructs its former behaviour when confronted with similar situations to the ones it has faced in the past. Such a computational description of memory is obviously rooted in Aristotle's acts of recollection, according to

[26] Maturana and Varela, 1972: 13; note that in biological autopoiesis, all living systems are autopoietic systems.
[27] Luhmann, 1988: 20, footnote omitted.
[28] Luhmann, 1993: 52.
[29] Maturana and Varela, 1987: 49.
[30] Steiner, 1975: 134.
[31] von Foerster, 1984: 296.

which when we remember, we undergo successive earlier changes until we encounter the one after which the change in question usually occurs.[32] Aristotelian theories have had a clear impact on network mnemonic theories, which posit the existence of nodes that connect concepts.[33] But the stauncher expression of computational memory comes from constructivism and biological determinism as seen through autopoiesis. King and Schütz refer to memory as the regular checks for internal consistency performed by the system itself.[34] But memory can also provide for changes, thereby expanding itself and the system. Memory is not always consistent: it includes contradictions and divergences. In such a context, one can talk about memory as *representation*, for memory cannot deliver 'truth' but simply descriptions of it.[35] Such a margin of uncertainty offers the necessary room for impromptu acrobatics, thus enabling the system to deal with novelties intelligently. For, intelligence is essentially the ability to perform new combinations of existing notions. Memory, just as learning, is an operation of selection, which can be conceived as difference, a coupling of two sides: an internal side that links habitually, and manages to link with a velocity analogous to the recurrence of the event, and an external side that links intelligently, in a velocity analogous to the procedural expertise of the system. Contemporary mnemonic studies offer the analogy of Internet engines:

> [n]o single individual can successfully navigate the vast spaces of the Internet's database. Instead, intelligent agents navigate and search that information space for their human users, using techniques modelled on the associative processes of human memory.[36]

In this case, the intelligent agents are less intelligent than the human users: the former can operate only habitually, whereas the latter both habitually and intelligently.

Systemic intelligence is tested through asymmetries. Indeed, learning is advanced with asymmetrical positioning of known positions. Explaining how the legal system learns, Jacobson writes: 'cognitive openness introduces asymmetries into the legal system. New cases present new problems of norm-application, hence norm-formation.'[37] A system in perfect accord with its environment, that is a system free from environmental perturbations, finds itself in a point-for-point mirroring of complexity with its environment. This is not only impossible — since, axiomatically, the environment is more complex than any system[38] — but also undesirable, since

[32] Aristotle, 1972.
[33] I find the best introduction to associative and network memory to be Anderson and Bower, 1983.
[34] King and Schütz, 1994: 140.
[35] Radstone, 2000.
[36] Locke, 2000: 30.
[37] Jacobson, 1989: 1673.
[38] Luhmann, 1995.

the system would never learn. The introduction of asymmetry in the form of environmental complexity is what obliges the system to learn to adjust to new forms of perturbations aided by memory and intelligence. And intelligence is inseparable from the environment, because it is there where the locus of search is. According to Baecker's comments on Luhmann,

> intelligence starts where an entity is able to take its own lack of knowledge into account and to search for the knowledge it lacks in other entities which presumably are in a better position to bring forth the knowledge sought.[39]

To put it differently, the selection of environmental perturbations that are relevant to the system is a reiteration of the usual distinction between self-observation and external observation. Naturally, external observation is the reconnoitring foray of the system into its environment, which will probably result in a recurrence of mutual observations necessary for the system's learning and memory building. This recurrence has already been identified as *structural coupling*. But structural coupling is not an orderly exchange of observations and cognitive opportunities. It is mainly a source of disorder that constantly tries and tests the system's structures.[40] Thus, structural coupling offers both regularities and asymmetries, thereby both confirming and modifying the system's structures.

Thus, memory represents the aggregation of procedures selected to be retained by the system. The rest — that is, the non-selected — is discarded into the environment and stands a fair chance never to be selected again because of the need to *forget*, which is concomitant to the act of remembering. Forgetting is always and irretrievably in the past and it can only manifest its presence *in absentia*. In a way, the forgotten lies in a slice of the environment as alienated from the system as possible, in a veritable wasteland, conceptually and geographically distanced from the system that needs to forget. This does not mean that the forgotten can never be selected. Indeed, this partly is the purpose of this essay: to show how the forgotten in the form of waste can cross the forbidden boundary and be reselected by the system. It is in that sense that the environment of an autopoietic system is included in the system itself, making the difference an instance of contingency. Here, the boundary between the system as the bastion of present certainty, and the environment as the wasteland of the system is questioned and its contingency is brought forth. A fusion is attempted between, on the one hand, the undesired waste as it lurks in the space of uncertainty of the environment, and on the other, the self-sufficiency of the system that discards in order to survive. Alterity lies in the environment and never in the system. The system, however, can never reach outside itself. Thus, alterity will have to be comprehended by the system and within the system. This is why the environment must return to the system. The systemic environment operates as the

[39] Baecker, 2001: 62.
[40] Luhmann, 1992.

deposit of the forgotten, non-selected part of a selection. By reintroducing it, the system faces an internal inevitability: the uncertainty of certainty. It is only in this manner, though, that a system may stabilise itself as an inclusive structure.

III URBAN WASTE

Waste is what is discarded during and after a process. A process in autopoiesis always involves selection. Waste, therefore, is the non-selected part of the selection. This is not all that there is to waste, though. The non-selected is contingent, hence it is still within the cognitive domain of the system and can always be selected later on. Waste does not form part of the cognitive domain of the system as modified by the system's evolution and memory. Waste is labelled by the system as undesired and stands little chance of being considered for selection. Waste is what is discarded.[41] This may seem unduly 'clean-cut' and exclusionary of other candidate values, such as the possibility of waste being retained in and despite the system; waste as misery never to be shed; or waste as repression. While these and other possibilities are inherent in a systemic definition of waste, one should be reminded that any binary selection is good for as long as it is, and any attempt to freeze contingency can only last for a fleeting present moment with little guarantee from a re-enacted past and even less guarantee for an identical future. One should be reminded that doubting the operational binarism of a system in autopoiesis, while epistemologically adventurous, offers little more in terms of desired ambiguity or multiplicity than what is already reserved for in the operations of the autopoietic tools themselves. Keeping with the binary way of defining a concept does not denote certainty: if anything, it exposes the ambiguity of every present selection in all its unreliable comparability and predictability.

Thus, waste, being the opposite of usable for the system, is submitted to temporal, geographical and conceptual distanciation from the system. Systems deal differently with their waste but they all have this in common: they all produce waste and it is to their benefit to be rid of it as timeously and efficiently as possible. The problem with storing waste in the system is that it creates symmetries that cannot be resolved. The paradox that ensues when both parts of the selection are retained within the system cannot be deparadoxified with another selection, and then another *ad infinitum*,[42] because the system will be obliged to make the same selections and obtain the same result again and again. There is no margin for different questions. The needle on the record is stuck and the same musical phrase returns again

[41] See for example, art 1, Directive 91/156/EEC, definition of waste: 'waste shall mean any substance or object in the categories set out in Annex I which the holder discards or intends or is required to discard.'.

[42] Teubner, 2001.

and again. In the meantime, the system cannot learn because its memory is clogged with unresolved bifurcations.

A further problem with waste comes precisely from its distanciation. By making it scarce, the system positions its waste in a cognitively inaccessible part of its environment. Waste, of course, is being amassed there, usually as part of different systems, which do not perceive it as waste but as part of their own systemic structure. In the meantime, the memory of the initial system is evolving according to the retained selections. When the perturbations from the environment become impossible to ignore, in other words when waste forces itself in the cognitive domain of the system, the system is unable to cope relying only on its memory and learning abilities because memory is of the system and, as such, it retains only the selected. The system will have to learn anew how to cope with its discarded non-selections. This does not necessarily mean that the system will not manage. The effect may range from a disintegration of the system to structural redefinitions within the system that will alter the system while maintaining its identity.

Faithful to Luhmannian definitional methods, I will define waste as the value at the antipodes of *usable*. The binarism can be tangibly explained in the urban context. Urban waste is what is not usable by the urban system; hence it is discarded. The city assigns its waste to its hinterlands, pushes it out of its geography and denies any intimacy with it — or, at least this is what it tries to do. Urban waste is not assigned to urban memory, for memory is present and waste is by definition past. The city tries to forget its waste and to carry on becoming only by retaining a small portion of it as an *aide mémoire*. This urban memory converts waste immediately from past to present, from memory to being: in other words, the memory of the system transcends the binary border and converts waste into usable, through processes such as reusing and recycling. What has not been selected by the system as usable is discarded geographically and denied any memory — that is, any possibility to be present and within our cognitive domain, for, according to Maturana,

> [t]he physical space defined as the space in which living systems exist…is epistemologically singular because it defines the operational boundaries of our cognitive domain.[43]

Spatial dislocation is a certain way of denuding something from any memory it may carry: the decontextualisation of the object ('Who are you? I know you from *somewhere* but I cannot *place* you!') apart, movement leaves memory behind, for, as Bachelard puts it, 'memories are immobile, solid only if they are spatialised.'[44] Bachelard famously sees home as the prime locus of memory, where intimacy exists in mnemonic propinquity and immobility. Space is widely recognised as the residence of memories, more so than time, as Pierre Nora's legendary *Les Lieux de Mémoire* painstakingly try to

[43] Maturana, 1999: 162.
[44] Bachelard, 1989: 28.

show, where from a politicised and largely national historicity we are eased into a past remembered as place.[45]

So, the further we transfer waste, the more we denude it from its memory — and memory here should be read intentionally as the link between the body and the space around it.[46] The further afar waste is from the body, the less remembered it is. Merleau-Ponty's take on memory shows how memory resides both in the 'body-subject' and the space around it as container of objects and processes to be remembered.[47] Bergson defines memory as 'the state of our body', explaining that it is through our bodies that memory becomes the 'progression from the past to the present.'[48] As Casey appositely writes,

> in the actions of the customary body, we observe the continuance of time in place — a continuance that connotes not merely maintenance but active incorporation. In this way the past becomes our true present; it loses its identity as a separate past (a past of another time and place) through its precipitation into the present of bodily behavior, which enacts the past rather than picturing it. And this presentiment of the past is nowhere more active or more evident than in bodily memory of place.[49]

If the body is taken away from its intentional mnemonic object, any memory will be much harder to evoke. This means neither that our cities are clean, nor that we cannot remember the bin in our kitchen. It simply means that, in urban autopoiesis there can be no place for waste.[50] Waste *was*, and if it *is*, it is part of another system, geographically elsewhere, and it is no longer waste but communication of another system.[51]

If the Bachelardian home is the locus of immobile memories, then contemporary cities must be the locus of forgetting in all its fleetingness and transience. Forgetting is an operation that enables the system to evolve cognitively by discarding the non-selected. Frow sums it up eloquently:

> ... the past is a function of the system: rather than having a meaning and a truth determined once and for all by its status as event, its meaning and its truth are constituted retroactively and repeatedly. Data are not stored in already constituted places but are arranged and rearranged at every point in time. Forgetting is thus an integral principle of this model, since the activity of compulsive interpretation that organizes it involves at once selection and rejection.[52]

[45] Nora, 1984–93.
[46] Casey, 1987: 48.
[47] Merleau-Ponty, 1962: 130.
[48] Bergson, 1988: 239–40.
[49] Casey, 1987: 194.
[50] If urban autopoiesis can be defined as the circularity between the body and the city; see Zeleny and Hufford, 1991.
[51] 'Communication' here is meant in the Luhmannian (1995) sense, as the faculty of social systems, and in distinction to 'perception', which is the faculty of humans (psychic systems). Communications are produced by systems and can be loosely understood as the internal elaboration of external facts.
[52] Frow, 1997: 229.

Cities reject more because they select more. Their presentocracy means that they forget — they assign everything to achronicity — because of the facility of selection. In his work on the fetishisation of commodities, Baudrillard describes cities as the space of 'limitless promotion of needs',[53] where 'the dictatorship of fashion' demands an excessive production of present and encourages instant forgetting. In fact, the whole orientation of the urban system is towards the production — but not the consumption — of waste. The production of waste, and not the production of goods according to a clearly Marxist Baudrillard, is the main indicator of abundance, affluence and social pre-eminence:

> waste even appears ultimately as the essential function, the extra degree of expenditure, superfluity, the ritual uselessness of 'expenditure for nothing' becoming the site of production of values, difference and meanings on both the individual and the social level.[54]

The urban system forgets as soon as it consumes, spits out before it chews, throws its objects in the past before they are even aired in the present: '[w]hat is produced today is not produced for its use-value or its possible durability, but rather with an *eye to its death*.'[55] The city operates in a perpetual state of dissatisfaction where only the gadget after the one there is now will do — and gadgets oblige with their in-built obsolescence, and perpetuate a state of conservative affluence, without memory and without cognitive opportunities. The city selects to reject, and its selections are constantly fed by the desire to forget. Overproduction of waste creates an imbalance in the basic circularity of autopoiesis by favouring a hydrocephalous becoming that grows to the detriment of being. The circularity is frozen by an overabundance of selections for the sake of rejection.

A way out of such unidirectional development is found in the process of recycling. Recycling can be safely described as the city's best attempt to allow crossability of the border between being and becoming. Based on its mnemonic abilities, a city that recycles attempts to re-enact the past as present. Memory is the opposite of forgetting, and although a great deal of waste produce is expelled and forgotten by the urban system, some materials escape their fate as waste and are selected by the system by way of re-use or recycling. The processual nature of memory means that, given certain conditions, the system can perform the passage from waste to usable more readily. In memory, the temporalities merge, since memory is always a present re-enactment of the past. Of course, the memory of the system is selective — since forgetting is also operationally necessary — and only operates along the already existing mnemonic structures, with all the usual implications for its cognitive openness as a system. In other words,

[53] Baudrillard, 1998: 65.
[54] Baudrillard, 1998: 43.
[55] Baudrillard, 1998: 46, original emphasis.

memory evolves on the same lines as any other system, which includes mutual observations and structural couplings between systemic memories. Accordingly, the mnemonic mutuality between the city and other systems (amongst which notably the legal system and general education) enables the structures of recycling to perpetuate.[56]

However, the basic feature of recycling is what has been hailed as its 'symbolic role in beginning to change the nature of western societies and the culture of consumerism.'[57] Indeed, while actual recycling is at disproportionately low levels when compared to waste disposal,[58] its representation of the crossability of the binary border has acquired symbolic dimensions. This becomes particularly relevant in view of the relevance recycling has for packaging waste — to wit the EC Directive on Packaging and Packaging Waste,[59] which provides for 50 to 65 per cent of the weight of packaging waste to be recovered. Packaging waste apparently contributes 50 per cent of the volume of the total household waste in western societies.[60] It seems that controlling packaging waste through recycling is tantamount to a battle of symbols: affluence versus nostalgia, excess versus utility. Recycling is the counterpart of the Baudrillardian irony, which promotes waste's positive function as the main indicator of social well-being. To the above, recycling's ability to fuse temporalities must be added, for recycling presentifies the past *and* encompasses the future. The latter not only because of its reliance on memory, but also in that any decision on recycling strategy takes into consideration — however inadvertently — the interests of future generations[61] as included in the Brundtland definition of Sustainable Development, namely

> the development that meets the needs of the present generation without compromising the ability of future generations to meet their own needs.[62]

Recycling emphasises the role of memory as the systemic operation that brings together the temporalities of the system under the security of the notion of repetition. Because of its symbolic rather than actual importance, recycling can afford to ignore all the familiar doubts about its economic and environmental appropriateness,[63] and guiltlessly embrace the elasticity between usable/waste.

[56] Specifically on the law, it is significant that recyclable matter is still considered waste for the purposes of the EC Directive 91/15 on waste, since, the term 'to discard' also includes consignment for recovery. It is there where the memory of the system comes in and re-selects the expelled waste by crossing the binarism usable/waste.
[57] Gandy, 1994: 1.
[58] Haughton and Hunter, 1994.
[59] Directive 94/62/EEC.
[60] Gandy, 1994: 25.
[61] Alder and Wilkinson, 1999: 308. Of course, the introduction of intergenerational equity brings along further prioritisations of needs along the lines of renewable and non-renewable sources, which simplify any recycling decisions.
[62] WCED, 1987.
[63] Alder and Wilkinson, 1999.

IV LAW'S WASTE

Law is 'wasteful' because it is obliged to select. Law cannot refuse to apply itself on a case. It is bound by expectations and self-expectations. People expect the law to be present when called for; the law expects itself to learn from its selections. These expectations form a series of inescapable black boxes in which the balance of lawful/unlawful is determined. There is no alternative outside the black box. What we do not know about Schrödinger's cat is only analogous to what the cat does not know about us. The law can only come out of the box once the selection is made, and only to fall into another selection in another box. As Schütz remarks, 'as opposed to his Roman forebears, the modern judge who declares *non liquet* breaks the law.'[64] The law cannot abandon itself. Thus, the law is obliged to select.[65] Selections are asymmetrical, in that they prioritise one branch of the bifurcation over the other. The non-selected is abandoned as inconsistent with the system's memory. The non-selected does not enter the memory of the system but is expelled to the system's environment with a slim chance of being reselected, because of its conceptual distanciation from the system. The non-selected part of the selection is law's waste.

Law's waste follows the usual fate of any systemic waste: it is forgotten. The system forgets, not only because otherwise its selectional mechanisms become clogged, but also because it needs to be rid of the uncertainty inherent in every selection. However, a clarification is needed: strictly speaking, what becomes waste is not the non-selected part of the legal decision as such but *its possibility of having been selected.* This possibility is embodied in the selected as intentional inclusion of its selectability. In other words, every selection implies an intentional link with the selected, which is being internalised in the selected as the possibility of its being selected. Such possibility is the processual expression of selection as internalised by the selected. Conversely, waste is the process with which something has not been selected and has consequently been rejected by the system as waste. This process is intentionally internalised by the non-selected, just as the reverse process is internalised by the selected. The contingency of the non-selected is reduced because it is discarded in such a way that it no longer fits the binary code of the system. When the legal decision finds an act unlawful, the non-selected 'lawful' is no longer object of the question 'lawful/unlawful'. It is past the black box of uncertainty of outcome and it has come up the other end. The law moves on, plunging into further black boxes, while the possibility of the act being 'lawful' is left behind because it can no

[64] Schütz, 2000: 113. See also Luhmann, 1993.

[65] The law cannot use the 'rejection value', that is a third value that negates the binary code as the basis of choice (Luhmann, 1986b). Law cannot describe itself with such a margin because of fear of disintegration.

longer involve the system.[66] Law becomes unengaged with this conceptual distanciation — which is the equivalent of the urban system's geographical distanciation. Such a distanciation exemplifies the legal system's expectations of certainty. If the law could not select with the requisite temporal or conceptual certainty, then the law would not be the law as it describes itself at present.[67] As Christodoulidis writes,

> [t]he law provides a constancy peculiar to it alone. This is due to the function law has in society of stabilising expectations, of controlling normativity, of guaranteeing that its expectations will not be discredited if disappointed, that Alter is bound by the legal norm and will bear the consequences if she defies it.[68]

Such a responsibility is what keeps law apace with its self-description: law binds expectations temporally and guarantees certainty infinitely. The law feels the need to forget for fear that the non-selected will return and compromise the certainty that law expects of itself. Law expels its waste and forgets about it because law's waste questions law, shakes its very processes, threatens with disintegration. As a matter of survival, the legal system casts its waste away from its cognitive domain, deep into an unthematised horizon that succeeds selection, reducing uncertainty by retaining only certainty.

Reduction of uncertainty is another form of deparadoxification perpetually performed by the system. Paradoxes can be threatening for the system — for example, law's fundamental paradox is whether the code itself is lawful or unlawful.[69] Not asking itself such a question — not applying the code to itself — is the legal system's prime concern. The same concern applies to the paradox of every selection/legal decision — because a selection is a unity of difference between contingencies that cannot be selected simultaneously.[70] The only way out of the paradox is the introduction of asymmetry between selections, which results in a temporary postponement of the annihilating effect of the paradox. In the legal system, postponement is performed by the courts — and this is what, according to Luhmann, gives the courts their 'central' position in the management of law, in contradistinction to other forms of legal communication, such as the legislature that correspond to the 'periphery' of the system.[71] Luhmann was quick, though, to dispel any impression of hierarchy between centre and periphery, since hierarchy is a misinterpretation

[66] In the event that the *same* act returns to the system asking once again the question lawful/unlawful, the system will accept it only if it is a *different* act, that is a different uncertainty in a different black box, for the law does not engage with identical questions but only with variations of the first question and only in some cases where the judicial hierarchy allows it. If a *similar* act irritates the system, the system will respond by employing its memory and deliver the outcome of its selection accordingly.
[67] And what is wrong with this? See below.
[68] Christodoulidis, 1998: 107.
[69] Luhmann, 1993.
[70] Luhmann, 1993: 307.
[71] Luhmann, 1993.

of autopoietic circularity.[72] It is simply that the courts are the elements of the legal system that deparadoxify law's fundamental paradoxes, not least because their operation itself is based on a constant need for deparadoxification — that of the legal obligation to decide;[73] but also because courts are the guards of systemic memory, or else the facilitators of its evocation. The courts bring together the past, present and future by reproducing past and already assimilated computations in order to decide a case in the present, and by taking into consideration the future consequences of their decision.[74] The courts — just as memory — are also intentional in that they link an internal with an external element. This is better observed through the concept of *programme*: the courts are the main applicators of the computation between an *if* and a *then*, or else a fact and a legal rule.[75] The conditionality of the application (*if ... then ...*) is what a programme is. This conditionality renders the programme more flexible than the binary code and facilitates a more practice-informed application of the code. When a court employs a programme, it links the internal self-referentiality of the code with the avenue of external connection as provided by a programme.

The same internal/external differentiation can be witnessed in another Luhmannian binarism, that between *redundancy* and *variation*.[76] Variation is the systemic accommodation of surprise, whereas redundancy is akin to the memory of the system. While there is little doubt that the system accommodates surprises according to its memory, variation triggers not only evocation but also new combinations — in other words, intelligence. Redundancy, on the other hand, is the process of banalisation of external perturbations that takes place in strict accordance with the system's memory. The system is expected to balance both functions without compromising either its ability of cognitive openness to innovations, or its structural unity. In balancing, the system takes into consideration two kinds of consequences: the intrasystemic consequences which refer to future legal decisions, and the external consequences, or the effects a decision has on the legal environment.[77] It is not as if redundancy and variation have respectively internal and external consequences, or that the legal system can consciously select which mode of reaction it will employ. Rather, the connection is one of contingently balancing one binarism against the other without any prioritisation.

I suggest that the law is in fact prioritising its internal self-reference over external check for consequences — and this *contra* Luhmann's concerns about a historical overgrowth of external reference.[78] While such behaviour is understandable in view of the supposedly unsettling effects of uncertainty

[72] Luhmann, 1993: 302.
[73] Luhmann, 1993: 320.
[74] Luhmann, 1993: 308.
[75] Luhmann, 1989b; 1998; 1993.
[76] Luhmann, 1995b.
[77] Luhmann, 1995b: 294.
[78] See the methodological discussion in Luhmann, 1995b: 296–97. See also Baxter, 1998: 2030.

as expressed by law's waste, it is restrictive of the system's cognitive abilities. When the court applies the conditionality of a programme to a correlation between event and rule, it may encounter surprises (asymmetries), with which it deals by evoking its memory and employing its intelligence. In so doing, the system checks internally and externally for the consequences of its selections. Now, waste lies in the environment of the system. Waste, however, represents a threat to the consistency of the system, since it introduces the uncertainty of paradox. It is in the interest of the system, therefore, to turn its back to its environment and concentrate instead on its self-reference. Of course, waste is isolated, lying outside the cognitive domain of the system. Thus, the system is able to carry on evolving cognitively, assuming surprises and checking its redundancy, without having to expose itself to the wastelands of the forgotten. In so avoiding, however, the system does not allow its redundancy to be questioned, nor does it expose its past selections to cognitive re-evaluation. This inevitably leads to more internal checks, and the more comfortable the system is in its structures, the more complacent it becomes.

Legal complacency comes under criticism by Ladeur, who finds Luhmann 'a bit too old fashioned' with regard to the 'iffishnes' (if/then) of Luhmannian legal operations.[79] Ladeur comes from a network-based theoretical background, to which he links autopoiesis. The offspring is a pluralistic, anti-Universalist, self organisational theory that questions some of the more conservative aspects of Luhmannian autopoiesis, offering in their stead a much more market-orientated, liberal approach.[80] Ladeur's general suggestion is that, since state law in postmodernity is no longer what it used to be, and its substitution with organisations is progressive but inevitable, the only viable way out is the self-organisation of these organisations. In view of all the theoretical exposés of legal globalisation, one cannot but accept the fact that state law is no longer the only source of law. However, this is something that Luhmann seems not to have come to terms with.[81] For Luhmann, the description of the legal system corresponds to state law and any variation would probably not be accepted, such as Ladeur's contracts and other individual legal acts. Admittedly, this is one form of law — or indeed the form of law to which every system that employs the same lawful/unlawful code subscribes. But accepting other sources of legality — in other words, expanding the conceptual boundaries of the legal system — is simply a natural consequence of the lack of a vantage point in the autopoietic state of things: '[a] distributed order of decisions as a compensation for the impossibility of the position of the ideal observer of society.'[82] The autopoietic universe is a-centric, non-hierarchical, indescribable in its totality. If we accept that there

[79] Ladeur, 1999: 26.
[80] The desirability of combining autopoiesis and network theory has also been suggested by Murphy, 1997.
[81] Teubner, 1997, however, arrives to his salvation by accepting globalisation.
[82] Ladeur, 1999: 22.

is one legal system that, as legal systems go, offers the certainty of legal overview, then we accept the existence of a viewpoint that offers the Law of God as the indisputable, all-knowing, all-describing but not all-revealing observer. This egocentric thematisation of autopoietic space is the commonality between utopia and reality, because it describes itself as both 'good-for-all' and beyond descriptions. I find preferable, therefore, to use instead the concept of 'reality', as the boundary between utopia and reality. 'Reality' can be defined as the pragmatically operable state of systemic co-existence, as perceived by each system that partakes of that co-existence. 'Reality' in this sense expresses the evolutionary surprise of communication in view of the incommunicability of the systems. As such, it propagates an a-centric, diffused subjectivity, which, although the only available description, does not describe itself as such, because of the constant surprise of surrounding communication. In its diffusion between internal closure and external surprise, 'reality' accommodates the postmodern idea of legal pluralism without assuming the vantage point of an *über*observer. Thus, while the legal system accepts as part of it only legal communications, it is cognitively open to new forms of legality. As Ladeur puts it,

> I think autopoietic theory should not be regarded — as Luhmann regards it — as the one and only scientific construction of modern law, but rather as a concept for the description of post-modern law because it is more open to plural concepts of law.[83]

This openness does not nullify state law but re-evaluates its operations. It is thus that adaptation becomes a matter of survival for state law. It is thus that law needs to include the uncertainty of certainty, whether this law is state or organisational. So, Ladeur's suggestions are apposite if one accepts that state law is as competent a legal source of selection as any.

Along with the fragmentation of legal institutions, Ladeur also points to the surrounding conditions of uncertainty, variably attributed to technology, science, demise of linear causality, society itself and so on,[84] that contribute to the 'postmodernisation' of society and increasingly question the foundations of law.[85] In view of institutional (internal) fragmentation on one hand, and constant conditions of (external) uncertainty on the other, the legal system is faced with the need to take recourse to a greater openness towards its environment through what Ladeur calls *modelling*:

> [t]he search for new, permanent, stable rules is made impossible, its place must be taken by strategic model formation under conditions of uncertainty: as a standard of correctness, only the 'viable', self-confirming practice can be valid, which has to be explicitly attuned to learning, in a provisional rationality of experimenting with relationing-possibilities. In such a context characterised by

[83] Ladeur, 1999: 33.
[84] Ladeur, 1995b; 1999.
[85] Ladeur 1999, 1995, 1995b, criticises both the need for legitimisation as explained by Habermas, 1987, and the idea of a universalistic, positive law as propagated by Luhmann.

> complexity, modelling distinguishes itself from the norm, as from prognosis, in that it integrates through a multi-factor prospective method specialist knowledge and action, thus, does not presuppose the separation of knowledge (norm) and practical application.[86]

In other words, no separation between internal and external reference, and certainly no prioritisation of the former can be accepted under the present conditions of indeterminacy. What in this extract Ladeur calls 'modelling', he later calls *proceduralisation*, or else 'experimental relational rationality'[87] which involves internal learning on the basis of partial, fragmentary knowledge. As he writes characteristically, the legal system

> ... should be more oriented at establishing new kinds of procedural rules stressing flexibility, innovation, experimentation, incentives for long-term horizons of decision-making ... within a strategy oriented at managing the unexpected through the generation of learning capabilities.[88]

This occurs not with pre-established norms and goals but with patterns, which emanate not from 'the illusionary goal of attaining justice in concrete cases'[89] but from experimentation and internalisation of uncertainty.

So, Ladeur does not share Luhmann's concerns about too much external reference; on the contrary, he positively encourages it, if it is for law to proceed with its balancing act between redundancy and variety. External reference involves not only the cognitive domain of the system, but also an expansion of the latter to include what the system habitually has been avoiding for fear of paradoxical outcomes; in other words, law's waste. Waste, defined as the ostracised possibility of the other branch of selection being selected, brings forth the two main legal paradoxes: how to choose from a unity? Further, is the selection between lawful/unlawful itself lawful? Waste calls into question both the rule-like structure of the legal system and the legal system itself. One way to deal with waste — law's preferred avenue — is by forgetting it, and thus postponing the paradox until the next selection. The other way, as indirectly suggested by Ladeur, is by embracing it and succumbing to the very questions that may disintegrate the system. From there, two things can happen: either the legal system will disintegrate indeed and will have to invent itself anew, or it will evolve cognitively and become operational, having managed to adapt to an era of internal and external uncertainty.

There is perhaps a way for the system to pave the way for the latter contingency before the former knocks on its door, and this is the *procedural* reintroduction of law's waste to the system. This involves a progressive temporal inversion from past-to-present and present-to-future, to present-to-past. Such an inversion requires a level of flexibility unbeknown to law, which will probably be channelled not to its code but its programmes.

[86] Ladeur, 1995: 30, footnotes omitted.
[87] Ladeur, 1999: 19.
[88] Ladeur, 1995b: 14.
[89] Ladeur, 1999: 19.

Programmes are adequately flexible to accommodate the procedural aspect of the inversion, which demands a progressive, experimental pattern formation that is linked to a constant check for external and internal consistency. The only problem may be that the flexibility of a programme is temporally orientated towards the future, without any possibility of reapplication to the past or differentiated application in the present, because such an application would seemingly abandon the characteristic intentionality between internal and external reference. But programmes can be programmed according to the code.[90] Here, programmes will not be required to deviate from the code but only to reinforce its contingency through a reconsidered fusion of temporalities. As I have already mentioned, if present for the law is the lair of certainty, then the forgotten past should be the wasteland of uncertainty and doubt. The past, however, can present itself as a cognitive opportunity for mnemonic re-evaluation: the law can look back and face its waste. The cognitive consequences of such turning back can be as freezing as they are bracing: looking Euridice in the eyes may make the law come to terms with its limitations and its self-assured capacity for certainty. Indeed, the legal system's boundaries will shrink if its waste is brought back to its cognitive domain, and this can only lead to a re-evaluation of the expectations and the expectations of expectations of the system. By inverting the temporal orientation of legal selections, thereby reintroducing past non-selections (that are excluded from memory and the system as waste) as contingencies, the legal system internalises uncertainty, hence its environment. I am not suggesting a case-by-case re-examination of the law's past non-selections — here I will side with Ladeur when he dismisses case-by-case justice as illusionary — but a reintroduction of the other side of redundancy. If redundancy is the operation of the system with which stabilised grounds and patterns are reactivated[91] — ie, the memory of memory — then its flipside will not be variety as external reference, but the *memory of forgetting* as the negative internal formula, which is activated whenever an irritation, similar to the one that led to the construction of memory appears in the cognitive domain of the system. Since memory is processual, memory of forgetting will be not what the selection was or was not, but *how the selection did not take place*. The memory of forgetting reactivates the contingency of the alternatives and the paths that lead to their rejection. In so doing, it instils doubt in the form of regular revisiting of choices made and done with.

The difference from a generic version of reflexive control[92] is that here self-control is combined with post-decision monitoring. In other words, the legal system claims a greater share in what has axiomatically been considered a predominantly public media domain, namely the questioning of legal selections. Except that the legal system is better equipped to look at the processual

[90] According to Luhmann, 1989b, programmes are given conditions for the suitability of the selection of operations.
[91] Luhmann, 1993b.
[92] Such as the one described by Orts, 1994 and 2001.

development of past selections, which is the focus of the memory of forgetting. Therefore, the suggested inversion can only take place, at least initially, in the courts, since they are considered the 'centre' of legal communications, obliged by the law to apply its code.[93] Of course, such inversion will question the centrality of the courts itself, since a process of demythologisation of the judicial ability to deliver certainty will be in operation. Regardless of their described position, however, it is debatable whether courts can pull off such changes while feeling their own foundations shake. Programmes can be of help here only if external reference, which is strictly determined by the cognitive domain of the legal system, is so constructed as to include waste. This, however, presupposes, on the one hand, a broadening of external reference, which, if one listens to Ladeur and Luhmann, is already happening anyway; and on the other, a parallel debilitation of the border between the values of the code, even if this traditionally tends to harden when the selection has already taken place. In short, memory of forgetting addresses precisely the contingency of the boundary, and reinforces it by encouraging cognitive trips to past selectional processes. To return, therefore, to the role of the courts, such inversion will place before them the double challenge of maintaining both their centrality, and the self-description of the system as the locus of irreversible certainty. As a result, courts may see their centrality taken away from them to be re-instituted as 'periphery' of the alternative, which allows for more external reference and less preconstituted norms. Forms that can accommodate revisiting of the process can be norms constructed in such a way that they include uncertainty in the form of 'fuzzy' conditionality.[94] Or even forms that are not quite norms but informal arrangements, 'soft' legal hybrids, mediation, self-organising mandates, economic instruments of internalisation and so on, all of which have already been suggested by other authors.[95] At its most basal form, memory of forgetting can be envisaged as the second-order dealing with dissenting judgements, which, although deprived of precedent power, they offer the possibility of a post-decisional self-check.

The obvious question of how the system is expected to decide what to remember and what to forget is simply another instance of the paradoxical decision tree of each system, whereby one selection leads to another *ad infinitum*.[96] The paradox can never be solved; only postponed. With every selection, a new set of memorables and forgettables is created, constantly posing the same questions to the selecting system. Remembering not to forget is another selection imposed on the system by itself, an endogenous irritation in view of potential problems with the future of the system in question: wastelands perilously surround the system and induce, if not

[93] It is interesting to note that the centrality of the judicial features only in Luhmann's later descriptions of the legal system (1993b). Ladeur, 1999: 27, explains that the shift is due to 'the weakening of the rule-based universalistic paradigm of law'.
[94] Flournoy, 1994; Tarlock, 1994.
[95] Teubner, 1996; Shelton, 2000.
[96] Luhmann, 1993b, refers to the decisional tree when dealing with risk decisions.

solutions, at least an unease that may lead to an internalised and (self-) imposed imagining of change. The change can only come from inside, through the bodies of permanence. The question of how the legal system will react to such imaginings is a matter of empirical observation. The system reconfigures its internal and external references according to its autopoiesis. The advantage of autopoiesis is that it is a relevant and flexible tool of description and explanation of even non-prescribed evolutionary probabilities. Its disadvantage, of course, is that it cannot prescribe such probabilities to the system. It is only the system itself that can prescribe anything to itself, and this only if it is in accordance with its autopoiesis.

On the whole, courts may have a greater role in the inversion, but at the end it will be the legal system as a whole that will have to find another way of managing its paradoxes and allocating new ones. Then, the main paradox of the legal system may be how order is achieved without law.[97] There is little doubt that inversions such as the ones suggested above bring doubt, confusion and uncertainty. Which means that the law will no longer be the beacon of certainty that traditionally has been. Which means that the law will temporarily increase its internal references to reflect and adjust, and then will open up its cognitive domain to ideas and practices that may suggest that, in fact, law has never been the traditional beacon of certainty it thought itself to be.

V CROSSING

What is excluded can be reinserted. What is forgotten can be recalled. What is crossed can be re-crossed. Autopoiesis offers the necessary tools for a contingent dealing of binarisms, not only because the values can fluctuate, but mainly because of the possibility of including the environment (alter) in the definition of the system (self). The environment here has been embraced by the system in its capacity as the locus of the memory of the forgotten. To put it from a different point of view, the environment is constructed so as to include those parts of the system that the system itself no longer desires. This is somehow against the systemic grain, but at the same time it is less daring than it seems. It only suggests a reintroduction of these elements to the systemic cognitive domain, since anyway, they already are in the broader systemic environment. The necessity of waste production, however, (which, autopoietically speaking, is nothing more than the production of asymmetries that follows every selection) prohibits the actual reintroduction of the undesired. Both systems described above, namely the city and the law, distanciate themselves from their waste, they push the latter to their environment hoping to forget about it and to stop it from clogging their selectional mechanisms. While this is understandable in view of the paradoxical consequences of waste retention for the system, waste overproduction leads to a loss of cognitive opportunities for the system.

[97] Ellickson, 1991.

In the domain of urban waste, the process of recycling has been indicated as a tangible way of waste re-introduction to the system. In the legal domain, things are not that simple. Law's perceived self-description as a landmark of certainty and conclusiveness can be at stake. Thus, it has been suggested that the environment enters the system procedurally in the form of a reversed mnemonic investigation. With every selection, the ensuing schism between the selected and the non-selected (or the remembered and the forgotten) impassionately echoes a universe in difference. Such universe can only be expressed in halves, each half perpetually wanting and striving to postpone the paradox of the bleeding self. When the self remembers, the alter is remembered and forgotten in a displaced simultaneity that winks playfully at the illusions of unity. The selected is constantly receding or proceeding, a mere instance of the autopoietic *différance* that allows seemingly solid labelling and operational stability for the system. In 'reality', however, this labelling is simply a bridge that attempts to span the cavernous Erebos underneath the isolation of the self. Such labelling offers to the system the requisite certainty of selection, the blinding permanence of the always contingent but presently unshakeable 'marked' space of selection. The system cannot operate without this. Present is what it is, and if it were not for the gaping temporalities of past and future, unity, certainty and symmetry would be the order of the day. Thankfully, it is only the illusion of these utopian graces that lurks behind every selection, rendering it necessary for the autopoiesis of the system. Thus, while the system bathes in the certainty of each selection at each point of its becoming, temporalities make sure that this certainty is adequately precarious for the system to carry on learning from its surrounding asymmetries. The ability to describe the world as solidly segregated yet contingently united is an advantage that autopoiesis abundantly offers.

Since certainty of selection is a requisite for the stability of the system, systemic memory has an instrumental role. Seen from the reverse point of view, the memory of the process of waste production is how the system checks on itself and its operations for consistency. This means that the system is never granted open access to its environment. Environment and system remain intransparent and essentially antithetical. Even in view of the fact that part of the systemic environment was a part of the system, the connection between the two remains one of difference. The environment is never assimilated by the system, even if the system is caught at its most accommodating. Hence, the boundary between the two remains solid and in place. Likewise, waste production remains an inevitable part of the operations of the system and a safe indication of the systemic becoming. However, by acknowledging the fact that the environment includes cognitive opportunities, not only in the form of future risks, but also in the form of past selections (in the sense of the process rather than the result), the system broadens its systemic boundary, enhancing thereby its mnemonic openness and allowing for unpredicted twists in its evolution. The fluctuation of contingent values between past and present shakes up both the system and its simulated environment. The environment becomes a riskier place, historically burdened with the ghosts of pasts forgotten, but at the same time more proximate and more available to the system. From this apparition of the past in the systemic cognitive domain, the system unfolds and allows the ingress of waste, which could have never been of use to the system, had it not left the system in the first place.[98]

REFERENCES

Alder, J and Wilkinson, D, *Environmental Law and Ethics*, London: Macmillan, 1999.

Anderson, J and Bower, G, *The Architecture of Cognition*, Cambridge, MA: Harvard University Press, 1983.

Aristotle, *Περι Μνημης*, *De Memoria et Reminiscentia*, trans R Sorabji, London: Duckworth, 1972.

Bachelard, G, *La Poétique de l'Espace*, Paris: Quadrige, 1989.

Baecker, D, 'Why Systems?', 18 *Theory, Culture & Society* 1, 59–74, 2001.

Bankowski, Z,'How Does It Feel to be Alone? The Person in the Sight of Autopoiesis', in D Nelken (ed), *Law as Communication* Dartmouth: Aldershot, 1996.

Barthes, R, *Roland Barthes par Roland Barthes*, Paris: Seuil, 1975.

Baudrillard, J, *The Consumer Society: Myths and Structures*, London: Sage, 1998.

Baudrillard, J, *Simulacra and Simulation*, trans S F Glaser, Michigan: Ann Arbor, The University of Michigan Press, 2000.

Baxter, H, 'Autopoiesis and the Relative Autonomy of Law', 19 *Cardozo Law Review* 6, 1987–2090, 1998.

Beck, A, 'Is Law an Autopoietic System?', 14 *Oxford Journal of Legal Studies*, (1994), pp 401–18.

Bergson, H, *Matter and Memory*, trans N Paul and S Palmer, New York: Zone Books, 1988.

Bourdieu, P, *Outline of a Theory of Practice*, trans R Nice, Cambridge: Cambridge University Press, 1977.

Casey, E, *Remembering: A Phenomenological Study*, Bloomington: Indiana University Press, 1987.

Christodoulidis, E, *Law and Reflexive Politics*, Dordrecht: Kluwer Academic, 1998.

Cotterrell, R, 'Sociological Perspectives on Legal Closure', in A Norrie (ed), 1993.

Ellickson, R, *Order Without Law: How Neighbors Settle Disputes*, Cambridge, MA: Harvard University Press, 1991.

Foerster, von, H, *Observing Systems*, California: Intersystems Publications, 1984.

Frow, J, *Time and Commodity Culture: Essays in Cultural Theory and Postmodernity*, Oxford: Clarendon Press, 1997.

Flournoy, A, 'Coping with Complexity', 27 *Loyola of Los Angeles Law Review* 3, 809–24, 1994.

Habermas, J, *The Theory of Communicative Action, ii. Lifeworld and System*, Boston: Beacon, 1987.

Jacobson, A, 'Autopoietic Law: The New Science of Niklas Luhmann', 87 *Michigan Law Review*, 1647–89, 1989.

[98] To recall Pascal, 'I wanted to write what I forgot, but instead I write that I have forgotten', quoted in Barthes, 1975.

King, M, 'The Truth about Autopoiesis', 20 *Journal of Law and Society* 2, 218–36, 1993.
King, M, 'The Construction and Demolition of the Luhmann Heresy', 12 *Law and Critique* 1, 1–32, 2001.
King, M and Schütz, A, 'The Ambitious Modesty of Niklas Luhmann', 21 *Journal of Law and Society* 3, 261–87, 1994.
Ladeur, K-H, *Social Risks, Welfare Rights and the Paradigm of Proceduralisation*, 95/2 EUI Working Paper, Firenze: European University Institute, 1995.
Ladeur, K-H, *Post-Modern Constitutional Theory: A Prospect for the Self-Organizing Society*, 95/6 EUI Working Paper, Firenze: European University Institute, 1995b.
Ladeur, K-H, *The Theory of Autopoiesis as an Approach to a Better Understanding of Postmodern Law: From the Hierarchy of Norms to the Heterarchy of Changing Patterns of Legal Inter-Relationships*, 99/3 EUI Working Paper, Firenze: European University Institute, 1999.
Lempert, R, 'The Autonomy of Law: Two Visions Compared', in G Teubner, (ed), 1988.
Locke, C, 'Digital Memory and the Problem of Forgetting' in S Radstone (ed), 2000.
Luhmann, N, *The Differentiation of Society*, trans S Holmes and C Larmore, NY: Columbia University Press, 1982.
Luhmann, N, *A Sociological Theory of Law*, trans E King and M Albrow, Boston: Routledge & Kegan Paul, 1985.
Luhmann, N, 'The Coding of the Legal System', in G Teubner and A Febbrajo (eds), 1986.
Luhmann, N, 'The Unity of the Legal System' in Teubner, G (ed), *Autopoietic Law: A New Approach to Law and Society*, Berlin: Walter de Gruyter, 1988.
Luhmann, N, 'Law as a Social System', 83 *Northwestern University Law Review*, 136–50, 1989.
Luhmann, N, *Ecological Communication*, trans J Bednarz, Jr, Cambridge: Polity Press, 1989b.
Luhmann, N, 'Closure and Structural Coupling', 13 *Cardozo Law Review*, 1419–42, 1992.
Luhmann, N, *Das Recht der Gesellschaft*, Frankfurt am Main: Suhrkamp, 1993.
Luhmann, N, *Risk: A Sociological Theory*, trans R Barrett, New York: Aldine de Gruyter, 1993b.
Luhmann, N, *Social Systems*, trans J Bednarz, Jr, Stanford, California: Stanford University Press, 1995.
Luhmann, N, 'Legal Argumentation: An Analysis of its Form' trans I Fraser, ed W T Murphy and G Teubner, 58 *Modern Law Review* 3, 285–98, 1995b.
Luhmann, N, *Observations on Modernity*, trans W Whobney, Stanford, California: Stanford University Press, 1998.
Lyotard, JF, *The Postmodern Condition: a Report on Knowledge*, trans by G Bennington and B, Massumi, Manchester: Manchester UP, 1984.
Maturana, H, 'The Organization of the Living: A Theory of the Living Organization', 51 *International Journal of Human and Computer Studies* 2, 149–68, 1999.
Maturana, H and Varela, F, *Autopoiesis and Cognition: the Realization of the Living*, Dordecht, Holland: Reidel Publishing, 1972.
Maturana, H and Varela, F, *The Tree of Knowledge: the Biological Roots of Human Understanding*, Boston: Shambala, 1992.

Merleau-Ponty, M, *The Phenomenology of Perception*, London: Routledge & Kegan Paul, 1962.
Morin, E, *La Méthode II: La Connaissance de la Connaissance,* Paris: Seuil, 1986.
Munch, R, 'Autopoiesis by Definition', 13 *Cardozo Law Review*, 1463–73, 1992.
Murphy, W T, 'Modern Times: Niklas Luhmann on Law, Politics and Social Theory', 47 *The Modern Law Review* 5, 603–21, 1984.
Murphy, W T, 'Some Issues in the Relationship between Law and Autopoiesis', 5 *Law and Critique* 2, 241–64, 1994.
Murphy, W T, *The Oldest Social Science? Configurations of Law and Modernity*, Oxford: Clarendon, 1997.
Nelken, D (ed), *Law as Communication*, Aldershot, Dartmouth, 1996.
Nora, P (ed), *Les Lieux de Mémoire*, Paris: Gallimard, 1984–93.
Norrie, A (ed), *Closure or Critique: New Directions in Legal Theory*, Edinburgh University Press, 1993.
Paterson, J, 'Who is Zenon Bankowski Talking To? The Person in the Sight of Autopoiesis', in D Nelken (ed), 1996.
Radstone, S, 'Screening Trauma: *Forrest Gump*, Film and Memory' in S Radstone, (ed), 2000.
Radstone, S (ed), *Memory and Methodology*, Oxford: Berg, 2000.
Schütz, A, 'The Law With and Against Luhmann, Legendre, Agamben', 11 *Law and Critique* 2, 107–36, 2000.
Shelton, D, *Commitment and Compliance: The Role of Non-binding Norms in the International Legal System*, Oxford: Oxford University Press, 2000.
Steiner, G, *After Babel*, Oxford: Oxford University Press, 1975.
Tarlock, D, 'The Non-Equilibrium Paradigm in Ecology and the Partial Unravelling of Environmental Law', 27 *Loyola of Los Angeles Law Review* 3, 1121–44, 1994.
Teubner, G, *Law as an Autopoietic System*, trans A Bankowska and R Adler, Oxford: Blackwell, 1993.
Teubner, G (ed), *Global Law without a State*, Aldershot: Dartmouth, 1996.
Teubner, G, 'The King's Many Bodies: The Self-Deconstruction of Law's Hierarchy', 31 *Law and Society Review*, 763–88, 1997.
Teubner, G, 'Economics of Gift — Positivity of Justice: The Mutual Paranoia of Jacques Derrida and Niklas Luhmann', 18 *Theory, Culture & Society* 1, 29–47, 2001.
Teubner, G and Febbrajo, A (eds), *State, Law, Economy as Autopoietic Systems*, Milano: Giuffré, 1986.
Tromans, S, 'Alternatives to Landfill — Can the Planning System Deliver?', *Journal of Planning and Environmental Law*, 257–64, March 2001.
World Commission on Environment and Development (WCED), *Our Common Future*, Oxford: Oxford University Press, 1987.
Weisberg, R, 'Autopoiesis and Positivism', 13 *Cardozo Law Review*, 1721–29, 1992.
Wolfe, A, 'Sociological Theory in the Absence of People: the Limits of Luhmann's Systems Theory', 13 *Cardozo Law Review*, 1729–45, 1992.
Zeleny, M and Hufford, K, 'All Autopoietic Systems Must Be Social Systems (Living Implies Autopoietic. But Autopoietic Does Not Imply Living): An Application of Autopoietic Criteria in Systems Analysis', 14 *Journal of Social and Biological Structures* 3, 311–32, 1991.

5

The Spaces of Irony

CLAIRE VALIER[1]

The ironic nothing is the dead silence in which irony walks again and haunts (the latter word taken altogether ambiguously) (Kierkegaard, 1841/1989: 258).

SØREN KIERKEGAARD'S STATEMENT, made during the course of his treatise on irony, means more, much more, than it says. Irony, this dead man walking, jests while it haunts (in the vernacular used by the philosopher, the verb *spøger* carries this double entendre). Haunting, joking, this doubled figure is an unlikely one, for there is, it seems, something improper about the dead man's jesting. Apparently the Copenhagen faculty did not take kindly to Kierkegaard's sprightly dissertation. Although he anticipated censure of its ease of style and apparent frivolity, Kierkegaard submitted his work for examination. His apprehensions were not unfounded, for the professors appointed to evaluate the work didn't know what to make of it. The defence of thesis was, by all accounts, a heated affair. This is a telling incident, which speaks of the pitfalls of irony as much as of its pleasures. Pointedly, the critical potential of irony, as well as its problems, lies in the fact that irony exists only in and through its demonstration. Irony, one might say, is the performative par excellence. As a consequence, it is relatively ineffectual if I tell you what irony is and what it can accomplish. Happily, the situation is somewhat improved if I show you. However, this remark should immediately be qualified, for the very same demonstrative aspect of irony imparts upon it an uncertain status. In the instant example, there was consternation over whether Kierkegaard's theses constituted a work on irony or a work of irony. The very idea that his text was, at one and the same time, both, was quite unpalatable to the faculty. To present an

[1] I would like to thank Ronnie Lippens for organising a fruitful and highly enjoyable workshop in Oñati, Andreas Philippopoulos-Mihalopoulos for presenting an excellent précis of my paper, and Louis, Richard, Rolland and Simon for their helpful comments. The research upon which this essay is based benefited from the award of a grant by the British Academy. I am grateful to the Fellows and their excellent administrative staff for their support and assistance.

ironical dissertation on the concept of irony, however sparkling a performance, was for the examiners an incomprehensible departure from the established norms of scholarship. Irony is not only disruptive of academic discourse. More broadly, it is a risky mode of address, courting controversy. Perhaps writing about it is equally foolhardy. Yet there is more to the story of Kierkegaard's thesis than the merely cautionary, for its very out-of-placedness permits irony to attain potent effects, to provoke immediate and intense reactions in its audiences.

Now just because irony can be compelling, it does not follow that the ironic is an authoritative mode of address. Look again at the epigraph to this text of mine. Following his comment upon the dead silence of irony, Kierkegaard immediately marks the ambiguity of his statement. Ironically enough, he makes it clear that he intends this ambiguity! So the clarification turns out to be equivocal, indeed its placement in parentheses only underlines the equivocal textuality of the entire dissertation. I point this detail out because it illustrates the non-exegetical character of irony, which is neither instructive nor commanding. Basically, the ironist does not communicate didactically because irony is an abstention from determinate meaning. The ironic text places a question mark over the very notion of authorship. As Sartre remarks in *L'Etre et Le Néant*, 'in irony a man annihilates what he posits within one and the same act.' Irony is hence not only a negation of the said, but also of the saying. It is, one might say, a negation of iteration itself. However, this radical reflexivity makes for no less persuasive a rhetorical device.

Returning to the out-of-placedness typically associated with irony, this leads me to reflect upon the topic of ironic discourse, to consider the question of its sitings, its contours and spaces. Where, indeed, does the out of place take place? Standard treatises on rhetoric generally inform their readers that the figure of irony simply consists in saying the opposite of what one really means. Unfortunately, this commonplace definition will not do at all, for accompanying the implication that I do not (really) mean X, there is no affirmation that I thereby mean Y. It is not the case that irony simply substitutes an unsaid for that which is said. Oh no, the matter is much more slippery than that. The 'is and is not' of Kierkegaardian irony after all does not conform to a binary logic of the either/or. A more precise statement would be that irony happens, it comes about, in a space somewhere *between* the said and the unsaid. This borderland locus can produce surprising effects, at a minimum making visible the multiple meanings of an event. A matter of double vision, the ironic challenges an utterance or an image in its customary meaning. It undermines the authority of this privileged meaning by staging a confrontation with the spectral presence of other possible meanings. In this way, a subtle interplay between the literal and the subtextual is made visible. Some would go further still and say that in irony, the contingency of all language and the inalienable polysemy of the image are performed.

This in-between and interstitial space, within which irony performs its spectral work, calls for, and calls upon, the attendance of a critical audience. Indeed, irony only exists 'as such' in its interpellation of this audience. It is of course the ironist, be this the critic, cartoonist or writer, who begins to open up the space of irony. It is the ironist who first offers this invitation:

> I say this silence or, better, construct this space
> So that somehow something may move across
> The caught barriers of language to you and me
> (Graham, 1970/1996: 50).

Yet let me say it again: no irony without an audience. Beyond the originating act of the ironist, irony comes about, it happens, in and through the interpretation made by the listener, reader or viewer. The coming into being of this audience that makes a double reading is the moment of irony. Constructing this space which is the space of irony, the barrier between said and unsaid becomes a site of communication, a portal through which movement takes place across a boundary. This co-mmunication is a moving with, rather than a moving together. In this way, ironist and audience become fellow travellers, travelling companions if you like. The apparent motility of irony is noted by Northrop Frye (1957: 40), when he writes that irony is 'a pattern of words that turns away from direct statement or its own obvious meaning.' Characterised by this motion of turning away, and of moving across, this space is a space of passage. As a space of the 'somehow something', it is also a space of possibility. Note the irresolute, if hopeful, tone of this 'possibility', a perhaps, a maybe, an opportunity which is, nevertheless, devoid of all certainty. In turning away, there is no final place, no terminus towards which irony travels. One might add that if it has no destination, there is an initial route, a redirection, with the turning from the literal towards the figurative. Nevertheless, the moment of departure does not envisage an end to the journey. So, the ironic reader does not anticipate the stasis of narrative closure, the resolution of determinate meaning.

As I mentioned above, the ironic address can generate powerful feelings in its audiences. We should therefore note that the space of irony doubles as both a semantic and an affective space. As well as seemingly saying something, hinting at more than it says, the ironic moves us (that is to say, it is emotive). Given all that I have said so far, you can imagine that the space of irony is neither a place of solace nor of reassurance. If anything, it is discomforting, unsettling, and leaves us uneasy. At one point Kierkegaard characterises the ironist as vampiric. There is much to be said for this gothic analogy. The ironist needs an audience and draws upon the reader or viewer. Furthermore, the seduction of the ironic reader is an initiation into the pleasures and dangers of an illicit space. In locutory terms, the invitation is an 'aside', which leads one apart from the everyday and the commonplace.

Feeling the bite of the vampire, the cut of the ironist, then, is a risky business. To put the matter more prosaically, irony puts us on edge. At its sharpest it is incisive; it is cutting and sometimes wounding. Of relevance here, I believe, is Kierkegaard's (1841/1989: 256) comment that 'the moral categories are too concrete for irony.' One might surmise that irony is associated with the staging, with the provocation even, of moral ambiguities. It slips and slides around and in-between the perceived solidities of apparent certainties. This wounding force of irony provides a cogent mode of critique, able to strike at the heart of contemporary culture.

Irony is, by nature, interlocutory. Because it first acknowledges what it then proceeds to question, irony is a dissenting mode of address. It looks to the customary meaning only to turn away from it, and for me, this gives the ironic mode considerable political purchase. In fact, as well as constituting a distinctive kind of speech act, for Kierkegaard irony is a mode of engagement in public life (Cross, 1998). He used this device to counter the social production of stereotypes, and taken as a whole his corpus mounts quite some critique of the emergent mass society. The usefulness of this dissident rhetorical device in cultural and political critique has not been lost upon others. For instance, Lauren Berlant (1997) suggests that the fantasy nation form both produces normative political subjectivity and creates public spaces of exaggeration, irony, or ambivalence. Relatedly, she writes of a pervasive rhetoric of citizen trauma in the public culture of America, which, she argues, produces a 'cartoon version of the shaken nation.' The new figure of the victim-citizen addressed by a range of criminal-legal practices is, I believe, the product of what Berlant (1997: 2) names politics by caricature, which she describes as, 'a farce-style moral and civil war between icons and hyphenated stereotypes.' This politics by caricature constructs what Berlant sees as 'extreme images of personhood' which nevertheless, she tells us, constitute modal points in the identity politics of western societies. Her analysis charts the ways in which a number of alternately demonic and idealised images and narratives came to dominate the official national public sphere of the US. It seems to me that this politics by caricature instantiates within the realm of legal practices what we might as well call a cartoon justice. This may well secure a popular mandate for punitive measures, but it also permits spaces of irony to be opened up. These have the potential to be transformative, for while irony opens out new discursive spaces, these are not safely located outside of, and at a distance from, the established, the mainstream and the canonical. No, spaces of irony open out from within, and turn us away from, we ironists, the dominant culture.

The hegemony of politics by caricature is undercut by the cartooning of the political. My attentions in this essay are directed towards one specific site of ironic communication, namely, the editorial cartoon. In *Crime and Punishment in Contemporary Culture* (Valier, 2003a), I argued that if we are to pursue justice we must address the historically specific, and changing,

Priestley, Independent, 25.11.1997

relationships between punishment, culture and communication. The cartoon is, as Randall Harrison (1981) has written, a caricature of modern mass communication. It seems to exemplify the fast-paced and increasingly visual character of communication, its typically disposable soundbite messages, and its blurring of information with entertainment. It is my belief that editorial cartoons supply a readily accessible space, within which the cartoon justice of today is exposed to debate and ridicule. This much is evident in Priestley's excellent cartoon, 'Judge for Yourself', which sends up the hotly contested issue of public opinion in criminal sentencing, as it was played out in Myra Hindley's case:[2]

The viewer poll in the cartoon makes explicit the relation between infotainment and punitive populism, and the mockery that this makes of the ideal of participatory democracy. Relatedly, the absurdly unconstitutional position of a politician setting tariffs is sent up by the surreal caricature of 'Jumpin Jack Straw' (England's Home Secretary at the time). The ascribed status of Hindley as 'icon of evil' is undercut by the show's own polling number, 666, the number of the beast. All in all, this cartoon of Priestley's demands a response from the viewer, a response which is more than laughter, for it turns ridicule to political advantage. This black humour is deadly serious.

[2] *R v Secretary of State for the Home Department, ex parte Hindley* [1998] 2 WLR 505, QB 751; [1998] AC 539; [2000] 2 WLR 730, 2 All ER 385.

In this chapter, I am going to look into the iconoclastic force of irony, its smashing capacity to question the evidences of the self-evidently iconic. Irony, as I have been demonstrating to you, is a trope in which the border between the said and the unsaid is called into question, becoming a site at which dominant truth claims are called to account. This particular tropological strategy calls upon critical audiences to distance themselves from some commonplace notion. For the usual modes of interpellation and address an alternative idiom is substituted. On this occasion my reflections address the strident discourses surrounding the execution of its first federal prisoner in four decades by the United States of America. I critique the state of unitedness of this vengeful 'America', convoked through powerfully emotive images of national trauma and of closure through imposition of the death penalty. Funnily enough, the word 'closure' connotes all the notions of semantic and narrative finality which irony upsets.

This chapter looks at some images connected with the killing of Timothy McVeigh, the Oklahoma City bomber. This particular case is emblematic of a number of changes in criminal justice philosophies and practices, occurring in similar forms across several western jurisdictions. The case is also, relatedly, associated with battles of various kinds over images.[3] Days before the execution, an internet entertainment company sued the authorities for the right to show a live public webcast of the event.[4] Their demand, levied 'as citizens and as victims', was rejected by the court. However, Congress passed a special motion to permit survivors and relatives of the dead to witness the killing of prisoner 12076–064 by live satellite feed in Oklahoma City, 650 miles from the death chamber.[5] The execution was delayed by ten minutes while engineers fixed a technical glitch in the transmission. After McVeigh had been declared dead, the American President brazenly announced, 'today, every living person who was hurt by the evil done in Oklahoma City can rest in the knowledge that there has been a reckoning.'[6] Today we are regularly presented with emotive 'iconic' images. These are appropriated into punitive discourses when an authoritative and retributivist

[3] The McVeigh case was central to several important changes in American criminal justice procedures. Congress passed the landmark Effective Death Penalty and Anti-Terrorism Act 1996, which was introduced to make the death penalty more 'robust' through substantial habeas corpus reform. An 'effective' death penalty was linked by this statute to a diminished ability of the federal courts to enforce the constitutional rights of state prisoners (Steiker, 2001). Secondly, new victim participation legislation was passed, overriding decisions of the trial judge and the US Court of Appeals, in the Victim Rights Clarification Act 1997.

[4] *Entertainment Network Inc vs Harley Lappin, Kathleen Hawk Sawyer and John Ashcroft*, TH01-0076-T/H.

[5] Congress passed 18 USC § 3510(a) and 42 USC § 10608, and revisions were subsequently made to the Department of Justice *Guidelines for Victim and Witness Assistance*. Details of the transmission to Oklahoma City were outlined in 'Arrangements for Victim Viewing of McVeigh Execution', Attorney General's Statement, April 19 2001, (202) 514–2007.

[6] George W Bush, 'Statement on Execution of Timothy McVeigh', White House Press Office, 11-6-2001.

interpretation of them is promulgated. This interpretation is grounded in a strident narrative, in which trauma is necessarily followed by 'closure', a state which can only be attained through the imposition of maximally retributive punishment. This discourse is indeed strident. It openly excludes dissenting voices including, for instance, the voices of those crime victims who do not support the death penalty. How can we counter this potent aesthetic? What alternative ways can we find of engaging critical audiences? In this essay I take a look at two striking works by the Pulitzer Prize-winning editorial cartoonists Doug Marlette and Steve Benson. Both of these were published in mainstream daily newspapers, as well as on the internet. They initiate what to my mind is a highly effective critique of the mass subject invoked as the subject of the killing state, as well as more broadly questioning the very iconicity of iconic images.

The McVeigh case occasioned a flurry of activity from editorial cartoonists.[7] A cartoon is a representational or symbolic drawing that makes a satirical, witty or humorous point. The editorial cartoon typically appears in a newspaper, periodical, or website, and uses a single panel to present one specific scene in snapshot. These images are indeed graphics, making political commentary in black and white, eschewing colour and shading to make a trenchant and sometimes caustic point. Cartoons have been used to great effect as a campaigning strategy, for instance during the struggle for women's suffrage (see Sheppard 1994; Atkinson 1997). They have also taken a prominent place in electoral politics, employing wordplay, ridicule and vulgarity to lampoon political figures and their electorate (see Blaisdell and Selz, 1976; Edwards, 1997). These pictures do their work through a combination of persuasiveness and personal affront. As one cartoonist put it, 'our job is to foment rebellion and try to make people nauseous at breakfast' (Meyer, cited in Borromeo, 1984: 9). Books about cartoons often make this provocative intent overt in their title, for instance *Communication to the Quick* or *The Bite of the Print* (Harrison, 1981; Getlein, 1964). During their history political cartoons have been subject to both ad hoc censorship and more systematic legislatory control. For instance, in the early twentieth century several states of America introduced anti-cartoon legislation. California's law of this kind was passed in 1899, and remained on the statute book for fifteen years. It prohibited the publication of any drawing reflecting adversely upon the 'honor, integrity, manhood, virtue, or reputation of any individual.' In some countries political cartoonists continue

[7] Sixty cartoons on the McVeigh execution, and thirty more on the death penalty in general, are archived at www.cagle.slate.msn.com. An annual selection of American editorial cartoons can be found in the book *Best Editorial Cartoons of the Year* (for instance, Brooks, 1999). Those interested in British political cartoons can consult the extensive collection at the Centre for the Study of Cartoons and Caricature, University of Kent, which has a useful online catalogue.

This cartoon is reproduced by the kind permission of Doug Marlette, Tribune Media Services©

today to be tortured, sent to prison, exiled and assassinated.[8] The existence elsewhere of these violent forms of repression should not however detract from our understanding of the barbed and dangerous impact of political cartoons in general.

Berlant, you may remember, described the obsessive production within American public culture of alternately idealised and demonised figures. Many cartoons on the McVeigh execution dramatised the very prosaic rendering of the condemned man as evil, depicting him being welcomed into hotel hell by the devil. Others focused on the audience, and sent up the idealised iconic figures of the television viewer in a sports bar, or, as in the editorial cartoon below by Doug Marlette, at home with the family.

This cartoon is absolutely loaded with ironic counter-meaning. As you can see, the device of caricature, which comically exaggerates and distorts a person's distinctive features, is used to great effect by Marlette. In this instance, the image of the audience depicts a generic family unit. The family tableau shown here is every bit as revealing as the classical scene of *Las Meniñas*. The cartoon shows up in bold relief the primary constituency addressed by the politicians who claim that we should centre criminal justice upon victims. The framing of the OKC bombing as a specifically

[8] Details of these events are listed according to country on the Index on Censorship site at the following URL: www.oneworld.org/index_oc/Cartoon/.

national tragedy foregrounded images of dead children and their grieving parents. The bombing, which took place on Patriot's Day, decimated the America's Kids Daycare Centre, killing nineteen babies and children. In the hours following the bombing, televised images of bleeding and dead infants being pulled from the ruins were broadcast far and wide. President Clinton took the opportunity to state, 'we were for a moment once again family, outraged and heartbroken' (cited in Linenthal, 2001: 111). As we will see, the term 'heartbroken' is quite significant, evoking as it does the profundity of trauma to the very 'heartland' of American public culture.

In the Marlette cartoon, the national citizens, the audience addressed as this 'America', hailed and greeted by the television anchor, occupy the fantasy space of domestic entertainment and harmony. This indexes nostalgic evocation of the suburban space of pleasurable consumption *and* normative nuclear familial relations associated with the advent of mass television ownership (see Spiegel, 1992). This domestic snapshot also satirises the heteronormative politics of the family, which one might evoke by mere mention of the Defence of Marriage Act. The cartoon sends up all those institutions, instruments, images and ways of understanding that make the hetero-familial both coherent and privileged. The national family, the 'America' hailed, welcomed, and which recognises itself here as the audience, is privatised, coupled, gendered (in a spoof on the division of labour, she handles, quite literally, childcare; he drinks, ready for the office, his coffee) and hetero-reproductive. This is all written here in black and white. The cartoon makes explicit what Berlant and Warner (1998) identify as typically unmarked, as invisible and tacit, as the basic idiom of the social and the personal.

The cartoon also makes ironic commentary upon the mass subject invoked by discourses of trauma and closure. Like the imagined audience in the Priestley cartoon, the goggle-eyed bozos staring at the television screen prompt reflection upon debates about western public spheres. In his fascinating text *The Present Age*, Kierkegaard characterised the democratised culture of his day as productive of a phantom public sphere, writing:

> In order that everything should be reduced to the same level, it is first of all necessary to produce a phantom, its spirit a monstrous abstraction ... and that phantom is the Public (Kierkegaard, 1846/1962: 59).

According to Kierkegaard, this phantasmatic character of the public came about as the press engendered a realm of idle talk, curious yet ultimately disinterested amusement, and opinionated irresponsibility. This 'monstrous abstraction', he argued, is produced in the form of anonymous spectators, who are constituted as citizens through their consumption of mass media. People become riveted voyeurs, whom, Kierkegaard complained, feel themselves bound by no commitments. The ironic idiom was, in a way, his means of undercutting the superficiality of the public of his day. Over the last decade, notions of the phantom public sphere have undergone a critical revival since the publication of an edited collection upon the subject (Robbins, 1993). This stimulating text looked back to Walter Lippman's use of the phrase, when he argued in 1925 that the formation of citizens into the responsible, well-informed public of participatory democracy was deeply problematic. The Robbins book addressed the ways in which the subject of mass culture is invoked, an analysis also taken up by Hal Foster (1996) in his essay 'Death in America.' Foster writes that the mass subject of modern democracies is convoked both through a body, for instance that of a celebrity or a politician, and as a body, for instance as a collective traumatized by the same event. He terms this latter collectivity the 'psychic nation':

> a mass-mediated polis that is not only convoked around calamitous events (like the Rodney King beating or the Oklahoma City bombing) but also addressed, polled, and reported as a traumatic subject (Foster, 1996: 55).

This phantomatic public sphere is constructed through mass-mediated death and disaster. Convoked, addressed, polled, and reported in wounded nationality, the images in and through which this kind of mass-mediated polis is constituted seem to have a sacrosanct quality about them. Editorial cartoons, however, are typically irreverent. As you can see, Marlette's image directly sends up the *esprit de corpse* which the privileged traumatic subject of western culture supposedly lives out.

The deeply emotive familial nationhood evoked within today's criminal justice practices is evident. Days after the Oklahoma City bombing, President Clinton issued a highly indicative press statement. This message proclaimed a national day of mourning, and then swiftly announced that the government would seek the death penalty for the bombers. Here the traumatic subject is also addressed as the subject of the killing state. Throughout the case these two interpellatory forms continued to be juxtaposed. The trial itself featured searing testimony from survivors and the relatives of the deceased, far in excess of the detail needed to prove the corpus delicti or to establish the guilt of the accused. In addition, forty victim impact statements were admitted during the penalty phase, and (unusually) these included those from rescue workers as well as survivors and relatives of the dead. Four police officers gave testimony about their rescue efforts in the immediate aftermath of the blast. This entailed what the defence were to call 'graphic and gruesome' testimony about finding and removing the grievously injured and dead from the rubble. The police officers also spoke of psychological suffering that they had endured due to witnessing the scenes of carnage, terror and death. The jury, several of whom cried during the victim impact testimony, unanimously recommended that McVeigh be executed. During the minutes that it took to kill this man, ABC's *Good Morning* programme showed footage of survivors and relatives reading the victim impact statements that they had presented to the court. For the prohibited images of execution was substituted the figure of the traumatic subject, authorising maximal retribution as just deserts for loss and suffering. It was through these extreme images of national familial trauma that US citizens were interpellated into a retributive community of grief.[9]

In the Marlette cartoon, 'Closure' corresponds to restoration of the 'safe' familial space of secure meanings. Entertainment Network Inc, the company suing for the execution webcast, claimed that their proposed transmission could 'help to bring a sense of closure to this event for all of the Americans who were outraged and traumatised by this heinous crime.'[10] The national trauma of the attack was officially described as having 'literally brought home the impact of terrorism for Americans' (Department of Justice, 2000). This official report described the huge shock for Americans to discover that they are not immune from massive-scale attack within their own borders. The report states that the shock was further magnified by the specific location of the attack, a deadly wound inflicted right there in the 'heartland' of the country. The national trauma was hence depicted as one of anxiety, loss and fear because the bombing, 'changed the Nation's general sense of safety and insecurity.' In comments like 'OKC looks like Beirut', the bombed city was imagined as an alien landscape. The attack was described as the kind of thing that happens in 'hybrid' cities like LA and New York, but not in middle America, 'far from the country's urban edges, deep in the farm belt, a quintessentially secure and American landscape' (*Life*, 1996). The Marlette cartoon can be seen as a space of irony exposing the familial politics of the wounded 'heartland way', so evident in the memorialisation of the bombing and the demand for the death penalty. As Victoria Johnson (1999) has shown, commemorative television programmes related recovery after the bombing to the reconstruction of a mundane family life. She relates the imagined pastoral of Oklahoma to an idealised turn towards the home, in a privatised and familial model of citizenship. For Johnson, coverage of the anniversary of the bombing was infused with a fantasy politics of 'the normal.' She argues that typical narratives and images of victimhood and recovery constructed a mythical heartland landscape. This was the scene of privatised citizenship, based in the

[9] Steve Bell's striking cartoon 'George Bush and Timothy McVeigh' ironically dubbed the dead terrorist, depicted as strapped martyr-like to the gurney, 'King of the Closures' (*The Guardian* 12-06-2001). This image can be accessed through the newspaper's online cartoon archive at the following URL: www.guardian.co.uk/cartoons/stevebell/0,7371,531759,00.html.

[10] ENI Press release (undated) 'The McVeigh Execution and Entertainment Network, Inc.'

observance and display of traditional gender roles within the heterosexual nuclear family. She hence argues that the notion of the heartland is less concerned with a specific bounded geographical locality, than with evoking the symbolic geography of a specific American pastoral ideal. This, she explains, is centred on a privatised ethic of church and family. The imagined rural safe space, inhabited by good citizens with an 'innocent' communal sensibility, injured by the bombing, is also evoked by the 'sacred' space of the Oklahoma Memorial. Within an hour of McVeigh's death, a plaque marking his execution was installed in the timeline. Yet as we shall see, the supposedly sacred character of the icons of the OKC bombing, and their intimate connection with address to the vengeful traumatic subject, has been hotly contested.

In addition to addressing the ways in which the subjects of mass culture are convoked, the contributors to the collection, *The Phantom Public Sphere* emphasised the multiple character of publics, with the formation of both dominant publics and subaltern counterpublics. These latter were envisaged as oppositional spaces opened up by subordinate social groups. More recently, Michael Warner (2002) has further elaborated upon the notion of counterpublics, writing that they are not limited to the subject positions generally associated by theorists with subalternity. Interestingly, he argues that counterpublic spaces are not only spaces of resistance and agitation as concerns ideas and policies, but also develop distinctive speech genres and modes of address. He characterises dominant publics as spaces that take for granted their discourse pragmatics, and that misrecognise, as universality or normalcy, their expansive address. By contrast, Warner relates the counter- or oppositional status of counterpublic spaces to the novelty with which sociability with strangers and its reflexivity is imagined. I believe that irony can contribute to the alternative idiom that generates and sustains counterpublic spaces. The notion comes with that of doubled audiences. Simply put, there is one audience that gets the gag, and another which does not, which is also the one being sent up. So, the ironist takes with him a discerning listener, or, to prefer a Kierkegaardian locution, one who is 'in the know.' The family figured in the Marlette cartoon, the unreflexive grinning blockheads, are those who refuse to read ironically. Kierkegaard argues that the subject of modernity is an ironic subject. One might remark that however much ironic reading is an ever-present possibility, encouraged by the existential conditions of western modernity, it is one that some people cannot countenance. As well as the Kierkegaardian ironic subject, an equally noticeable figure is the subject of resentment. This is the subject that moves from the wound to revenge. This bitter, resentful and vengeful figure is at the heart of the traumatic subject of today, a subject that nostalgically seeks closure. Irony however, is a refusal of nostalgia, 'that fantastic longing for direct and absolute truths, for primal innocence, for transparent immediacy' (Shakespeare, 1998: 97). The characters drawn by Marlette are the subjects of mass culture, interpellated as members of the dominant public. They happily, gleefully almost, misrecognise themselves as 'America itself' through the expansive address of the television anchor. At the same time, the cartoon works as a space of irony, a space of passage within which a critical audience can recognise itself in turning away from the brute literality of the term 'Closure.'

The Marlette cartoon evokes what we might call iconic unmarked citizens. It shows up the tendency of official and mainstream discourses of criminal victimhood to construct a generic traumatic subject, or privileged vengeful mourner. These discourses frame privileged forms of victimhood in certain ways. They create images of the idealised victim, a figure who is preferably unmarked by the indices of subaltern status, and always constructed as innocent. This idealised victim, or his/her surviving relatives, ideally always demand strong measures of protection and tough penalties. This tendency is not limited to the sphere of criminal justice policy and practice. For example, Berlant more broadly relates the coupling of suffering and citizenship to the production of generic people, those iconic citizens, the white middle class family.

This frequent appeal to the generic traumatic subject gives me pause to reflect a little upon the iconicity of iconic images. Indeed, one could posit something like an iconomy, an economy of icons. Addressing this iconomy, we might think about who profits from these iconic images, for whose consumption they are particularly destined, in what circuits they are distributed and in what ways they are coded to interest their target audiences. This line of thinking moves away from that generalist register in which one remarks that iconic images are simply 'for everyone,' that they are in themselves 'of and for the people.' The notion of an iconomy departs then from Marshall McLuhan's description of the icon as 'an inclusive compressed image' (McLuhan, 1964/2002: 118). For instance, he emphasised the power of television images to involve *all* members of the nation, describing the coverage of JF Kennedy's assassination and funeral as emblematic of the medium's ability to involve the whole nation in moving depth. For him, (1964/2002: 180), 'TV simply involved everybody in everybody more deeply than before.' However, more recent scholarship emphasises that the spectacles which produce 'iconic intimates' rely upon illusions of reciprocity, participation and dialogue, creating what actually only amounts to a hallucination of nearness (Bhabha, 1998). Furthermore, rather than involving everybody in everybody, iconic images both appeal to a mass subject, and are the focus of a number of competing readings. The mediated nature of iconic images renders them vulnerable to irony's edge, that is, to a profound questioning of their very iconicity. This exposes and challenges the particular viewing relations by which they function as icons. Basically, the ironic reading undercuts the relations of spectatorship that permit icons to operate within a familiar vocabulary and set of symbols.

Ever since Northrop Frye's classic text *The Anatomy of Criticism*, the ironic mode has been linked to the portrayal of the hero within a scene of absurdity. The iconic image of the OKC attack, awarded a Pulitzer prize, was an amateur's photograph of a firefighter cradling the lifeless and bloodied body of a dead baby covered in dust, dirt and debris in his arms. This image was immediately identified as 'an American icon', as 'an American emblem for the sorrow of April 19' (Linenthal, 2001: 145; Hamm, 1997: 50). Not only did the image of Baylee Almon and the firefighter become the most popular memorial idea for remembrance of the tragedy of OKC, it was also the subject of an extensive memorabilia, including T. shirts, belt buckles, key chains, necklaces, statues and phone cards (Linenthal, 2001). A controversial cartoon by Steve Benson, composed in protest against the sentencing of McVeigh to death in June 1997, redrew this 'American icon.' The resulting image was quickly denounced by a number of parties, including the Oklahoma Governor, as 'offensive' 'repulsive' and 'disgusting.' Alfred Whitehouse, President of the International Association of Fire Fighters, complained that the cartoonist had taken an image of heroism and twisted it into something obscene. Benson however defended the 'brutal honesty' of his cartoon.

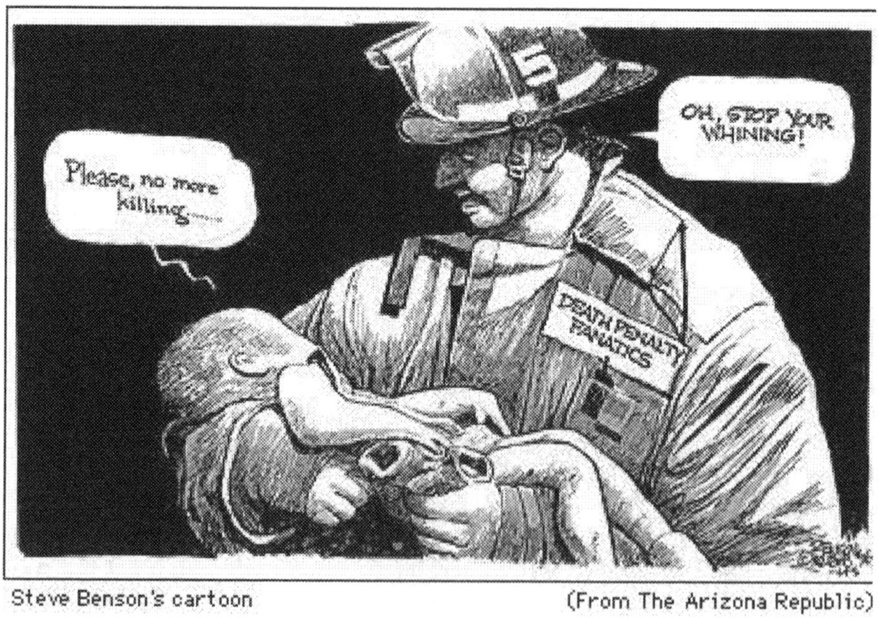

Figure 2 Copyright© Arizona Republic 1997. This cartoon is reproduced by permission of Steve Benson and UFS Inc.

This cartoon created quite a furore, with its very direct demand that its viewers take up a position vis à vis the appropriation of the iconic OKC image into a pro-death penalty agenda. The cartoon also exposes uncomfortably the relations of spectatorship central to iconicity, dramatising its very constructedness. The ready rejection of this image as 'disgusting' is a visceral response akin to the energetic condemnation of Marcus Harvey's painting of Myra Hindley, upon which subject Alison Young (2000) has published a fascinating paper. Nevertheless, the vocal consternation at the cartoon only further underlines its critical impact.

In addition to the contested politics of victimhood there was, as part of the killing of McVeigh, a related battle over hero status. Something of this battle is played out in the Benson cartoon. A common device in irony is the naïve hero, a credulous figure. In the cartoon, for the name-tag is substituted the label 'death penalty fanatics', just as for the identity of the individual firefighter, Chris Fields, was substituted the symbolic figure of heroism through tragedy. A fanatic is one marked by an intense, uncritical devotion. The 'sorrow of April 19' is rewritten here as the opening scene of a revenge movie, similar in a way to *Collateral Damage* (Warner Brothers, 2001). In this film, Arnold Schwarzenegger plays a family man and firefighter who seeks revenge after the authorities fail to bring to justice the Colombian rebel who bombed a building, killing his wife and child. The hero turns avenger, but in doing so can he remain hero? Critics fiercely objected to the series of proximities imagined between firefighter-hero and vigilante. The Benson cartoon superimposes both incarnations of the action-hero.

Moving from one man in uniform to another, the Benson cartoon calls up the contested status of Timothy McVeigh as war hero and self-styled American patriot. Berlant (1997: 2), you may remember, described politics by caricature as, 'a farce-style moral and civil war between icons and hyphenated stereotypes.' Farce, a comic genre, engages its audiences through the performance of ludicrous confusions, improbable situations, and the display of exaggerated and stereotyped characters. These are all features of the McVeigh case. He was, as some of the popular books put it, *One of Ours*, an *American Terrorist*, an *All-American Monster* (Serrano, 1998; Michel and Herbeck, 2001). Not only was the OKC bomber an American citizen, he was also a decorated Gulf War veteran, trained by his government to defend the nation against its enemies. McVeigh, who saw action during Operation Desert Storm, was the man from the combat zone, a top gun who killed the distant enemy. Yet he brought back from that deadly exchange, from that dangerous and foreign wild zone, a fury at America's extravagant violence. His attack on the federal government building was also designed as revenge for the excessive use of force against 'enemies within' at Waco and Ruby Ridge. Opposing stay of execution the government were keen to depict him as 'an enemy of the

Constitution.'[11] Immediately after the death penalty was passed, Congress rushed through legislation to prevent him from being buried with military honours in the sacred space of a national cemetery, to forestall this desecration of the space designed to remember and honour the nation's official war heroes.[12] McVeigh's last statement was read outside the prison after his death, its words the text of a nineteenth-century poem:

> Invictus
> Out of the night that covers me,
> Black as the Pit from pole to pole,
> I thank whatever gods may be
> For my unconquerable soul.
> In the fell clutch of circumstance
> I have not winced nor cried aloud.
> Under the bludgeonings of chance
> My head is bloody, but unbowed.
> Beyond this place of wrath and tears
> Looms but the Horror of the shade,
> And yet the menace of the years
> Finds, and shall find, me unafraid.
> It matters not how strait the gate,
> How charged with punishments the scroll,
> I am the master of my fate:
> I am the captain of my soul
> (WE Henley, 1875)

Into the cacophony following the execution came this stern poem, with its ideas of stoicism and forbearance through adversity and suffering. In the context of its use as McVeigh's last statement, it also reads as resolutely unapologetic, as a determination to stand by his convictions. The secular idiom of 'Invictus', with its message of indomitable self-determination, levels a challenge to the dogmatic rhetoric of righteous vengeance, evil and damnation. In the world of politics by caricature, idealised generic victims are demarcated against stereotyped villains. Yet the figure of McVeigh contains elements of both hero and enemy. The Benson cartoon makes evident the constructedness of both heroism and notoriety, that these are a question of imputation more than they are inherent qualities.

The firefighter cartoon at Figure 2 demonstrates clearly the caustic effect, the bite and the cut, of irony. Responding to enraged denouncers, Benson stated, 'art is intended to grab you in the gut and to twist', and explained that

[11] *United States of America v Timothy James McVeigh*. Brief of the United States Opposing Stay of Execution.

[12] The text of this legislation is contained in the Death Sentence and Veterans Benefits Act 1997, 38 USC §2411.

his cartoon was intended to bring about introspection and self-examination (cited in Moore, 1997). Quite unimpressed with this explanation, Whitehouse for the firefighters retorted,

> at a time when the healing process has begun and all of those who were touched by the Oklahoma City bombing are trying to bring closure to this tragedy, Mr Benson and United Features Syndicate by their callousness, have opened some deep wound.

Well, in a way, this objector has hit the nail on the head, for irony disrupts the (violently) therapeutic register of 'closure.' As I mentioned above, there is a certain traumatic force of irony, which particularly proceeds, I believe, from its staging and provocation of moral ambiguities. Relatedly, Kierkegaard speaks of 'the wound of negativity', the wounding character of irony, of this nothingness that calls borders and limits into question, which disrupts the myths of innocence and immediacy (Shakespeare, 1998). The Benson cartoon makes plain the cutting edge of irony. Paul de Man (1969/1983; 1977/1996) emphasised this disturbing aspect, arguing that irony produces the permanent interruption of narrative. He added that ironic consciousness is not reassuring, pointing to its tendency to gain momentum and unravel all customary distinctions. Irony is neither curative nor reconciliatory. Ultimately, it defers closure.

The Marlette cartoon shows the home restored as a surreally safe and cosy site for the domestic consumption of distant violence. The figures, these couch potatoes, are Berlant's infantile citizens. Naïve, passive and infantilised, they are also the consumers of this televised entertainment. They are the index market for the Toyota and Outback Steakhouse advertisements that punctuated the coverage of McVeigh's execution. The Marlette and Benson cartoons put on display, but also question, the Baudrillardian subject, the subject who is saturated with information and images, riveted by the latest kind of reality TV. Baudrillard argues that the media implode into the mass consciousness, obliterating distinctions between public and private, and replacing them with an increasingly pervasive media space. The subject, he claims, is reduced to a terminal within an all-consuming circulation of the hyper-real. Hence for Baudrillard, new media bring the neutralisation of meaning and the emasculation of politics, with the collapse of all critical distance. Though Baudrillard's work is usefully provocative, I do not believe that the media are always already anti-mediatory. As you will have gathered from this essay, I prefer to work with a notion of doubled audiences. There is, as I have hoped to demonstrate to you, much critical mileage to be gained from addressing the figure of an ironic reader, from calling upon one who can, and will, read between the lines.

REPRISE

Today there is a pressing need for strategies by which we can critique the profusion of iconic images, so pervasive in daily life. This essay has pursued an ironic reading of iconic images, a reading to which you, after all, have been a party. I believe that this kind of subaltern reading can play an important part in the constitution of critical counterpublics. Through the opening up of spaces of irony, we can engage with the dominant culture, we can camp on its terrain, but at the same time we can perform acts of disaffiliation.

Ironic spaces are one way in which the critical distance that Baudrillard claims is an impossibility can be engendered. Because irony is sited in the in-between, on that edge which is also a point of passage, the spaces of irony are media. As media, they occupy a middle position, they effect a conveyance and a communication. The ironic is therefore a space which mediates, and it constructs an alternative media space. It is, of course, only one among a number of possible strategies, which might also include the penning of 'trade books' and the practice of photojournalism (for the latter, see Valier, 2003b).

The ironic is a mode of address suited to the formation of counterpublic spaces, those sites in which an alternative idiom develops. These new discursive spaces engage with the mainstream and dominant public sphere, seeking to reinscribe its terms. Irony contributes to this task, as a device by which dominant discourses can be challenged in their habitual and hegemonic vocabularies, for, as Rorty (1989: 74) points out, 'the opposite of irony is common sense.' Because irony unfolds within a logic of repetition and negation it counters the iterative construction of dominant terms. As an effective counterfoil to the populist appeal of commonsense, irony suspends the assumed commonality of that which is called the common*place*. It points towards other spaces, turning away towards an elsewhere. Here it is then, this space of passage, this 'dead silence', this space of communication constructed between you and I:

> ...I say
> This silence here for in it I might hear you
> (Graham, 1970/1996: 50).

REFERENCES

Atkinson, D 1997. *Funny Girls: Cartooning for Equality*. London: Penguin.

Berlant, L 1997. *The Queen of America Goes to Washington City: Essays on Sex and Citizenship*. Durham: Duke University Press.

Berlant, L and Warner, M 1998. 'Sex in Public' *Critical Inquiry*. 24: 547–66.

Bhabha, H K 1998. 'Designer Creations.' In Merck, M (ed), *After Diana: Irreverent Elegies*. London: Verso.

Blaisdell, TC and Selz, P (eds), 1976. *The American Presidency in Political Cartoons 1776–1976*. Berkeley: University Art Museum Press.

Borromeo, T 1984. 'Political Cartoonists' *feed/back*. 4: 8–13.

Brooks, C 1999. *Best Editorial Cartoons of the Year*. Gretna, Louisiana: Pelican.

Cross, A 1998. 'Neither either nor or: The perils of reflexive irony' in Hannay, A and Marino, GD (eds), *The Cambridge Companion to Kierkegaard*. Cambridge: Cambridge University Press.

Department of Justice. 2000. *Responding to Terrorism Victims: Oklahoma City and Beyond*. Washington, DC: United States Department of Justice.

Edwards, JL 1997. *Political Cartoons in the 1988 Presidential Campaign. Image, Metaphor and Narrative*. New York: Garland Press.

Foster, H 1996. 'Death in America' *October* 75: 37–59.

Frye, N 1957. *Anatomy of Criticism*. Princeton, NJ: Princeton University Press.

Getlein, F 1964. *The Bite of The Print. Satire and Irony in Woodcuts, Engravings, Etchings, Lithographs and Seriographs*. London: Jenkins.

Graham, WS 1970/1996. 'The Constructed Space' in *WS Graham, Selected Poems*. London: Faber and Faber.

Hamm, MS 1997. *Apocalypse in Oklahoma. Waco and Ruby Ridge Revenged*. Boston: Northeastern University Press.

Harrison, RP 1981. *The Cartoon. Communication to the Quick*. Beverley Hills: Sage.

Johnson, V E 1999. 'Fertility Among the Ruins: the "Heartland", Maternity, and the Oklahoma City bombing' *Continuum* 13 (1): 57–75.

Kierkegaard, S 1841/1989. *The Concept of Irony, with Continual Reference to Socrates*. Princeton, NJ: Princeton University Press.

Kierkegaard, S 1846/1962. *The Present Age*. New York: Harper and Row.

Life 1996. 'Oklahoma City' *Life*. January 1996: 42–46.

Man, P de 1969/1983. 'The Rhetoric of Temporality' in *Blindness and Insight: Essays in the Rhetoric of Contemporary Criticism, Second Edition*. London: Methuen.

Man, P de 1977/1996. 'The Concept of Irony' in *Aesthetic Ideology*. Minneapolis, MN: University of Minnesota Press.

Michel, L and Herbeck, M 2001. *American Terrorist: Timothy McVeigh and the Oklahoma City Bombing*. New York: Harper Collins.

Moore, M T 1997. 'The Hazards of Using Powerful Images From Real Life in Editorial Cartoons' *USA Today*. June 20 1997.

Robbins, B ed 1993. *The Phantom Public Sphere*. Minneapolis, MN: University of Minnesota Press.

Rorty, R 1989. *Contingency, Irony and Solidarity*. Cambridge: Cambridge University Press.

Serrano, R 1998. *One of Ours: Timothy McVeigh and the Oklahoma City Bombing*. New York: WW Norton.

Shakespeare, S 1998. 'Books About Nothing? Kierkegaard's Liberating Rhetoric' in *Kierkegaard and Freedom*. Basingstoke: Macmillan.

Sheppard, A 1994 *Cartooning for Suffrage*. Albuquerque: University of New Mexico Press.

Spiegel, L 1992. *Make Room for TV: Television and the Family Ideal in Postwar America*. Chicago: University of Chicago Press.

Steiker, J 2001. 'Did the Oklahoma City Bombers succeed?' *Annals of the American Academy of Political and Social Science*. 574: 185–94.

Valier, C 2003a *Crime and Punishment in Contemporary Culture* London: Routledge.

Valier, C 2003b 'Tourist Trap' *Public Culture* 15(2).

Warner, M 2002. 'Publics and Counterpublics.' *Public Culture*. 14(1): 49–124.

Young, A 2000. 'Aesthetic Vertigo and the Jurisprudence of Disgust' *Law and Critique*. 11: 241–65.

6

The Subject of Surveillance: Notes on Mann's 'Heat' and Kieślowski's 'Three Colours: Red'

RICHARD JONES

THIS CHAPTER AIMS to investigate questions relating to surveillance, the visual, power and knowledge, in a way that emerges out of but also seeks to transcend the well-known model proposed by Foucault (1979; Gordon 1980; see also Dreyfus and Rabinow 1982). Specifically, I will draw from psychoanalytic theory and psychoanalytically-influenced sociology, as well as from psychoanalytically-informed film theory. Film theory offers a useful resource for interrogating the visual world because of its preoccupation not only with visual representation but also with visual reception, interpretation, and power relationships. In order to help reflect further on these themes, I will discuss two films — Michael Mann's *Heat*, and Krzysztof Kieślowski's *Three Colours: Red*. My argument is that these various resources suggest a way of thinking about surveillance which represents a departure from the Foucauldian and Foucauldian-Marxist paradigms (Foucault 1979; Garland 1985; 1990; 2001; S Cohen 1985) in which modern power/knowledge configurations are held closely to relate to surveillance, the optical, the visual. In this chapter I will attempt to contribute to the development of the line of thought introduced by A Young (1997), Valier (2000), and others, which attends to certain Foucauldian themes but which engages with them from a psychoanalytically-derived perspective.

FROM DISCIPLINE TO THE GAZE: BEYOND THE PANOPTICON

Recently, a number of writers from within criminology and sociology have sought to reconsider the applicability of Foucault's (1979) seminal, post-structural work on 'discipline' and disciplinary power (Bogard 1996;

Deleuze 1995; Jones 2000; Mathiesen 1997; Bauman 1999). While Foucault's post-structural approach in general has long come under criticism from writers from opposing theoretical camps, this newer work considering the applicability of Foucault's model of disciplinary power has sought to question not the power/knowledge hypothesis in general, but instead whether the disciplinary historical phase has been 'superseded,' or is presently in the process of being superseded, by another paradigmatic mode of power which has reshaped or is currently reshaping other societal institutions, practices, and knowledges. (Readers will recall that Foucault's *Discipline and Punish* sketched three successive historical modes of power-knowledge — the monarchical, the classical and the disciplinary — and the question for some Foucauldian scholars has been whether the third of these has been or is being replaced by a fourth. Successive modes do not eliminate earlier modes entirely, but do achieve paradigm status.) Such claims have often been cast in terms of the question as to whether there may presently be a shift from 'disciplinary' to 'post-disciplinary' societies; at other times, the terminology is in terms of a shift from 'Panopticism' to 'Post-Panopticism' (Boyne 2000), favours the latter terminology, though disputes that such a transformation has happened.) Another term which has been proposed as capturing the qualities of the post-panoptic era is the 'synopticon' (the many seeing all, but it is the many here who are the controlled) (Mathiesen 1997). Broadly speaking, the arguments advanced by Bauman, Deleuze and Bogard can be seen as having certain links with the 'new penology' hypothesis advanced by Feeley and Simon (1992; 1994), and with the 'Anglo-American' version of the Foucauldian 'governmentality' thesis. Despite their many differences, what these various approaches share in common is that they identify the central limitation with Foucault's disciplinary surveillance model as being one of limitation of scope (whether operational or historical), and as such they do not directly engage with the question as to the adequacy of Foucault's disciplinary surveillance model itself.

These attempts to identify characteristics of contemporary surveillance and penal practices and ideologies have provided interesting and imaginative ways of 'updating,' as it were, Foucault's work which had captured something of the qualities of bureaucratic-administrative penal and policing regimes but which had seemed less well-placed to identify qualities of surveillance in a world featuring electronic, computer and bio- technologies. Indeed, the very desire to 'update' Foucault's work on power/knowledge arguably also led to too uncritical an approach to some of its central claims. In particular, the post-disciplinary work seems to too quickly assume that Foucault's claim, that the modern human sciences are founded on the 'illumination' of spaces so as to facilitate the study of individual humans (and hence the objectification of these human subjects), means that knowledge generation in such spaces is relatively unproblematic.

Foucault's speculation as to the relationship between seeing, knowing, and capacity/ability, by drawing upon the linguistic relationship between the verbs for the same in French (voir, savoir, pouvoir), is grounded in his analysis of the institutions of modernity. For Foucault, 'power and knowledge are not external to one another. They operate in history in a mutually generative fashion. Neither can be explained in terms of the other, nor reduced to the other' (Dreyfus and Rabinow 1982, 114). Dreyfus and Rabinow argue that '[i]n many ways this is the most radical dimension to Foucault's work', not only because it rejects the common idea that power can be 'possessed', but because it reflects a sophisticated epistemology and methodology (which Dreyfus and Rabinow term 'interpretive analytics'), positing a world which the social scientist can only analyse and critique from the inside, as it were (1982, 114; see also their Chapters Five and Seven more generally on this point). Jay (1994) has argued that Foucault's work can be understood in terms of a wider pattern of the 'denigration' of vision within twentieth century French thought. In an article published in France in 1975 which has certain parallels with *Discipline and Punish*, the psychoanalyst Jacques-Alain Miller (1987), also writing about Bentham's Panopticon, describes it as a 'temple of reason' in which there are 'no shadows and nowhere to hide ... totalitarian mastery of the environment excludes everything irrational: no opacity can withstand logic' (cited in Jay 1994, 382). Striking at the Panopticon, then, was a way of striking at 'the older Enlightenment project of linking reason and illumination' (Jay 1994, 382). In Foucault's similar but more social and political project,

> vision could be damned for its role in the construction of an ideological notion of the ego, [and] could also be deemed complicitous in the complementary apparatuses of surveillance and spectacle so central to the maintenance of disciplinary or repressive power in the modern world' (Jay 1994, 383).

In this respect, as Jay argues, Foucault privileges the realm of vision in *Discipline and Punish* in order to attack it and to reveal its complicities within practices of domination:

> the occularcentrism of those who praised the 'nobility of sight' was not so much rejected as reversed in value: Vision was still the privileged sense, but what that privilege produced in the modern world was damned as almost entirely pernicious (Jay 1994, 384).

In a rather different take on the discipline/post-discipline debate, Valier (2000) has argued that a psychoanalytical reading of the scene of punishment 'renders the question as to whether contemporary penality can be described as "post-disciplinary" somewhat premature' (2000, 379; abstract). Her argument, which I find persuasive in many respects, begins with the claim that

Foucault's model of disciplinary punishment was always intrinsically flawed, and continues by arguing that this can be revealed through the study of certain artistic representations of prison and punishment. For Valier, the effect of a psychoanalytic reading 'is to render problematic the viewing subject's relation to [various] images of prisoners', such as to suggest that subsequent viewers of artistic depictions of the scene of punishment are in fact 'implicated within its staging'. The reason for this, for Valier, is that the paintings of the scenes of prisoners, as gazed upon by the artists, necessarily involve a returned gaze by the prisoners, and that, moreover, as viewers of a painting, standing in the artist's viewing position, we are somehow compromised, made complicit with, the original scene. In turn, she writes,

> [t]hese reflections lead me to question Foucault's thesis that penality demonstrates a power-knowledge relation that may be characterised as disciplinary in its effect and modelled heuristically as panopticism (2000, 380).

Valier quotes Pollock's comments on one of the paintings in question: 'the return of the gaze ... provocatively disrupts the relations of viewing and surveillance [...] The viewer enjoys the place of the third look as protected witness, on the edge of a voyeurism where the threat of the spaces and their populations is evoked but contained' (Pollock 1988, 36, cited in Valier 2000, 384). But, Valier argues, in fact 'no safe position of this kind can be taken up', because the 'viewer cannot be secured against the intensity of their desires' and because '[v]oyeurism is an unstable *fantasy* of control' (2000, 385–86, emphasis in original). Drawing from Melanie Klein's object relations theory, Valier suggests that processes such as those of 'projection' and 'introjection' should alert us to the possibility that we as viewers of scenes of punishment may be involved in the spectacle, and in non-straightforward ways. A point left moot in Valier's argument is whether there is *always* such a collapse in viewing representations of prisoners, or whether this is to be found only in particular images, including those on which she focuses in her article. Additionally, her argument leaves unresolved the degree to which this 'collapse' is an effect of, or at least is encouraged by, specific painterly techniques of representation used by the artists in question.

While Valier's suggested psychoanalytical approach (the Kleinian, with its emphasis on the intrasubjective) is not one I will adopt here, nevertheless, her article seems to me to suggest and help open up a range of possibilities for sociological and criminological study. More specifically, firstly, it makes a good case for the possible use of artistic works as the focus for theoretical, conceptual reflection. Secondly, even if we do not subscribe to Kleinian psychoanalysis, it establishes that psychoanalytic theory in general problematises a number of key elements in the scenes of surveillance and punishment, including the supposed coherence of the subject; its motivations; and, relating to the first point about artistic and linguistic representation, provides the analytical tools for examining the construction of subject positions. In terms of visual culture, for example, psychoanalytic theory provides such starting points as the concept of 'the gaze'. Thirdly, she shows that psychoanalytic theory provides an alternative resource for the study of the role of optics in penality and social control to that suggested by Foucault. Fourthly, she suggests a way of moving forward the investigatory study of 'panopticism' beyond the rather now sterile debate over panopticism/post-panopticism, by suggesting a way of bypassing this argument. As is alluded to in the second point above, what I propose to take as the field of study to which this theoretical approach may be applied, is an extended field encompassing not just the scene of punishment, but also scenes of surveillance more generally (which extend to policing and social control).

SEMIOTICS AND THE STUDY OF VISUAL CULTURE

The critical sociology of visual culture has a reasonably long history. An interest in the use of appearance to sell commodities can be found in work by Simmel, Kracauer and others (see Frisby 1985, for a good introduction). The Frankfurt School in general, and Adorno in particular, had a (highly critical) interest in the mass media, and a highly analytical interest in high art. But it is perhaps with Roland Barthes' groundbreaking work on semiotics-classic applications of which can be found in his *Mythologies* (1973) collection of short essays (dating from the 1950s and 1960s) — that the modern era of 'decoding' visual meaning can be said to have begun.

Barthes was particularly interested in visual representation. Following Saussure (1983), he argued that every visual image could be thought of as a 'sign' conveying meaning, and that the sign could be thought of as having two key components, namely the 'signifier' (the element conveying meaning) and the 'signified' (the thing or referent being represented). Signs can themselves be referred to by other signs (one sign here becoming the signified of the second sign), so that meaning can be thought of in terms of 'chains' of meanings. Advertisers, Barthes thought, could exploit already-existing associations (for example, by showing images of fresh vegetables alongside a jar of factory-made pasta sauce in an advertisement, they might be able to suggest the sauce was 'fresh' or 'natural'), or could innovate by introducing new associations in the hope these would be accepted by the viewer. Since visual meaning could be aggregated from chains of signs, so too could it be decoded by the critical visual analyst.

Semiotics/semiology is a useful approach for analysing visual media, but not without its limitations. As well as issues to do with representativeness of the sample analysed (see Rose 2001, 97), and the possible subjective-ness of the interpretation offered, more fundamentally there is the issue of the extent to which it actually constitutes a critical approach. Its critical moment depends to a large extent on the positing of the presence of an ideological system, in which such sign chains as are seen to exist are essentially ultimately understood as a mystificatory and ideological construct. Without this (Marxist) background, the approach is simply a technique which could be (and indeed today is) used as much by advertisers to sell products as by sociologists to critically analyse their marketing.

It has been argued that psychoanalysis is simply another form of semiology (Bal and Bryson 1991). This has a certain plausibility in the context of applied psychoanalytic theory in fields such as film studies, though fails to capture the fundamental claim to truth to which psychoanalysis proper, like Marxism, makes, as well as the considerable theoretical sophistication of it various concepts and styles of approach. As is well known, psychoanalysis 'consists of a range of theories that deal most centrally with human subjectivity, sexuality and the unconscious' (Rose 2001, 100). As has also now been shown, in addition to the psychoanalysis of individuals undergoing a course of therapy with their analyst, psychoanalytic theory can be applied to visual and popular culture.

In a passage apparently influenced by psychoanalytic theory, though possibly also revealing how merely being attentive to subjects and subject positions may be sufficient to begin theorising the relationship between the audience and the film, Stuart Hall writes that:

> The articulation between viewer and viewed is ... conceptualised in this body of work ... as an internal relation. Indeed, the two points in the circuit of articulation privileged here — the viewer and the viewed — are seen as mutually constitutive. The subject is, in part, formed subjectively through what and how it 'sees', how its 'field of vision' is constructed. In the same way, what is seen — the image and its meaning — is understood not as eternally fixed, but relative to and implicated in the positions and schemas of interpretation which are brought to bear upon it. Visual discourses already have possible positions of interpretation (from which they 'make sense') embedded in them, and the subjects bring their own subjective desires and capacities to the 'text' which enable them to take up positions of identification in relation to its meaning (Hall 1999, 310).

Elements of this approach have become highly influential within a range of social and cultural studies fields, but in these fields have often been adopted and understood in a highly sociological way, which has pulled the above idea away from its more social-theoretical roots. In the more sociological variant, the tendency has been to adopt the account which Hall summarises well, and turn it into a 'social constructionism' theory, informed by left-liberal theories such as labelling theory, as well as from a form of ideological analysis taken from Marxist theory. In this work, although there is reference to 'subjectivity', this is usually a reference to 'ideologies' or 'beliefs'. The claim then typically becomes not one about 'the modern Western subject', but about differing social and political perspectives. Whilst such claims usefully draw attention to the presence of starkly different political ideologies within Western societies, and to the role of the media in maintaining such social and class schisms, in its social constructionism variant at least, the theoretical perspective does not offer substantial advances over labelling theory, semiotics, discourse analysis, and Marxist analyses of the media.

PSYCHOANALYSIS AND FILM THEORY

As Rose notes (2001, 101), film 'has proved particularly amenable to psychoanalytic interpretation, and from the mid-1970s through the 1980s the journal *Screen* carried many essays exploring particular films in relation to psychoanalytic ideas'. Films provide an unusually powerful artistic medium through which we can imagine and depict a world. Mulvey (1989, 25; cited in Rose 2001, 101) writes that

> 'playing on the tension between film as controlling the dimension of time (editing, narrative) and film as controlling the dimension of space (changes in distance, editing), cinematic codes create a gaze, a world and an object'. Lacanian psychoanalysis 'in particular seemed immediately relevant to analysis of representation in film', because his 'theory of the mirror phase, for instance, readily lent itself to analogy with the screen-spectator situation' (Kaplan 1990, 10).

One of the pioneers in the introduction of Lacanian psychoanalysis to film theory was Christian Metz in the 1970s (though Metz's work is also influenced by Klein). Metz was particularly interested in the origins of spectator pleasure and displeasure when watching films, and argued that it was a mistake to focus too much on the film's sequence of images and sounds. Instead, one should consider the film experience as a whole, and consider 'the phantasies, pleasures, and fears triggered in specific spectators by the film' (Stam 2000, 165). The question as to the aesthetic merits of a film should not be confused with the (now psychoanalytic) question: 'Why did this film please or displease *me*?' (Stam 2000, 165). (The 'me' in this question extends from members of the public to film critics themselves.) One of the features of Metz's work is that it addresses the question as to why viewers may enjoy watching films about what might otherwise seem to be unpleasant topics (for example horror movies or family tragedies). Metz's claim is that in a strange way these films may reassure the viewer (because they help us believe that others share our fears), and/or that within the Western world films satisfy viewers by luring them into

> identification (first with the camera and then with characters); voyeurism (observation of others from a protected position); fetishism (the play of lack and disavowal); and narcissism (self-aggrandising sensations of being an all-perceiving subject) (Stam 2000, 166, 168).

In this respect, his claim seems to be that film-goers go to watch films because of the pleasures afforded them, but that these pleasures are in certain respects both 'dark' and their satisfactions self-deluding.

Rose notes that 'Feminist film critics have of course been particularly concerned to see how films visualise masculinity and femininity in ways that disempower women, and how that visualisation then positions the audience in gendered terms', recognising at the same time that feminism's relationship with psychoanalysis has not always been an easy one (Rose, 2001, 102; see also the various essays in Kaplan 1990). One of the seminal feminist film theory essays of the 1970s was written by psychoanalytic film theorist Laura Mulvey. As Stam notes, her 1975 essay 'Visual Pleasure and Narrative Cinema' argued that 'cinema choreographs three kinds of 'gaze:' that of the camera, that of the characters looking at one another, and that of the spectator, induced to voyeuristically identify with a masculinist gaze at woman' (Stam 2000, 174). Drawing from Lacan and Althusser, Mulvey argues that cinema 'interpellates' the viewer as a (male) gendered viewing subject, viewing a narrative involving an active male subject and a passive female subject (who is also the object of the male gaze). While the implication of this, that women viewers are inevitably forced into masculinist subject positions, is one which attracted some criticism from other feminist film theorists, Mulvey's contribution remains immense in the field (see also Mulvey 1990).

Mulvey (1989) has also suggested certain more specific themes in the content and presentation of movies, which effectively serve male interests, and which derive from anxieties and complexes which can only be understood psychoanalytically. The first of these themes is voyeurism. According to Rose, for Mulvey, voyeurism

> is a way of seeing that is active; it distances and objectifies what is looked at. It is controlling and even sadistic ... a look that is only given to men by films (whether as characters in the film or as the film's audience). It deals with castration anxiety by investigating the woman and then punishing or saving her. Mulvey notes that this is typical of how the women in the film noir genre are represented; as threatening but ultimately guilty and weak (Rose, 2001, 110).

This can be achieved through the use of certain 'filmic techniques', including 'putting distance between the male and female protagonists of a movie', and 'putting distance between the female protagonist of a movie and the movie audience' (Rose 2001, 110). (Rose gives the example of scenes from Hitchcock's *Rear Window* to illustrate both cases.)

The second theme is 'fetishistic scopophilia' — 'when the female figure is represented simply as a beautiful object of display' (Rose 2001, 110):

> Again, this is a mode of representation directed both at the hero of the film and at the male spectator: she is on display for both of them. Her beauty is so overwhelming, often pictured in huge close-ups, so perfect that the threat of castration is assuaged as she is turned into a reassuring object in an intimate relation to the spectator (Rose 2001, 111).

Techniques by which this might be achieved in cinema include framing (especially close-ups of the face), lighting (again, especially of the (female) face), and camera movement (as in a classic establishing shot in *Rear Window,* in which, as Modleski argues, Madeleine is represented though camera movement as the 'mute, only half-seen object of man's romantic quest' (Rose 2001, 112; Modleski 1988, 92, cited in Rose 2001, 112).

The third concept identified by Mulvey as useful in the study of cinema is the Lacanian concept of the mirror stage. The mirror stage is a supposed child developmental stage during which babies (mis-)recognise themselves as coherent individuals when seeing their own reflection in the mirror. Mulvey's appropriation of the concept, in which the cinema screen is taken to be a sort of mirror, is with the aim of 'explor[ing] the representation of male figures in narrative cinema, and the ways in which the audience is positioned by that representation' (Rose 2001, 113). Mulvey's claim is that the male character is set free in a 'space corresponding to that of the mirror recognition' (the child's perception of three dimensional space in the mirror) (Rose 2001, 113), and that he is 'free to command the stage, a stage of spatial illusion in which he articulates the look and creates the action' (Mulvey 1989, 20; cited in Rose 2001, 113).

PSYCHOANALYSIS VERSUS SURVEILLANCE

According to psychoanalysis, the presence of the unconscious prevents the subject ever from being fully conscious or coherent. As Rose notes, 'the notion of the unconscious focuses attention on the uncertainties of subjectivity and on the uncertainties of seeing; psychoanalysis is especially interested in visual confusions, blindspots, and mistakes' (2001, 103). As such, the subject's perception of the world is never a straightforward matter of acquiring pure information. 'Psychoanalysis does not therefore concur with the modernist notion that to see is to know' (Rose 2001, 103) as is nicely expressed by Lacan's (1979, 93) comment that '[i]n this matter of the visible, everything is a trap'. This is perhaps one of the central points underpinning Valier's critique of Foucauldian Panopticism. While there is an apparent similarity between the Lacan quote and Foucault in *Discipline and Punish*, in which Foucault too writes that 'Visibility is a trap' (Foucault 1979, 200), in the latter's case, the trap is the supposed social and political snares which rely on the optics of the modernist seeing, knowing eye. For Lacan, on the other hand, the trap is precisely that things should not, cannot, be taken at face value, and that knowledge-production, or rather interpretation generation, can only proceed circuitously. For these reasons, cultural psychoanalysis and psychoanalytically-informed film theory would seem to present a challenge to the Foucauldian paradigm. In order to explore these issues further, I will now turn to readings of two movies. As against Denzin (1995) it is not my claim that the significance of popular movies is that they promulgate ideological constructs useful for contemporary society, but rather that some movies, as works of artistic imagination, may serve as a useful resource for theoretical reflection. As Young (1996) has convincingly argued, chains of meaning, of imagination, relating to crime do not dutifully respect society's boundaries — as between fictional and non-fictional representations, for example — but instead may appear, unannounced, across boundaries. Whereas at times this may appear a threat, for my present purposes it is something which may be exploited.

THREE COLOURS: RED

Kieślowski's *Three Colours: Red* is the final part of his acclaimed 'Three Colours' trilogy, and the last film he made before dying in 1996. The film is a meditation on themes relating to justice and surveillance, and offers, I would argue, a conception of 'omniscient surveillance', but a very different one from either the Foucauldian or Orwellian models. The film can be read as introducing a theme of particular interest here, namely the seduction of surveillance. The figure of surveillance-seduction, epitomised in the giant poster of the model Valentine, evokes but also differs from the giant, intimidating posters of the leader in Orwell's (1997) *Nineteen Eighty-four.* The seductive effect of the poster (which the judge — who represents surveillance — himself experiences) could perhaps be understood in terms of the 'synopticon', but should instead, I contend, be thought of in terms of seduction.

Maurer usefully summarises the plot of the film as follows:

> Valentine, a warm and open young model living in Geneva, is struggling with a possessive boyfriend who is always abroad. Her neighbour, Auguste, is about to take an exam to become a judge. Their paths nearly cross but never quite do. One evening, Valentine accidentally runs over a dog and, on finding its cantankerous owner indifferent, takes the dog home and cares for it herself. When it is better, the dog runs back to its home leading Valentine to

> discover its owner eavesdropping on his neighbours' telephone conversations. She leaves in distress. Valentine's reaction causes the old man — a former judge, Joseph Kern — to shop himself to the police. His case makes the newspapers and, on reading the scandal Valentine rushes back to the judge's home to tell him that she was not responsible for his denouncement. In their ensuing conversation he encourages her to take the ferry for her upcoming trip to England. Kern then accepts an invitation to one of Valentine's fashion shows and after the show Valentine guesses the judge's history — which has obvious parallels to Auguste's life. Valentine and Auguste (who has passed his law exam and witnessed his girlfriend making love to another man) board the same ferry but it capsises in a huge storm. There are only a handful of survivors: Auguste, Valentine, Olivier and Julie from *Blue* as well as Karol and Dominique from *White* (Maurer 2000, 85).

The film offers a different take on the relationship between surveillance and justice. When Valentine discovers that Kern's hobby is to eavesdrop on his neighbours' telephone calls and disapproves strongly, Kern's defence is that it allows him 'better' access to the truth than his court ever did. (Note too that in the continental system, the criminal court is inquisitorial rather than adversarial as in the Anglo-American legal tradition.) Yet the unreal and socially isolated nature of the characters, along with the ethereal quality of places and interactions, leads us to question whether some of the people we are watching 'actually' exist. It seems possible that one or more of them really exist only in the mind of another character. In an interview after Red was filmed but while it was still being edited, Kieślowski had the following to say:

> [...] Auguste in *Red* hasn't any feeling that a judge exists. The judge, of course, knows that Auguste exists. But we'll never be sure whether Auguste really does exist of whether he's only a variation of the judge's life forty years later.
>
> [...] Everything that happens to Auguste happened to the judge although, perhaps, slightly differently. [...] So, does Auguste really exist or doesn't he? Is Auguste repeating exactly the judge's life? (Kieślowski, ed Stok 1993, 217–20).

The uncertainty which the film opens up as to the ontological status of Auguste and the judge helps lend it a non-real quality in which characters and events take on a metaphorical quality. Kieślowski suggests in one of the quotes above that we don't know whether Auguste exists or not; but equally possible is that it is *the judge* who isn't there, not Auguste. Could the judge be a figment of Valentine's imagination? We rarely see the judge with anyone other than Valentine, except in a strange scene outside a courtroom in which the residents of the area are bringing a case against him for eavesdropping; and at the fashion show, he cannot be seen even by Valentine until afterwards, when he appears alone in the auditorium (though in a different place from where he claimed to have been sitting, a place on high from which he 'can't be seen'). This scene is clearly intended to echo his eavesdropping practices, but also serves to reinforce his status as a somewhat mysterious figure. A further possibility is that Valentine is in some way the creation of the judge; he seems to know her destiny, and she seems to exist somehow for him.

If the Judge is not a figment of her imagination, he is still perhaps a device to give eerie foreshadow to the future, because he seems a prophetic figure, echoing (or predicting) the future of the young Judge who appears to be in the same time as Valentine. In this respect, the film's take on surveillance becomes a very human but spiritual (or mystical) one, in which surveillance is likened to a sort of seeing into the future, particularly in terms of the possibility of knowing about human relationships, personal secrets and personal destiny. In one scene (reciprocated later in the film), the retired Judge correctly guesses that Valentine's brother is a heroin addict. When she asks him how he knew, he indicates that it wasn't divine omniscience, but rather that she betrayed the truth in what she said and how she behaved: 'It wasn't hard to guess'. Yet the film also makes suggestions that the retired Judge is a mystical, God-like apparition. Such a quality has been noted too by Maurer, who writes:

> Is Auguste a person in his own right? Or is he merely just an echo of Kern? And is Kern more than what he appears to be? Kieślowski likened him to a chess player; others have compared him to a God-like figure. He certainly seems omniscient, and perhaps has more of hand [sic] in bringing Valentine and Auguste together than he lets on (Maurer 2000, 86).

There is also a strong voyeuristic element to the film. As we saw above, voyeurism typically distances and objectifies woman, and is a look given only to men. The Judge is a voyeur of citizens in his community (though not only of women), through his eavesdropping, but it is in his screen relationship with Valentine that we see his voyeurism more properly. And a possible frustration and obsession of an old director is hinted at in a number of scenes; in one scene, Valentine rejects the advances of her photographer, who could be seen as a proxy for a film director. In another scene, the judge opens his arms as if expecting an embrace from Valentine, before admitting that he has realised that her lack of reciprocation derives from her (physical) revulsion for him. If we see the judge character as an echo of a (real) Auguste character, the generational time-shift can be read as trying to legitimate an otherwise somewhat distasteful sexual longing of an old man for a young woman. But perhaps most of all, the voyeurism can be seen in two scenes. The first is a fashion parade scene in which Valentine is made beautiful but distant, elevated on a cat-walk, removed from the judge. The second is the inversion (yet retention) of the extreme close-up device, but here through the device of extreme magnification, in this case, via a huge picture of Valentine's face in profile in a giant billboard advertisement, before which the judge stops his car to gaze. In both these cases, the beauty of the model entrances the judge, and her persuasive power over him is symbolised by his agreeing to follow her wishes that he abandon his surveillance of his neighbours; in fact he goes further, and turns himself in to the (legal) authorities. Whereas for Mulvey and Rose, the 'fetishistic scopophilia' witnessed here serves to assuage the threat of castration for the (male) characters and film-goers, it could be added that in its confrontation with law and surveillance, this voyeurism also takes on an overwhelming, hypnotic and nullifying quality. The model seems to be there solely for the judge (it is as though he conjures her up for himself; she is on display for him, and he seems to engineer or fantasise a life where she and he are there together), and yet it has the unforeseen effect of entrancing the law into submission, through a process even more powerful than surveillance: seduction.

SURVEILLANCE, TRAGEDY, AND THE GAZE: MICHAEL MANN'S *HEAT*

Michael Mann's movie *Heat* (a slang term for police) is a film obsessed with surveillance. It is also a film which explores the crude and violent justice of the paramilitary world of violent criminals. Although obsessed with surveillance, it is not the surveillance of an all-powerful state against an innocent individual or group we see depicts here, but rather the deployment of a raft of surveillance technologies by two, fairly evenly matched groups against each other: the police against the criminals. In this film, it is the similarities as much as the differences between the two forces which are emphasised. (Relatively unusually, the film features two, opposing male lead characters.) The film does not at all invoke feelings of Panopticism; if anything, the sentiment is of a punitive, pre-modern justice. A classic heist movie, the film is effectively a tragedy, offering, in the last instance, a mixture of a traditional romanticisation of the violent criminal with a fairly traditional moral message that 'justice' will prevail.

In its plot, the movie is about a technically sophisticated gang of armed robbers who undertake a series of audacious heists in present day Los Angeles. Two of the main characters in movie are a detective police officer, played by Al Pacino, and the leader of the armed gang played by Robert De Niro. In many respects, the film is not only about the relationship between these two characters, but also about the consequent relationship between criminals and a law-enforcement officers, and between crime and justice.

In 1996 the cinema magazine called *Sight And Sound* published a review written by John Wrathall of the film *Heat*. The review usefully provides a summary of the plot:

> Neil McCauley and his crew, Chris Shiherlis, Michael Cheritto and Trejo, plan the armed robbery of a security van carrying bearer bonds; the job goes

> perfectly, except that a new recruit to the crew, Waingro, shoots a guard. Afterwards, McCauley tries to kill Waingro, but he escapes. Vincent Hanna, a homicide cop whose third marriage is falling apart because of his devotion to his job, examines the scene of the crime and admires the professionalism of the job; the only clue is that one of the robbers was overheard calling a security guard 'Slick'. McCauley's associate Nate arranges to sell the bearer bonds back to their original owner, Van Zant, but the meeting in a deserted drive-in turns out to be an ambush; McCauley and his crew kill Van Zant's men and escape.
>
> A chance lead from the brother of one of Hanna's informers identifies Cheritto as the man who calls people Slick. Hanna puts Cheritto under surveillance and starts tracking the crew around Los Angeles as they prepare their next heist. Meanwhile McCauley, who prides himself on his lack of attachments, has met and fallen in love with Eady, a graphic designer who knows nothing about his criminal career, and with whom he plans to leave for New Zealand after one last job. While burgling a metal depository, however, McCauley realises that they are being watched and calls the job off; because they have not stolen anything yet, Hanna doesn't arrest them. Even though they know the police are on to them, the crew decides to carry out one final bank robbery.
>
> Following him one night, Hanna stops McCauley, takes him for a cup of coffee and tries to warn him off. The same night, the crew all shake off their tails, except for Trejo. The crew goes ahead without him, and the bank robbery they have planned goes smoothly; but after a tip-off, the police arrive as the robbers are leaving. A gun battle ensues in which Cheritto is killed and Shiherlis wounded. Aiming to settle scores before he leaves town on a plane arranged by Nate, McCauley traces the tip-off to Trejo, who has been tortured into betraying the plan by Waingro, who has been recruited by Van Zant to get revenge on McCauley. After tracking down and killing Van Zant, McCauley persuades Eady to leave with him that night. But, learning that Waingro is holed up in a hotel near the airport, he can't resist having a go. Although the hotel is staked out by the police, McCauley manages to kill Waingro, but Hanna spots him on his way out the hotel, chases him across the airport runways and shoots him down. Hanna holds McCauley's hand as he dies (Wrathall 2000, 239).

It has been the noted by various commentators including film critics that the film has a number of flaws. One of these is that its script is not particularly strong. Another is that its characterisation of women is very weak, with the women characters reduced to bit parts and even poorer lines. Nevertheless, the film also has a number of strengths. One of these is the way that it evokes the Los Angeles of the white professional classes in the 1990s, through Michael Mann's trademark used of stylised camera and lighting techniques, a clean sounding but also slightly melancholic background music track, but most of all the presenting of criminals, in this case armed robbers, as well spoken, calculating professionals wearing designer clothing and inhabiting the same urban field as that occupied by other, seemingly more legitimate, professionals. The movie is actually a remake of a television movie Michael Mann had made in 1989, *LA Takedown* (the same movie was also released on video under the titles *Made in LA LA Crimewave*; *Showdown in LA* and *Crimewave*). Later in his career, when he was sufficiently well established to be able to make the movie with some of the stars he wanted and with the glossy production values for which he was now famous, Mann was able to make the film in a way that drew heavily from the earlier version (changes included the renaming of the lead criminal from Patrick McLaren to Neil McCauley; the adding of various extra scenes; and a different ending).

Wrathall argues that *Heat* can be seen as the director returning 'to the urban terrain of his television series *Miami Vice* and *Crime Story* and his features *Manhunter* and *Thief* with a film which can be read as a compendium of his works to date' (2000, 239). As Wrathall points out Neil McCauley is 'single-mindedly devoted to his profession ... and only loses control of his destiny when he tries to buy himself what Hanna, when he confronts him in the coffee shop, dismisses as 'a regular-type life' (2000, 239–40). 'Vincent Hanna, meanwhile, is a variation on [the detective] from *Manhunter* in his talent for putting himself in the shoes of his prey and seeing what they see, and in the way this leaves him closer to those he is pursuing than those he is protecting' (2000, 240).

Heat can be seen as a film which imagines a certain sort of justice, a justice which is neither justifiable (extra-judicial execution) nor the norm in the West (which is not to say that it does not happen). It also imagines a certain sort of surveillance, one of a strategic battle between two, fairly evenly matched groups, rather than between a dominant and a sub-dominant group. The criminals are no fools — in technical expertise, at least — but neither are the police. The movie can be seen as being about the attempt of contemporary man to set aside his social obligations in order to gain economic riches (both in the sterility of the LA urban landscape, and the story of Neil), and the necessity of the futility of this attempt (the lives of all the LA residents in the story are dysfunctional; Neil ultimately cannot resist his humanity and his desire for a justice of his own which is also what leads to his downfall, and the ultimate 'justice' in the story's ending).

One of the popular attractions of the film at the time was the pairing together of the actors De Niro and Pacino in the same film (in fact, they had both been in the film *The Godfather Part 2*, but never shared a scene together). The two actors share certain similarities, both being Italian Americans, both having established their careers in quasi-realistic gangster or tough-guy films, and both emerging broadly speaking out of the American method acting school, at least in terms of their vocal delivery and flexibility with script minutiae. What is useful for us to notice, echoing

Wrathall's point above is that this similarity helps establish within the film a positional similarity between the two characters. Wrathall puts this quite nicely: 'Heat were a play, you could imagine De Niro and Pacino swapping the roles every night, like Olivier and Richardson in Othello' (2000, 241). Moreover, having two male leads helps establish one of the claims of the film, namely the supposed similarities between detective and criminal. In one scene, for example, we see 'near identical shots' of one character picking up his gun as he leaves home and the other putting his down as he gets back home (Wrathall 2000, 240). Indeed, as Wrathall points out, Vincent is able ultimately to track and kill Neil because the two think alike.

This duality helps us reflect on an aspect of contemporary surveillance. First, *Heat* usefully draws our attention to a different dynamic of power between police and criminals or suspects than the disciplinary surveillance model would have us believe. Whereas Foucault posits a model in which criminals and suspects may try to resist, but typically do so along the same line as the police power they are up against (and hence are doomed to lose the fight), *Heat* suggests an alternative form of the relationship (at least for certain locales) in which the two parties are involved in a more dynamic 'struggle' against one another. (From a more conventional perspective, Ekblom (1999) has suggested that situational crime prevention theory needs to take such a dynamic into account.) This duality also echoes a device in Michael Mann's earlier detective thriller *Manhunter*.

As Wrathall noted above, there are some thematic similarities between the two Mann films. In fact, a feature of his earlier film helps us understand better one of the key scenes in the later one. Prior to his Lacanian discussion of *Manhunter*, Žižek summarises its plot as follows:

> [It is] about a police detective famous for his ability to enter intuitively, through his 'sixth sense,' the mind of perverse, sadistic murderers. His task is to detect a particularly cruel mass murderer who slaughtered a series of quiet, provincial families. The detective reruns again and again super-8 home movies shot by each of the slaughtered families in order to arrive at the trait unaire, the feature common to all of them that attracted the murderer and thus directed his choice. But all his efforts are in vain as long as he looks for this common feature on the level of content, ie, in the families themselves. He finds the key to the identity of the murdered when a certain inconsistency strikes his eye. The investigation at the scene of the last crime shows that to enter the house, to break open the back door, the murdered used a kind of tool that was inappropriate, even unnecessary. The old back door has been replaced a few weeks before the crime with a new type of door. To break open the new door, another kind of tool would have been far more appropriate. So how did the murderer get this piece of wrong or, more precisely, out-of-date information? The old back door could be seen clearly in scenes from a super-8

home movie. The only thing common to all the slaughtered families in then the *home movies themselves,* i.e., the murderer had to have had access to their private movies, there is no other link connecting them. Because these movies are private, the only possible link between them is the laboratory where they were developed. A quick check confirms that all the movies were developed by the same laboratory, and the murderer is soon identified as one of the workers in the lab (Žižek 1992, 107).

For Žižek, the 'theoretical interest of this denouement' lies in the way the crime is solved-through studying the 'form' rather than the 'content' of the home movies, as he puts it (by which he means that the detective doesn't solve the crime through watching something the families say or do in their (banal) home movies, but rather through his realising something about the fact of the movies themselves). Moreover,

> the decisive turn takes place when [the detective] becomes aware that through the very screening of the home movies, *he is already identified with the murderer,* that his obsessive gaze, surveying every detail of the scenery, coincides with the gaze of the murderer. The identification is on the level of the gaze, not on the level of the content (Žižek 1992, 108; emphasis in original).

Žižek uses this scene to introduce the Lacanian understanding of the 'pervert,' and to suggest that Stalinist Communism can be understood as 'perverted' in this same, technical sense:

> There is something extremely unpleasant and obscene in this experience of our gaze as already the gaze of the other. Why? The Lacanian answer is that such a coincidence of gazes defines the position of the pervert. [...] This coincidence of the subject's view with the gaze of the big Other, which defines perversion, enables us to conceptualise one of the fundamental features of the ideological functioning of 'totalitarianism' ... [because] the perversion of Stalinist Communism consists in the fact that the view by means of which the Party looks at history coincides immediately with history's gaze upon itself ... it is history itself, its necessity, that speaks through [Communists'] mouths (Žižek 1992, 108).

Another way to understand why the coincidence of gazes is perverse in the Lacanian sense is to recognise that for Lacan, the normal relationship between gaze and eye is an 'antinomic' one: 'the eye viewing the object is on the side of the subject, while the gaze is on the side of the object. When I look at an object, the object is always already gazing at me, and from a point at which I cannot see it' (Žižek 1992, 109). Žižek goes on to quote from Lacan:

> In the scopic field, everything is articulated between two terms that act in an antinomic way — on the side of things, there is the gaze, that is to say, things

> look at me, and yet I see them. This is how one should understand those words, so strongly stressed, in the Gospel, They have eyes that they might not see. That they might not see what? Precisely, that things are looking at them (Lacan 1977, 109; cited in Žižek 1992, 109).

This sentence, which by conventional standards makes little sense, makes a little more sense when we recall Žižek's distinction between the eye (of the subject) and the gaze (of the object), and remember that 'the object' here means 'the image [which the subject] views' (see Žižek 1992, 114).

Žižek, with his interest in middlebrow cinema and fiction, suggests further ways of thinking about detective fables and of the role of the detective. The first is Žižek's argument that the role of the detective cannot be understood by either of the conventional interpretations (that the detective is the embodiment of scientific rationalism, or that he is the 'successor to the romantic clairvoyant, the man possessing an irrational quasisupernatural power to penetrate the mystery of another person's mind' (1992, 49). Neither 'a pure scientific procedure' nor pure 'intuition' alone are by themselves experienced as satisfactory detective processes by the reader/viewer of the detective story (1992, 49). Instead, Žižek argues, we should draw an analogy between the detective and the (psycho-)analyst. In particular, and following the Lacanian interpretation of Freud's (1991) work on dreams, Žižek argues that the best 'puzzles' in detective stories often feature a 'false solution', a scene which tricks ordinary police officers into trying to find meaning in a particular, unusual situation, but which can be solved by the detective through consideration not of the apparent whole scene, but of its anomalous details or even its absences.

> [T]he scene of the crime with which the [fictional] detective is confronted is also, as a rule, a false image put together by the murderer in order to efface the traces of his act: The scene's organic, natural quality is a lure, and the detective's task is to denature it by first discovering the inconspicuous details that stick out, that do not fit into the frame of the surface image (1992, 53).

Furthermore, the key point about this for Žižek is '*the structural necessity of the false solution* toward which we are enticed ... [because] it is only *through* them that he can arrive at the truth, for there is no path leading immediately to the truth' (1992, 54, emphasis in original). In this respect, Žižek is again suggesting a similarity between the detective and the analyst, but for our purposes, also raises potentially interesting objections to the Foucauldian model of knowledge acquisition through surveillance.

This point can neatly be applied to the scene in *Heat* in which the detectives find the tables turned on them, and themselves under surveillance:

> in one breathtaking sequence in *Heat* which evokes the voyeuristic, hall-of-mirrors feel of *Manhunter*, Hanna and his men watch McCauley's crew

> scouting out a refinery. When they've gone, Hanna stands exactly where they stood, trying to guess what they were looking at — before realising that they were looking at him, and that McCauley has now lured him into the open. The camera then pulls back to show McCauley taking his picture (Wrathall, 2000).

Whereas this scene could be interpreted in terms of establishing the similarities as between the two characters, and while this is of a certain significance, the more original interpretation would be to apply to this scene a similar type of interpretation as Žižek's interpretation of the above *Manhunter* scene. In the *Heat* scene, the puzzle is what it is that Neil and his crew have been looking at; they scan the horizon, but see no target of likely interest. So what was it they were looking at? The answer is nothing at all; knowing they were already being watched, the crew have 'acted out' a target reconnaissance, with the precise aim that the police, intrigued, will adopt their subject position, as it were, in order to try to see for themselves what it was the crew were just looking at. However, the 'object' that was being looked at was not some distant target; when the police adopt the subject position of the crew, they inadvertently put themselves in this same subject position which is in fact an object position. The scene satisfies the audience, precisely because here — in a moment of tactical failure but perceptual success — Vincent *realises* what has happened. It is only by virtue of a certain *modesty*, recognising the relative equality between the police and the crew, that Hanna can realise the problem that he and his colleagues are up against.

The scene is helped by two devices: cinematically, there are both first-person (subject) and third-person (object) type shots; in the narrative, the Hanna character glosses over the tenses of the situation in what *was* and what *is* being looked at by using the linguistic construct, 'You wanna know what *they're* looking at?', eliding the 'they were' and 'they are' and helping the scene flow. However, both the first-person type shots and the third-person type shots are not purely subjective of the two subjects, and retain an element of the traditional additional third-person privileged viewer position of mainstream cinema. The effect of this is that we see the whole scene acted out before us, and it is this further privileged position that helps reward the movie audience. This privileged audience position, witnessing the cunning and the appreciation of the cunning before us, echoes a key element in the scene we are watching: ultimately, the scene is only partly about the mutually connected practices of surveillance and counter-surveillance; it is partly about one-up-man-ship, about establishing a power over and dominance of the other party, for its own sake. While the regular detectives puzzle over what it was that the Crew were surveying, Hanna is able to solve the puzzle by recognising that the scene is anomalous because of what it is that is *absent* from the scene — any plausible object for surveillance, given the known professionalism and aspirations of the Crew. He solves the mini puzzle by realising that the only remaining object of surveillance is the police officers themselves. However, while this is just one mini puzzle in the film, it is a key one, because it establishes the nature of the relationship between the police and the criminals (a certain parity) but also shows very neatly how surveillance can be 'flipped around'.

Žižek argues that the detective's ability to solve such puzzles lies in the ability to see beyond the apparent (the deception of the false scene) by 'push[ing] it to the point of self-reference, ie to the point at which it becomes obvious that its sole meaning consists in the fact that (others think) it possesses some meaning' (1992, 57). The reason that the fictional detective was always going to be able to apprehend the murderer is that 'he will literally *catch the murderer in his deception*, ie that he will trap him by taking into account his cunning. The very deceit the murderer invents to save himself is the cause of his downfall' (1992, 57, emphasis in original). In this respect, Žižek is not abandoning the modernist project of deriving social knowledge through study of people, but is instead suggesting a mode of power/knowledge which is less straightforward. This, I think, offers the basis of a critique of, or at least sketches an alternative to Foucault's model of surveillance in which one knows from what one sees (the appearance is what it seems). Žižek argues that both the detective and the psychoanalyst are supposed by reader/patient as 'the "subject supposed to know" [...] — supposed to know what? The true meaning of our act, the meaning visible in the very falseness of the appearance. The detective's domain, as well as that of the psychoanalyst, is thus thoroughly the domain of meaning, not of "facts"' (1992, 57). This reveals a key difference between psychoanalytic interpretation and the more straightforward semiotic analysis of Barthes, namely psychoanalysis's contention that the 'basic feature of the signifier is its differential character: since the identity of a signifier consists in the bundle of differences from other signifiers, the absence of a trait itself can have a positive value' (1992, 57). Žižek suggests that,

> 'it is perhaps not by chance that the most famous of all Sherlock Holmes's dialogues is the following from 'Silver Blaze':
> 'Is there any point to which you wish to draw my attention?'
> 'To the curious incident of the dog in the night.'
> 'The dog did nothing in the night.'
> 'That was the curious incident,' remarked Holmes' (Žižek 1992, 57–58).

A similar situation to the one in *Manhunter* is at work, I would argue, in the above surveillance switch scene in *Heat*.

Finally, Wrathall has also drawn attention to the dark side of *Heat*:

> ... for a cop movie, *Heat* seems unusually suffused with an awareness of death. Hanna's wife Justine, who, like her husband, always wears black, keeps telling

> him that he is walking dead through life. When McCauley and Hanna meet, they compare their dreams — and both have been dreaming of death, of time running out .... and, in the film's only superfluous scene, Waingro announces himself as the Grim Reaper before murdering a prostitute — leaving Hanna, who in his wife's haunting words 'lives among the remains of dead people', to pick up the pieces (2000, 241).

One of the explanations for this preoccupation with death may be that the film is essentially a tragedy. All the crew end up killed, with the exception of Chris Shiherlis, who obtains his freedom only at the cost of abandoning his wife and child. Moreover, their deaths all carry a moral component: having betrayed the crew, Trejo is left for dead, and is finally 'compassionately' executed by Neil; Trejo's getaway driver stand-in for the bank-job, a probationer, dies at the wheel from police gunfire minutes after the robbery; Cheritto is killed by Hanna (himself a father of a young girl) with a single shot moments after grabbing a young girl to hold as a human shield (a moment which the film implies, is a reprehensible aberration by Cheritto, stepping outside the crew's own moral code); and Neil himself is killed by Hanna, after the former abandons his lover despite her having overcome her revulsion at discovering his true occupation and having agreed to leave LA with him, and after all the other wrongs Neil has done. Only Nate, advisor to but not member of the crew, remains untouched, establishing him as mere conduit of information, with a hacker morality, an informational omniscient who merely grabs information from the air (Neil: 'how do you get all this [inside] information?' — Nate: 'this stuff just flies though the air — you just gotta know how to grab it') (in fact, Nate is up to all sorts of white collar crime, as well as being an accomplice to the various robberies).

Moreover, in each case, the film is at pains to show that the character in question had a choice (with the exception of Trejo), and it is precisely their choosing to set off down a certain route which lends the fable its quality of tragedy. If their choices bear a certain inevitability, this merely serves to underline their tragic quality; the success of the film lies in fact in large part in establishing a certain inevitability to the choices while making the consequences seem unpredictable in their detail.

CONCLUSION

Michel Foucault was not unaware of the complexities of the modern subject, and indeed his entire body of work could be said to interrogate the question of subjectivity and knowledge. Writing towards the end of his life, he suggested retrospectively how the three main 'phases' of his life's work might really be seen as different aspects of the same thing, namely the 'modes of objectification which transform human beings into subjects' (Foucault 1982, 208). The first phase of his career, he says, was devoted to the study of the human sciences (both natural and social), and their various ways of objectivising the human subject. The second phase, including his work on surveillance and power, he characterises as being concerned with 'the objectivising of the subject'. His final phase was concerned with 'the way a human being turns him — or herself into a subject' (1982, 208).

'Thus,' he wrote, 'it is not power, but the subject, which is the general theme of my research' (1982, 208). If this increases the complexity of our engagement with Foucault on the question of the subject — as it surely does — at the same time his insistence that his work should be seen as involving three complementary phases, rather than successive phases superseding each other, would seem to increase rather than reduce the importance of his claims about surveillance and power/knowledge within his overall corpus.

As his retrospective synthesis above indicates, Foucault was aware of the need periodically to reinterpret earlier parts of his work, and was not above so doing. The central phase of Foucault's work (on power, knowledge and disciplinary surveillance) is thus open to re-working, in which the vexed question of the modern subject once again is at the fore.

In this chapter, I have investigated questions relating to surveillance, visuality, power and knowledge, in a way that has emerged out of, but has also sought to transcend, Foucault's theoretical model for understanding surveillance, and in particular for understanding the relationships between seeing and knowing. I have argued that analyses of the optical realm, which can be found highly developed within visual studies and film theory, offer a rich resource for the reconsideration of surveillance. The contributions of these fields are various, and operate in various registers, but in relation to surveillance focus in particular on the viewer (rather than just the viewed); on the gaze (and its return); and on the subject as involving an ongoing dynamic internal struggle (rather than consisting of a unitary whole). Whilst these fields have themselves sometimes too uncritically accepted the Foucauldian paradigm, this paradigm is seen to weaken in the face of psychoanalytically-informed work in which the relationship between the viewer and the viewed is less straightforward than Foucault would have us believe. Whilst his analysis of the bureaucratic institutional form remains unparalleled, his conception of human subjectivity is less persuasive today. Given the centrality of his conception of the subject and his account of knowledge-generation for all his discipline-inspired work (which extends to his work on 'governmentality'), we must ask whether cultural psychoanalysis does not in fact offer a better way of interpreting surveillance today.

REFERENCES

Bal, Mieke and Norman Bryson 1991. Semiotics and art history. *Art Bulletin* 73: 174–208.

Barthes, Roland 1973. *Mythologies*. London: Paladin.

Bauman, Zygmunt 1999. On postmodern uses of sex. In *Love and Eroticism*, edited by M Featherstone. London: Sage.

Bogard, William 1996. *The simulation of surveillance: Hypercontrol in telematic societies*. Cambridge: Cambridge University Press.

Boyne, Roy 2000. Post-Panopticism. *Economy and Society* 29 (2): 285–307.

Cohen, Stanley 1985. *Visions of Social Control*. Cambridge: Polity.

Deleuze, Gilles 1995. Postscript on Control Societies. In *Negotiations: 1972–1990*. New York: Columbia University Press.

Denzin, Norman 1995. *The Cinematic Society: The Voyeur's Gaze*. London: Sage.

Dreyfus, Hubert and Paul Rabinow 1982. *Michel Foucault: Beyond Structuralism and Hermeneutics*. Hemel Hempstead: Harvester Wheatsheaf.

Ekblom, Paul 1999. Can We Make Crime Prevention Adaptive by Learning from Other Evolutionary Struggles. *Studies on Crime and Crime Prevention 8/1:* 27–51.

Feeley, Malcolm and Jonathan Simon 1992. The New Penology: Notes on the Emerging Strategy of Corrections and its Implications. *Criminology 30 (4):* 449–74.

Feeley, Malcolm and Jonathan Simon 1994. Actuarial Justice: the Emerging New Criminal Law. In *The Futures of Criminology* edited by D Nelken. London: Sage.

Foucault, Michel 1979. *Discipline and Punish*. Harmondsworth: Penguin.

Foucault, Michel 1982. 'Afterword: The Subject and Power', in *Michel Foucault: Beyond Structuralism and Hermeneutics* edited by Hubert Dreyfus and Paul Rabinow. Hemel Hempstead: Harvester Wheatsheaf.

Freud, Sigmund 1991. *The Interpretation of Dreams*. London: Penguin.

Frisby, David 1985. *Fragments of Modernity: Theories of Modernity in the Work of Simmel, Kracauer and Benjamin*. Cambridge: Polity.

Garland, David 1985. *Punishment and Welfare*. Aldershot: Gower.

Garland, David 1990. *Punishment and Modern Society*. Oxford: Clarendon.

Garland, David 2001. *The Culture of Control*. Oxford: Clarendon.

Gordon, Colin ed 1980. *Power/Knowledge: Selected Interviews and Other Writings*. Hemel Hempstead: Harvester Wheatsheaf.

Hall, Stuart 1999. Introduction: Looking and Subjectivity. In *Visual Culture: The Reader* edited by J Evans and S Hall. London: Sage.

Jay, Martin 1994. *Downcast Eyes: The Denigration of Vision in Twentieth-Century French Thought*. London: University of California Press.

Jones, Richard 2000. Digital Rule: Punishment, Control and Technology. *Punishment & Society 2(1):* 5–22.

Kaplan, E Ann 1990. From Plato's Cave to Freud's Screen. In E Ann Kaplan (ed) *Psychoanalysis and Cinema*. London: Routledge.

Kieślowski, Krzysztof (ed Stok, D) 1993. *Kieślowski On Kieślowski*. London: Faber and Faber.

Lacan, Jacques 1979. *The Four Fundamental Concepts of Psycho-Analysis*. London: Penguin.

Mathiesen, Thomas 1997. The viewer society: Michel Foucault's 'Panopticon' revisited. *Theoretical Criminology 1(2):* 215–34.
Maurer, Monika 2000. *Krzysztof Kieślowski.* Harpenden, UK: Pocket Essentials.
Miller, Jacques-Alain 1987. Jeremy Bentham's Panoptic Device. *October 41:* 3–29.
Modleski, Tania 1988. *The Women Who Knew Too Much: Hitchcock and Feminist Theory.* London: Methuen.
Mulvey, Laura 1989. *Visual and Other Pleasures.* London: Macmillan.
Mulvey, Laura 1990. Afterthoughts on 'Visual Pleasure and Narrative Cinema' inspired by *Duel in the Sun.* In E Ann Kaplan (ed), *Psychoanalysis and Cinema.* London: Routledge.
Orwell, George 1997. *Nineteen Eighty-four.* London: Secker & Warburg.
Pollock, Griselda 2000. Vicarious excitements. *New Formations* 4: 25–50.
Rose, Gillian 2001. *Visual Methodologies.* London: Sage.
Saussure, Ferdinand de 1983. *Course in General Linguistics.* London: Duckworth.
Stam, Robert 2000. *Film Theory.* Oxford: Blackwell.
Valier, Claire 2000. Looking Daggers: A Psychoanalytical Reading of the Scene of Punishment. *Punishment & Society 2(4):* 379–94.
Wrathall, John 2000. '*Heat*' review. In J Arroyo (ed), *Action/Spectacle Cinema: A Sight and Sound Reader.* London: British Film Institute.
Young, Alison 1997. *Imagining Crime.* London: Sage.
Žižek, Slavoj 1992. *Looking Awry: An Introduction to Jacques Lacan through Popular Culture.* London: The MIT Press.

7

Make My Day: Images of Masculinity and the Psycho-Dynamics of Mass Incarceration

SIMON HALLSWORTH

'Well right now I don't feel too agreeable.'
Clint Eastwood, *High Plains Drifter*

INTRODUCTION

BY STUDYING THE gender dynamics at play in Clint Eastwood westerns of the 1970s and 1980s, penology can learn much about the psycho-dynamics that underpinned the reconstruction of the United States as a mass incarceration society. What such movies evince in their narrative structure, this chapter argues, is a mode of conflict resolution premised also upon the restoration of patriarchal authority to societies whose conflict resolution structures were perceived as essentially weak through having become fatally effeminised. In form, it contends, communal redemption in these movies is achieved through two means: first, by the promulgation of extreme displays of purified male violence; and second, by the repudiation of qualities associated with the feminine. What makes these movies useful as vehicles through which to study the United States' own punitive turn is the fact that the response of the neo-liberal state to crime conforms to a similarly gendered pattern. By using the insights derived from studying Clint Eastwood movies, this pattern can be revealed and the psycho-dynamics exposed.

Future historians will judge 1973 as a defining moment in the post-war history of the United States. For in this year its welfare state would reach the nadir of its development prior to a period of sustained decline from which it would not recover. It was also the year that witnessed the dawn of what would become in two decades a mass incarceration society. Finally, the movie *High Plains Drifter*, starring Clint Eastwood, was released. These were not disconnected events. For not only was the demise of the welfare state and the rise of the mass incarceration society intimately connected with the rise of what would become a Neo Liberal State, the preconditions necessary for both were beautifully prefigured in the action genre of which Clint Eastwood was the supreme exponent.

In what follows, I will suggest that, by studying the narrative structure of this action genre, penal theory can learn much about the preconditions that would give rise to the mass incarceration society the US would become. What such analysis will illustrate is that, to understand the genesis of its punitive turn, it is necessary to pay close attention to the gender dynamics at play in its formation. What is significant about Clint Eastwood's movies of this period is that these gender dynamics are revealed in a paradigmatic form in their narrative structure. By examining this structure and by observing as we do the way in which the Eastwood figure imposes order to threatened communities, so it is possible to understand something of the gendered forces that would impel the US in its punitive direction. Such analysis will also, or so it is my contention, inform an understanding of western punitiveness in ways that have been overlooked in recent attempts to theorise it. However, I take the opportunity to stress here that an analysis of gendered psycho-dynamics in the filmic and in the realm of penality in no way precludes other types of analysis. With this paper, I merely wish to highlight a particular mode of analysis of penality that, in my view, has all too often been ignored.

To develop this argument, I will examine two movies in which Clint Eastwood starred, then apply the insights gained by studying the gender dynamics at play within them to an analysis of the punitive turn in the United States. Prior to this and by way of introducing the framework that informs this analysis, I will begin by briefly sketching in the contours of my theoretical standpoint. Its implications for penal theory I consider in the final conclusion.

MASCULINITY AND THE PSYCHO-DYNAMICS OF PUNITIVE DISPOSITIONS

As the growing literature on America's mass incarceration society shows (see Hudson 2002 for an introduction) no single reason can be identified to explain its punitive drift. To understand its appetite for pain delivery we must rather study the interrelation of a number of different factors and this is what recent analysis in the field has sought to do (see Garland 2001; Young 1999). Though a range of deeper structural forces (such as changes in the post war economy, regimes of governance, the limitations of and failures of penal modernity) as well as more proximate causes (such legislative change, the behaviour of political elites) have been examined within the literature, it is my contention that an important aspect of analysis remains tangibly lacking. This is an account of the gendered dynamics that also inform punitive responses to law and order.

My point is this: penal change has typically been theorised, as crime traditionally has by reference to everything but what was so glaringly obvious about it. Namely that crime and its causes was always to do with males and their masculinity. It is my contention that the same problem inheres to penal theory as well. It studies entirely relevant factors in its approach to social control while typically ignoring the fact that the behaviour of its object of analysis is also about males and, not least, their masculinity. Gender, in other words, matters if we are to understand social control as much as if we study crime. This chapter is an attempt to rectify this deficit.

What is it then that an analysis of gender dynamics can contribute towards our understanding of punitive trends in the US? What it can illuminate, I believe, is something of the underlying motives that propel people to embrace punitive responses as a response to the threat posed by perceived crisis of law and order. It can also help us, I will suggest, understand something of the form that the punitive response subsequently takes. This then takes me to the crux of my argument.

In order to understand the US' punitive turn we must examine closely how threats posed to its integrity and structure, specifically by a perceived crisis of law and order, are interpreted and identify the responses that follow from this. Now it is my contention, that when we look at responses to threat what we see if not something that is shaped by instrumental considerations alone. What we must do is try and interpret the way threat resolution structures operate by reference to the way in which they are conceived within what must be viewed as gender order interpreted largely in the image of what O'Connell (1993) terms 'hegemonic masculinity'. Interpretation of threat it is my contention is always already gendered and to understand this threat resolution mechanism we must be sensitive to the highly gendered way in which threat is read, interpreted and acted upon within a predominately male dominated order.

In effect, when we look at the ascendancy of the right in the US, and when we consider where the nexus of power resides in its penal complex, what we observe are institutional complexes dominated by men who interpret the world through a gaze fashioned by their (particular) brand of dominant masculinity. To understand how this system responds to threat we must consequently examine this response in the light of their masculinity and the interpretative gaze on which it rests. Prior to examining how it responds to threat let us clarify the terms of this analysis further by exploring the characteristics of the kind of hegemonic masculinity which prevails in these intensively masculinised institutions.

The term 'hegemonic masculinity' is usefully defined by Connell (1993: 184) to signify, not only the ascendancy of masculinity in society in general, but the social ascendancy of a particular form of masculinity. Its source of power derives both from its ascendancy in the cultural realm and by the forms of domination it is able to exercise through the threat or actually of physical force not least as mediated through the repressive apparatus of the state which largely rests in its hands. As Connell argues its 'social ascendancy is achieved in a play of social forces that extends beyond contests of brute power into the organisation of social life and cultural processes' (Connell 1993: 184). In effect its strength is registered in its capacity to shape the way the world is both conceived and understood.

The structure of hegemonic masculinity is defined, again in Connell's terms, by reference to its general (and successful) subjugation of women, to its heterosexual orientation, its contempt and hatred of homosexuality and its subjugation of masculinities deemed incompatible to its self-image. While Connell certainly identifies key aspects of this masculinity it is in the work of Seidler (1994), I would suggest, that we find a more complex analysis of its self image and the forces that have historically acted to bring it in to being.

For Seidler, western masculinity became, from around the 16th century onwards, attached to a self-image in which it became associated with reason and the capacity to exercise it. The association of masculinity with reason also went hand in hand with a repudiation of what reason was not and this Seidler associates with nature and the feminine. Because masculinity alone possessed the faculty of reason and, by virtue of this fact, could fashion through science, bureaucracy and commerce a world defined in its image, so masculinity also claimed for itself a mantle of culture and, by extension, civilisation. And in a relational world this positive attribute came to be defined against what came to be represented as the formless savagery of a wild nature that must be tamed. Imperialism, colonialism, and the subjugation of nature were thus conceived within this image of the world as exercises designed to pacify and make civilised a natural order seemingly devoid of the values that the male order believed itself to personify.

Though Seidler does not directly address the relationship between male sexuality and the male proclivity for violence his work certainly informs an understanding of how it is positioned within dominant masculinity as he conceives it. At one level both violence and sexuality belong to a realm beyond the order of culture and by definition to the state of nature itself. At another they also express essential truths about masculinity and not least male prowess. On one hand then, violence and sexuality can be conceived within the order of hegemonic masculinity as something which, belonging to the state of nature, must be subdued and controlled. Seen this way in terms of its imaginary to be 'a man' is to be in control of libido and not least aggressive impulses. This is what a reasonable man is. This does not mean however that sexuality or violence are devalued because in another sense both embody qualities about masculinity and which can also be valued in and of themselves. Moreover, as Freud and Lacan had already observed, the possession of the phallus would stand within the symbolic order as a triumphant symbol of masculinity ascendancy more generally. In effect it would come to signify masculinity itself and every attribute masculinity would like to claim as its own. In the possession of the phallus so to was the distance and separation from women revealed and their social inferiority positively certified.

What happens then when this order of masculinity is under threat? How does it interpret the threat, itself in relation to this threat, and what response follows through from its interpretation? Now clearly if the threat is small and the recipient is strong enough to address the scale of the threat, then there is little by way of a radical psychic readjustment required. The threat is simply dealt with the means available. But what happens when the threat manifests itself in the form of a violence which is ranged against an order that conceives itself by virtue of that threat to be weak? It is this crisis situation, I will suggest, that takes us into the realm of more punitive responses and to understand the response we need to investigate more carefully how threat is internalised and interpreted within the strange and contradictory order of hegemonic masculinity as it responds to it.

My hypothesis is that when orders of dominant masculinity find themselves under such a crisis specifically then a particular threat resolution structure can be identified. In form it has a number of interrelated components. First the shift from self-identification with reason is replaced with a more pronounced readiness to use violence because being threatened erodes the limits of tolerance. In effect what is posed in the manner of threat will be returned in like kind: violence will beget violence. To become ready for violence however also entails purging from self (or indeed the social order) those attributes that are equated with weakness. For, to be threatened at all, must imply weakness in the order of society itself. Within the structure of hegemonic masculinity I would suggest that what this entails is an attempt to eliminate that which hegemonic masculinity codes and positions as the feminine. It must purge itself of these aspects, not only because they make for weakness but because, at the symbolic level, they signify castration which is weakness personified. At the same time, to ready oneself for violence also requires an attempt to purify those traits identified as most masculine. In effect, in its response to threat hegemonic masculinity will respond by redeeming the phallus by stressing in practice ultra masculinist traits. Shakespeare, in King Henry V, sums up what this entails in ways that clearly expose the phallic symbolism upon which this order of masculinity resides: in the speech the king delivers to his troops prior to battle he encourages them to

> ... stiffen the sinews and summon up the blood, disguise fair nature with hard favoured rage. Then lend the eye a terrible aspect. Let it pry through the portage of the head like a brass cannon. Let the brow overwhelm it, as doth a jagged rock overhang and jutty its confounded base (Shakespeare, *Henry V*).

In summary then, when confronted with threat, the order of hegemonic masculinity is structured in its response by its own order of being. The consequence is to adopt a mode of conflict resolution which embraces three aspects. (i) To confront threat with violence, where to prepare for violence entails (ii) suppressing elements of being identified with the feminine while (iii) purifying masculinity in the process. Threat resolution then can be seen in terms of this structure not only as entailing the destruction of an external enemy, but also as marking the redemption of the threatened order itself via a reassertion of phallic authority. This structure I suggest is typical to the order of hegemonic masculinity and can be observed as a stable aspect of its repertoire.

In the next section my aim will be to illuminate this mode of conflict resolution by examining how it operates in two selected 'lone ranger' style movies in which Clint Eastwood starred. Having illustrated this in my (selective) reading of these movies I will then apply the insights we can obtain from this to an understanding of the US punitive turn.

THEMES OF THREAT AND REDEMPTION IN THE EASTWOOD GENRE

To develop this argument let us examine the narrative structure of Clint Eastwood's movies, attending to the gender dynamics at play within them. To accomplish this I will limit my analysis to two films: the 1973 western *High Plains Drifter* (HPD) and the western *Pale Rider* (PR), in which Eastwood both starred and directed in 1985. Though in some respects different, these movies share a number of common features which make them useful for this purpose. Both films are, in the first instance, about communities who face what Girard (1979) terms a 'sacrificial crisis' — a situation characterised by a threat posed in the form of violence — and their existing conflict resolution structures are unable to resolve it. The problem of violence in both films is also the same and is expressed in the form of a destructive violence perpetrated by outlaw groups external to the community itself. The plot in each case also concerns the restoration of order to the threatened community through acts of generative violence perpetrated by the messianic figure of Clint Eastwood, reprising in each case his role as the 'man with no name'.

By examining the way threat is constructed in these films and by examining their characteristic mode of conflict resolution within them it is possible to observe the gendered assumptions at play in their construction as I have identified these in the section above. To begin with, in both films we are invited to perceive the threatened community as weak not only because those who challenge its authority are strong, but because I will suggest from within the hegemonic masculine order within which these narratives are positioned, these are orders constructed as *effeminised* in ways that prevent the males within it from responding to the threat effectively. This crisis, I will suggest, is then countered by a mode of conflict resolution premised upon the entry of a hero figure whose purified masculinity will redeem what is implicitly coded as symbolically castrated orders through a dramatic reassertion of patriarchal authority. By exemplifying in action a form of violence greater than that the community itself faces and by evincing in so doing a purified display of masculinity from which all traces of the feminine have been eliminated, so the threatened community is saved. In each case redemption is found not only through the destruction of the external threat but through the reassertion of phallic law evident in a final generative performance of violence.

Let us now attend to the dynamic of conflict resolution in these films in more detail looking as we do at the threats confronting the communities in question, their internal weakness and the path to redemption that will be charted through the entry of the Clint Eastwood figure.

In PR the threatened community is represented by a group of miners, who, along with their families, attempt to carve a good life for themselves in a harsh and unforgiving climate of frontier US. In HPD the threatened community is represented by the townsfolk of a small frontier town. The threat posed to these communities has both external and internally generated elements. Externally, each community finds its existence threatened by violent lawless male forces that emanate from and operate outside of the boundaries that define civilisation. In PR the threat to the miners is posed by an unscrupulous property speculator who, with the help of hired thugs, aspires to appropriate the miners' land. In HPD the threat is posed by a gang of outlaws, hell-bent on the destruction of the town and its people. This we discover is an act spurred by a desire for vengeance, fuelled by a distant dark event in which the townsfolk were implicated. In both cases, what unifies the violence is that it is externally generated and is posed in the form of a lawless masculinity freed from all civilised constraints.

If the threat posed to these communities comes in the first instance from an external source, it is compounded, in turn, by serious failings in the social order of the threatened communities. For in each case, what we see are communities who are vulnerable precisely because they do not possess the means necessary to confront the threat they face. To an extent this could be because they are composed of ordinary citizens and not professional killers. Such a view, whilst partially plausible, is nevertheless wrong. Because, what the narrative structure of these movies invites us to believe, is that these communities are vulnerable not because their citizens are incapable of proving protection, but because the men who would be expected to protect them *do not* provide this essential function. The implication in each case is clear, by the standards of hegemonic masculinity which informs the narrative structure of this genre, these communities face a stark crisis engendered by the failure of men to be men. In these films, the structures of law enforcement are emasculated, as indeed are the men who constitute the active principles of the law.

In PR the emasculated status of the men is evident from the beginning. In the face of even moderate levels of violence, we see miners pack their bags and leave the community. More, it is intimated, will immanently follow. Even when one of the miners does confront the forces of evil in a local town, he is summarily executed, not least because his momentary courage is stimulated by drink. By far the most potent index of the failure of men to be men however is dramatised in the figure of the miner's leader, who is presented as an embodiment of the liberal figure of the 'reasonable man'. A being who is both moderate and seemingly proportionate but who does not appear to possess (at least from the outset) what it takes to confront evil with the means necessary to negate it. This is a man defined by lack, in effect the lack of the phallus.

This is dramatised graphically in the film by the respective fate that befalls the women with whom he lives and who he would like to make his wife, and her daughter. In the case of the daughter the theme of emasculation is played out in a scene where one of the outlaws attempts to rape her. Until, that is, saved by the Clint Eastwood figure who we discover is also desired by the daughter's mother with whom he subsequently sleeps. It is an interesting vision being painted here of a man here who while noble is nevertheless emasculated. To use a grail analogy, what we are presented with in figure of the miner's leader is a kind of latter day fisher king incapable of protecting and looking after his own family, let alone embodying in action the active principle of phallic law necessary to ensure the protection of his community from the dark forces that confront it.

HPD also conforms to a similar narrative structure. The men who comprise the townsfolk are presented without exception as inveterate cowards. In flashbacks to a past event, we are invited to witness the spectacle of the towns' previous Marshall being brutally horsewhipped while the townsfolk turn their backs in the face of his desperate pleas for help. These are a people mired in cowardice and bad faith in equal measure. Such men, it is intimated, are not capable of establishing the law, let alone upholding it. This they delegate instead to various gangsters. As in PR the failure of the men within the community to actively embody the spirit of the Law is dramatised most acutely by their failure to keep their women. When Clint Eastwood enters the town in his incarnation as 'the man with no name', one of his first acts is to rape the wife of one of the towns prominent citizens. Shortly afterwards, he installs himself at the cuckolded husbands home. Communal impotence it is implicitly suggested must be countered by the entry of a more virile seed. The theme of emasculation is thereafter played out in the movie through the various indignities which the Clint Eastwood character (who we discover is a mysterious reincarnation of the previous sheriff), imposes upon the town folk. At one point he persuades them to paint their town red, and installs as its leader a hitherto despised midget in an act of carnivalesque inversion.

In these action movies the threat of external violence is itself aggravated by the emasculated status of the men who are supposed to defend them. These are social orders which are presented as symbolically castrated from the outset and in which, consequently, the law of the father essential to the construction of order itself is no longer held to prevail. These are orders in which a sacrificial crisis may be observed to have occurred. This is a situation which societies confront when they face the contaminating threat posed by an unlicensed violence, where the existing structures by which violence has traditionally been kept at bay had been seen to fail. It is in the context of such a crisis that a hero figure will arrive both as avenger and redeemer. It is precisely in this context that Clint Eastwood appears: 'inhumanely tranquil, controlled and assured' (Kael, 1996: 304) riding in from the very desert from which the original violence emanated. A mysterious stranger, untrammelled from the very beginning from such mundane symbols of domesticity as a family, wife, children, biography or, indeed, even a name. He is not simply a hero who embodies masculinity he is Masculinity in its most distilled and purified form

His function in both movies is the same. He appears as a messianic figure whose great and mythic acts will be such as to resolve the sacrificial crisis that the threatened communities confront. This redemptive function is revealed in two ways. The most obvious way in which this function is mediated is as nemesis of evil. He will and does destroy the forces that challenge the threatened communities, and this he accomplishes by directing against these outlaw forces a form of violence even more devastating than that which they pose.

His function however is not simply that of eliminating the evil that exists outside the community, for he is also there to redeem an emasculated community by re-imposing patriarchal authority where this authority no longer prevails. Under the aegis of his short reign, men must become men once again — or perish in the act. At the barrel of his gun, emblematic of the phallus, which, in Lacanian terms, symbolises the active principle of paternal authority, the Law is re-imposed upon a community such that it can become a community again. In effect, in the figure of Clint Eastwood, a purified masculinity is offered as the solution to a social crisis caused in part by a lawless masculinity, but a masculinity that could not be defeated because the social order it sought to threaten had itself has itself become effeminised. What Clint Eastwood signifies is therefore not only the nemesis of an external evil (bad men challenging the good community), but the imposition of male order to an emasculated community in a form of purified masculinity. A patriarchal order whose totemic emblem is the phallus the strength of which is graphically affirmed through a cathartic ritual of generative destruction, spectacularly dramatised in the extreme violence of the final show down.

NEO-LIBERAL RULE AND THE GENDERED DYNAMICS OF THE MASS-INCARCERATION SOCIETY

What makes these movies important is not only that they emerged at the precise time that the United States embarked upon the construction of its contemporary gulag (see Christie 1979; Stern 1998) but that their gender dynamics parallels those that underpinned the rise of its punitive response. To understand the latter therefore I propose to use the former. To accomplish this I will use this reading of Clint Eastwood's action genre to say something about the social conditions that would lead the US in the direction of its punitive turn. Just as the narratives of the movies discussed above are organised around the re-imposition of male law to symbolically castrated orders as identified in the opening section, so too are the same dynamics at play in the rise of the Neo-liberal state and its response to crime.

As in the Eastwood movies, the threat to American society was interpreted in the first instance as an external threat posed against the 'good' order by lawless male forces external to it. The failure to confront this threat was also compounded in turn by the internal weakness of the liberal welfare state which, I will argue, the neo-liberal state came in effect to consider as fatally effeminised. The form embodied in its subsequent punitive response can consequently be considered in terms that equate with the form of salvation delivered by the man with no name. What we can observe in the practice of the neo-liberal state is a mode of redemption premised upon the re-imposition of male law through purified displays of violent masculinity. A demonstration of masculinity moreover from which all traces of that which could be equated with the feminine have been systematically expelled. In this dramatic reinstatement of male authority so the symbolically castrated order of the welfare state is redeemed by the reassertion of a phallic male authority.

Let us now attempt to consider this argument in moves that parallel the way in which the discussion of Eastwood's movies proceeded. We begin here with an identification of the threat that would provoke the New Right in the direction of its punitive turn.

To understand the New Right construction of the crisis of law and order however we need to proceed by conceiving their pronouncements (methodologically) as structured from the outset by a specifically gendered perspective. As we shall see, this gaze upon the world not only selects and organises what is seen, it provides the means necessary for its interpretation by providing a discursive grid that allows what is seen to be described within a pre-established narrative that will order its final meaning. What I propose to do, therefore, is examine new right texts, not as indexes of reality — even though they aspire to present themselves as such — but as persecution texts which stand in an imaginary relation to the real relations they aspire to describe.

Most criminologists would agree that the punitive turn in the US was shaped from the outset as a response to what was represented as a profound crisis in law and order. While this might appear a necessary cause to which a concerted law and order response would appear justified we must, I believe, be more circumspect in our analysis of its discursive construction. Different spectators can, after all, interpret the crisis in very different ways. While for the left the rise of crime in the post war period has been identified with a range of socio-economic changes within capitalist society (see Hall 1980; Lea and Young 1984; Garland 2001), this was not the view on the part of the new right who made little by way of such casual connections in their analysis. In a manner akin to the way in which the outlaw groups in the Eastwood movies were represented as incorrigibly corrupt and evil, so to was crime identified with what would be represented as lawless males freed from all civilised constraint (see Wilson and Hernstein 1985; Murray 1990), and it is in this image, as a predatory urban underclass, that we see crime and criminality depicted in new right texts. In a move that also parallels the Eastwood movies there is also a sense in which these uncivilised lawless forces are also held to emanate from spaces external to the boundaries of civilisation itself. Instead of the barren wasteland of the Arizona desert what the imaginary of the right would conjure into being was an urban desert: the wild, denuded and dystopian wilderness of an inner city landscape. A space again configured as an outside and from where civilisation as such could not flourish because the forces of male authority that might sustain it were no longer visible. Here instead would be found a world where life was feral, and ordered by a state of nature depicted graphically in Hobbesian terms.

Though the good society was confronted in the first instance by a lawless threat external to it, this threat was compounded in turn by the failure of the existing conflict resolution systems to confront it. As in Eastwood's movies, the problem here was that the state could not confront this threat appropriately because it was considered to have become weak. In effect, what the new right and populist writers in the mass media would articulate in their persecution texts was the vision of a symbolically castrated order from which authentic and appropriate male authority were considered to have become eliminated. The threat in other words was as much internally generated as externally imposed from an outside beyond civilisation itself.

Again, in terms of methodology, what we must do here is consider new right commentary on the welfare state not as a representation of the real as concrete in thought, but as persecution texts, the nature of which is legible only in terms of the gendered dynamics that underpin them. If we now attend to the way the welfare state was represented, what the new right saw was a state ultimately perceived to have failed in its primary function of guaranteeing sovereignty. It had failed to exercise the authority necessary to ensure male order could be guaranteed to begin with. The implication here is that this was a state where authentic male authority was in crisis because in its welfare-state garb it had become fatally effeminised. As the media would testify time and time again, this was a state which could not guarantee that windows would not be broken nor control the predatory gangs who openly challenged its sovereignty and hence authority. This was an order in which, to deploy Giddens's (1993) imagery, the order of the phallus had become revealed as a penis, an altogether less virile symbol.

It is not surprising therefore that we find disciplines such as social work and welfarism, considered within the terms of new right discourse, as a kind of feminised activity that could only ever aggravate illegal acts, never contain them. Thus we find a well-worn litany of complaints made by the right and their supporters in the mass media: conditions in prisons are always too comfortable; rehabilitation does not work yet the liberal state continues to provide it; punishment is never severe enough and never matches the gravity of the offence. What these forms of critique imply is that the welfare state not only lets its enemies get away with murder, but also literally encourages them to do so and will not punish them when they do. Far from making people self reliant, it makes them dependant; far from ensuring effective governance through promulgating a respect for authority; it provokes instead a crisis of ungovernability marked by a debilitating disrespect for sovereign male authority.

These fears about the effeminisation of the state and the dire consequences for society that followed on from this can also be found in new right concerns about rising permissiveness, and not least in the perceived breakdown of the nuclear family and rising illegitimacy. What clearly outraged new right sensibilities was the idea of an emergent social order from which male authority was considered to have dramatically waned. This pervasive concern is perhaps best exemplified by the morbid fears and hatred the new right would express towards a figure they constructed as both scapegoat and folk devil — the unmarried mother. A demonic figure on to which would be projected their deepest fears. Fears about the limits to male authority in an order where it was felt to be in decline; or fears about the pre-oedipal state of nature that would ensue in a world where a paternal father dominating a traditional nuclear family was no longer the norm. Murray's identification of an underclass gives a flavour of where this kind of thinking derives: 'the key to an underclass is not an individual instance but a situation in which a very large proportion of an entire community lacks fathers' (Murray 1990).

The fact that the welfare state only ever practised a form of masculinised care anyway, and that this was itself beset by massive contradictions when it came to the function of realising its benevolent (modernist) ambitions, is largely beside the point. For what the new right conjured up, was a representation of the state as fundamentally emasculated. This was a state which, understood from within the terms of hegemonic masculinity which, I argue, provides the interpretative grid around which this crisis could be conceptualised, was one in which male authority was perceived to have been fatally compromised. The phallus as symbol and guarantor of the law no longer prevailed because the authority with which its exercise is symbolically associated was no longer felt to be present. Order as such was undermined because the conditions that could alone make it possible — male authority — had been eroded and usurped in the name of a creeping effeminising set of processes that would be projected onto the welfare state.

Let us now attend to the resolution of the imputed crisis of law and order that the emergent neo-liberal state came to implement. As I suggested above, the crisis of law and order was one premised upon a conception of crime as manifest in contaminating violence that could not be contained by an effeminised state. As in the Clint Eastwood movies, what the neo-liberal state posed as a solution was to reinstate legitimate authority through the imposition of responses that stressed ultra masculinist 'solutions' to the crisis of law and order as it would conceive it within its symbolic order. In practice, this response was organised around the promulgation of practices that both accentuated ostensibly masculine qualities and directly repudiated feminising trends as these were observed to operate in the context of its practice.

The accentuation and purification of the masculine can be observed in an array of policy moves initiated as part of the neo-liberal response to law and order from the 1970s onward. They are evident above all in the resurgence of what elsewhere I have identified as the values characteristic of postmodern penality (see Hallsworth 2002). These centre upon the relegitimation of pain as a legitimate penal strategy, and not least, the shift towards disproportionate and visceral patterns of sentencing. As in the Eastwood movies what is noticeable about these trends is not only that the threat to order redeemed by imposing a violence which exceeds that it confronts, but in the enactment of violent rituals, male authority is dramatically reaffirmed.

It is this shift in the production of a self consciously macho state that explains, I would suggest, the socio-genesis of policies such as 'zero-tolerance', 'tough-love', capital punishment, supermax and the bootcamp. What unifies these practices is precisely the masculinist logic that informs them. A logic, I would suggest, only legible in and by reference to the gendered dynamics at play in its formation. In effect, what each of these practices embody is not just the reassertion of state authority in general as Garland (1996) argues, but the spectacular and visible reassertion of a particular kind of patriarchal authority. These are ultimately the acts not just of a state in general or a capitalist state but a male capitalist state whose characteristic mode of practice is revealed in a repertoire of acts stressing spectacular displays of sovereign authority ultimately revealed in its will to violence. In this context the similarity between new right 'solutions' to crime with the purified figure of masculinity evident in Clint Eastwood's man with no name is, I would suggest, no mere coincidence.

The bootcamp experiment in the US, exemplifies this form of purified masculinity in a paradigmatic form. What it reveals, I would suggest, is a penal experiment which has little to do with meaningfully addressing crime (as most evaluation studies seem to prove). What it does signify however in the semiotics of its practice is a solution to crime organised around ultra masculinised practices. In this context note the calculated sadism of the guards, the accentuated simulation of a military establishment, the severe austerity of the locations and the very term bootcamp itself. What such a bizarre experiment exemplifies is not only what Simon (1995) suggests we consider a postmodern simulation offered in the form of a spectacle. This is a spectacle offered as symbolic consolation designed to allay deep-rooted fears of castration on the part of a state that perceives itself to have become fatally effeminised.

As Theweleit's (1984) seminal study of the German Freikorp demonstrates, institutionalised male violence expresses itself not only in violent deeds and action, but also in its flight from and repudiation of all it considers to embody the feminine. And this explicit repudiation can be observed graphically in many of the responses to crime initiated under the aegis of neo liberal rule. In the first instance it is noticeable in the display of violence that characterise many aspects of its practice. Capital punishment perhaps best illustrates this chilling instantiation of male rule. The repudiation of the feminine can however also be witnessed in the recurrent attack the Neo-liberal state would visit upon perceived 'soft' institutions. Particularly those perceived to embody the qualities its imaginary would associate with the kind of feminisation it would hold responsible for the erosion of male authority to begin with.

The militarisation of the US probation service and its transformation from a social service institution premised on an ethic of care to one reconfigured around risk management is a case in point (see Christie 1994: 114–15). Note in this context how, in the process of its 'modernisation', the probation service were eventually armed with guns. A practice which, read psychoanalytically, can be considered akin to the receipt of a phallus. A process designed to signify the reorganisation of the force away from the feminised ethic of social work that had hitherto characterised it. No room here, one could note, for the kind of 'different voice' articulated for example (at around the same period of time) in the feminist work of Gilligan (1982).

Another example of the repudiation of the feminine is evident in the invention of penal regimes from which all traces of care and compassion have been carefully and systematically eliminated. The conditions that prevail in supermax provide one example of this trend (see King 2000) while the institutionalised violence that underpins the bootcamp experience described above exemplifies another (see Simon 1995). Stern's graphic description of the American supermax prison at Marion Illinois indicates clearly what happens when compassion is explicitly denied as a virtue.

> There the prisoners have an average sentence of more than 40 years. In the cells the furniture is immovable and there is no soap dish, toilet seat of toilet handle, as all of these can be made into weapons. The cells have cement floors painted grey. The building is designed so that the prisoners will not be able to see other cells or the Rocky Mountains through the small windows (Stern 1998: 55).

Prison Rights Watch (quoted by Stern) summarises the unrelentingly cruel conditions facing the prisoners within this regime. Again what bears noting here is just how far the flight from the feminine (and nature) can go and just how terrifying remain the spaces where masculinity can take itself in the process of its attempt to purify itself of contaminating feminising tendencies.

> When an inmate is outside of his cell he is handcuffed and a box is placed over the handcuffs to prevent the lock being picked; his legs may also be shackled. Inmates are forbidden to socialise with each other or to participate in group religious services. Inmates who throw food or otherwise misbehave in their cells are sometimes tied spread-eagled on their beds, often for hours at a stretch, while inmates returning to their cells are often (inmates of the control unit, always) subjected to a rectal search; a paramedic inserts a gloved finger into the inmates rectum and feels around for a knife or other weapon or contraband (Human Rights Watch 1993: 3).

The annihilation of spirit and not least of life itself in the realisation of this extreme vision of purified masculinity is also graphically evident in this description of the US state penitentiary at Pelican Bay:

> All trees and greenery are shaved off the earth. Concrete, asphalt and gravel have replaced the redwoods. There is not a living thing in reach of ... the prisoners (Elvin 1992: 5).

In these sections we see conjoined two issues which together betray the gender dynamics integral to such formations. First note the use of rectal searches which, in another context, can also be considered identical to what elsewhere could be called forced rape — here revealed as an institutionalised normal practice. A strategy of male power which, as many feminists have argued (see Brownmiller 1976; Segal 1990) remains intrinsic to male domination. Note too the sheer austerity of the conditions described. What has been accomplished in these carceral spaces is something from which anything that might be equated with nature and natural rhythms has been eliminated, all the way through to ensuring that inmates cannot even see 'the rocky mountains'. In its elimination of all that it codes as the feminine and in its negation of nature what purified masculinity establishes it could be noted is an architecture of death in its repudiation of life.

Finally the repudiation of the feminine can be seen as intrinsic in the politics of the family — particularly the sustained attack on single parents and not least in attempts to role back the welfare state in the name of a more muscular policies emphasising 'tough-love' or work-fare. Again what we can observe in these initiatives: reducing benefits for single mothers, attempting to strengthen the nuclear family etc. are not only aspects of a wider war on the poor, but attempts to strengthen the role of patriarchal authority by strengthening the hand of fathers in reconstructed family units.

CONCLUSIONS AND IMPLICATIONS

This chapter is not written as yet another grand narrative, designed to explain the contemporary punitive turn in its entirety. It has rather been written as an attempt to understand an aspect of it that has not in my view been adequately theorised, namely the gender dynamics at play in its formation. As I have sought to show, when we examine the kind of penal response that the new right imposed as a solution to the crisis of law and order, both interpretation and solution owed much to a gendered conception of the world. From the very outset the crisis of law and order was always already interpreted in gendered terms, and it was in profoundly gendered terms that the neo-liberal state responded. When the neo-liberals generated their own specifically repressive response to what I have defined above as this sacrificial crisis occasioned by the crisis of law and order, what we see in the repertoire of responses chosen was a specific reassertion of hegemonic masculinity. In effect what the neo-liberal state sought to impose was a regime in which a purified order of ultra masculinity became posed as solution to its own crisis. When we look at the form of penal regime that the neo-liberal state has created in its image, we must therefore see in its peculiarly brutal and repressive formations, an expression of the hegemonic masculinity around which it was constructed.

What is interesting about the Clint Eastwood movies is that in their narrative structure they already prefigured precisely the same solution to the same crisis that the neo-liberal state would pose. This symmetry it could be argued was not accidental for both the neo-liberal state and the movie industry are themselves beholden to a similar series of gendered capitalist dynamics and it is these that in each case give meaning to the acts and events that this paper has sought to discuss. What makes both similar is that both are beholden to and informed by the way in which the western gender order operates. Both, in effect, reflect the way the world is conceived within this gendered order in which hegemonic masculinity prevails. Unsurprisingly given that this order is itself profoundly structured by the assumptions of hegemonic masculinity, the interpretative grid upon which it relies only reflects the world as seen from within the terms made possible by its gaze. To look at this a different way, what I am arguing here is that the forces that could imagine a story line such as HPD or which could conjure into being a penal experiment such as the bootcamp, emanate from the same epistemic space. A world, that is, imagined in terms framed by the male imaginary in the context of a social order interpreted in its image.

What such analysis does throw into question however, and here it does stand in part as critique, is what might be regarded as the typically instrumental accounts of penal change and development that typically prevail in the criminological literature. That is, theories which explain penal change as a more or less rational response to given problems such as high crime, insecurity, the limits of liberal rule etc. Accounts that move within this genre include all approaches that account for penal change in terms of the shift towards new regimes of regulation and control or which conceive change in terms of new strategies of governance. While I accept that these explanatory narratives offer many insights into many aspects of recent penal change, the problem I have with them remains precisely their emphasis upon instrumental rationality as an organising motive driving penal change and development forward. What the analysis here offers is a way of looking at contemporary penal practice in ways that also recognise far more heterogeneous motives at play in their development and not least motives that might not be necessarily recognised by actors involved. These impulses however simply cannot be seen with the epistemic spaces available to more rational approaches, precisely because the irrational has no place within the terms of analysis available to them.

Reflecting back on the argument I have sought to develop, two potential lines of criticism could be directed against its assumptions. First that it presents a seemingly a-historical structure of conflict resolution; and second, not unrelated to this, it ignores societies where, in recent decades, not least, under the impact of feminism, gender has been 'on the move'. With regard to the former then what I have tried to identify is a structure of conflict resolution which is and remains typical to the way this particular form of hegemonic masculinity responds and continues to respond to crisis. In orders which remain dominated by and shaped largely in the image of this form of masculinity, then the structure as such still persists, not least, because it remains attached to a particularly resilient (fissured and contradictory to be sure) identity form.

Nor has its self-identity as such been particularly dented by feminist attempts to unravel its structure and contest its authority. This is not, however, to suggest that in other social realms — the cultural sphere, for example, has not been challenged or changed significantly as a consequence. In the grim order of authoritarian politics and not least the penal industrial complex, what we dealing with are institutions which were always heavily masculinised and which remain so today. If feminism can in anyway be connected with America's punitive turn then its role remains marginal and contradictory. On one hand the demand of feminists that male predators should be punished chimed well with the punitive dispositions that were already in evidence from the 1970s onward. On the other, the resurgence of feminism also helped provoke the right to reinstate more traditional conceptions of masculinity in the face of challenges elsewhere directed against it.

While the analysis I have attempted here does attempt to engage with the issue of gender, I remain highly conscious of the limits of the analysis offered here. I would also recognise and affirm here the subsequent need to initiate the theoretical spadework necessary to demonstrate more comprehensively the precise relation between the gender order and penal process. This remains however the task for a future project in penal theory.

REFERENCES

Brownmiller, Susan 1976. *Against Our Will, Men Women and Rape*, Harmondsworth: Penguin.

Christie, Nils 1988. *Crime Control as Industry: Towards GULAGS Western Style*, Routledge: London.

Elvin, J 1992. 'Isolation, Excessive force Under Attack at California's Supermax', *National Prison Project Journal*, Vol 7, No 4.

Garland, David 1996. The Limits of the Sovereign State: Strategies of Crime Control in Contemporary Society. *The British Journal of Criminology*, 36: 445–71.

Garland, David 2001. *The Culture of Control*, Oxford: Oxford University Press.

Connell, Robert 1993. *Gender and Power*, Cambridge: Polity Press.

Feeley, Malcolm and Simon Jonathan 1992. The New Penology, Notes on the Emerging Strategy of Corrections and its Implications. *Criminology* 30(4): 452–74.

Feeley, Malcolm and Simon Jonathan 1994. Actuarial Justice: the Emerging New Criminal Law, in *The Futures of Criminology*, edited by David Nelken. London: Sage.

Giddens, Anthony 1993. *The Transformation of Intimacy: Sexuality Love and Eroticism in Modern Societies*. Cambridge: Polity Press.

Gilligan, Carol 1982. *In a Different Voice*. Cambridge, Mass: Harvard University Press.

Griffin, Susan 1981. *Woman and Nature: The Roaring Inside Her*. London: Women's Press.

Girard, Rene 1979. *Violence and the Sacred*. Baltimore: John Hopkins University Press.

Hall, Stuart 1980. *Drifting into a Law and Order Society*. London: Cobden Trust (3–17).

Hallsworth, Simon 2002. The case for a Postmodern Penality. *Theoretical Criminology*, 6(2): 145–64.

Hudson, Barbara 2002. Punishment and Control in *The Oxford Handbook of Criminology*, edited by Mike Maguire, Rod Morgan and Rob Reiner. Oxford: Oxford University Press.

Human Rights Watch, (1999) *Prison Conditions in the United States* No 1–5632–046–4.

King, R 2000. The Rise and Rise of Supermax: An American Solution in Search of a Problem. *Punishment and Society* 1(2): 163–86.

Kael, Pauline 1996. *Conversations with Pauline Kael*, edited by W Brantley. Mississippi: University Press of Mississippi.

Lea, John and Jock Young 1984. *What is to be Done About Law and Order*. Harmondsworth: Penguin.

Murray, Charles (1990) *The Emerging British Underclass*. London: Institute for Economic Affairs.

O'Malley, Pat 1999. Volatile and Contradictory Punishment. *Theoretical Criminology* 3 (2): 175–76.

O'Malley, Pat 1994. Risk, Power and Crime Prevention. *Economy and Society* 21(3): 252–75.

Segal, Lynn (1990) *Slow Motion: Changing Masculinities, Changing Men*. London: Virago.

Simon, Jonathan 1995. They Died with their Boots on: The Boot Camp and the Limits of Modern Penality. *Social Justice* 22(1): 25–49.

Stern, Vivian 1998. *A Sin Against the future: Imprisonment in the World*. Boston: North Eastern University Press.

Seidler, V 1994. *Unreasonable Men: Masculinity and Social Theory*. Routledge: London.

Theweleit, K 1987. *Male Fantasies* (Vol 1). Cambridge: Polity Press.

Young, Jock 1999. *The Exclusive Society*. London: Sage.

Weston, J 1980. *From Ritual to Romance*. Bath: Chivers.

Wilson, J & Hernstein, R 1985. *Crime and Human Nature*. New York: Simon and Shuster.

8

Imagining Justice at the Cradle of Modernity: Re-Visiting Huizinga

RONNIE LIPPENS

IN HIS LONG essay, 'Art as Prophecy', Francis Haskell (1993: 389–432) wrote an account of how historians have in the past looked at how visual art, painting in particular, often can be used as a predictor of things to come. The prophetic as well as revolutionary force in paintings and drawings by David, for example, during the nineteenth century, have often been recognised by historians who, with hindsight, felt that David's works, much more than any contemporary political tract, were able to foreshadow the events of the Revolution. It's not so much the substantial contents of visual artworks but rather the formal characteristics that seem to be carrying this 'prophetic' force. It's as if historical change tends to show itself first in emerging forms, visual form in particular, before it also emerges in strings of words. Whether these forms find their way through an artist's conscious deliberations, through his or her rational, logical deductions, or whether they emerge on the waves of the unconscious, is not an issue here. The prophetic force of (some) visual works of art, according to many nineteenth-century historians as well as to Haskell, who quotes them favourably, seems to be due to artists',

> 'exceptional sensitivities rather than to their abilities at making clever guesses or to their faculties of reasoning', even to 'a sort of mystical talent, of which the artist himself is unaware and which can, by definition, be detected only with hindsight' (1993: 430).

Prophetic force, in short, is first and foremost a matter of the senses, the primordial amongst which seems to be vision, the realm of images, imagery, indeed imagination. We do not know whether this claim rests on some kind of truth, *really*. If anything, this claim should, according to its own premises, rest on an image, indeed on imagination itself. As newness, or change, or simply as something that emerges, this claim should be flowing within the bounds of an image in or through which it is imagined that sensitivity, visual sensitivity in particular, comes first, before words string into sentences and into claims. This image could very well be one of bodies that, as nodes of sensitivity, and driven by sensuous desires, emerge and disappear on the historical scene, during which process they trace forms that only post hoc, 'with hindsight', they can reflect upon using strings of words that form during, or in the wake of, historical experience.

Surely it can never be our intention here to show how this *particular* imaginary fully covers historical process and experience. Such a case, for reasons that are well known by now, would be impossible to make. However, what can be shown here is that any particular vision on historical process and experience that does not take account of vision, of images, imagery and imagination as important, although perhaps not necessarily primordial locations where social change announces itself, is equally *bound* to be partial or worse, problematic. Historical change, or newness, if you wish, necessarily has to take place, that means, it has to emerge and develop some *where*, within spatial bounds and limits, and it's precisely those bounds and limits that tend to emerge as lines in images, as boundaries of imagination. One aim of this essay is to illustrate this by way of a re-reading of Johan Huizinga's *The Waning of the Middle Ages,* a by now classic book that, although it aimed at a reconstruction of the cultural 'spirit' of the late Middle Ages, never quite managed to take seriously the many images and imagery it referred to.

This chapter also aims to argue how lines (in images) and boundaries (of imagination) are always particular and on the move.[1] They are particular because they are always the scene (the *seen*, in a way) of a particular eye, of an eye located in time and space. And they are on the move, at times slowly, at other times rapidly so. The eye always sees accumulations of history and space. It sees hybrid clusters of lines and boundaries, some of which will tend to announce newness emerging from the living remnants of previous histories and fragments of other geographies. What is seen by the eye or imagined by the 'mind's eye', ie particular scenes of movement, although particular to a particular point in time and space, can therefore never be reduced to a specific set of particularities. Imaginary boundaries, their lines and bounds hold imaginary material from a diversity of histories and

[1] I would like to thank all contributors to this volume for the many comments and suggestions made during our seminar. I also wish to thank Alessandro di Giorgi, Stephen Farrell, Evi Girling, Ruth Jamieson, Susanne Karstedt, Nick Lee, and Richard Wild for having offered highly appreciated comments during another presentation of this essay. Some of their suggestions have slipped onto the above pages. All remaining errors and flaws, of course, are entirely the author's.

geographies, and it is there, in this particularly hybrid mix, that historical change, or newness, may be showing through. It is hoped here that this chapter will be able to illustrate this, once again by way of a re-reading of Johan Huizinga's *The Waning of the Middle Ages*. Huizinga, who read Burgundian cultural products as expressions of a late, though essentially Medieval spirit (which, to a certain extent it was), did not make a sustained effort to scrutinise visual art works of the period, and did therefore not *see* how, in Burgundian visual art, lines and boundaries were on the move. In other words, he did not see how the imaginary boundaries of or within Burgundian visual art, painting in particular, however particular to Burgundy, also provided space for movement and newness. In them, historical change already announced itself quite conspicuously, also, and I'd say, precisely at places where Huizinga himself thought it was absent. We hope to be able to illustrate this by having a closer look at some of the paintings which Huizinga himself referred to in his book, but failed to analyse extensively. We will be looking at images of what roughly could be called scenes of justice. Indeed, it is often in scenes and visions of justice that the sensitivities of what Ernst Bloch (1986) once called 'forward-dawning' hope towards social and political formations first seem to crystallise into lines and shapes.

HUIZINGA'S *THE WANING OF THE MIDDLE AGES*

Johan Huizinga's *The Waning of the Middle Ages* is a classic in both historical as well as cultural studies. Since its first edition in 1919, the book has been inspiring historians, art historians and art critics, scholars and students working within the humanities as well as in social sciences more generally. The book still is a continuing source of inspiration. Only recently (1997) Chicago University Press published a new (and for the first time, complete) translation under the title *The Autumn of the Middle Ages*, a title which, by the way, is a literal translation of the original Dutch title, *Herfsttij der Middeleeuwen*.[2] Huizinga, in his magnum opus, set out to rethink medieval studies. Closely reading a wealth of 15th- and early 16th-century cultural products (chronicles, poetry, popular songs, romances, paintings, and so on) he managed to evoke the cultural dimensions of the late Middle Ages, and, simultaneously, to unsettle much of the received historical wisdom. Huizinga focussed on the 15th-century cultural produce of the then dukedom of Burgundy which, at the time, included the

[2] All references and quotations in the essay at hand are from the fully illustrated 22nd edition (1997) of *Herfsttij der Middeleeuwen* (Amsterdam, Contact). Translations are mine.

Low Countries, the most significant and culturally 'hegemonic' region of which may arguably have been Flanders. The book's highly evocative and literary style seemed to have broken new paths, linking historical studies (at the time largely a place of dates and kings, or, alternatively, of Henri Pirenne-style political economy) to cultural analysis. Although 19th-century historians such as Jacob Burckhardt (1860) had been breaking new ground before him, culture, after Huizinga (who always showed a keen interest in anthropology), became firmly part of a historian's archive. Prefiguring post-war authors such as Michel Foucault, or Edward Said (1978), Huizinga was able to demonstrate how cultural production (in the broadest sense) could offer a clear window to the soul of an historical age, much more so than a list of dates and names and events, much more so than a constellation of economic developments and political moves. In that sense, the book also prefigured the 'cultural turn' that has marked the humanities and social sciences since about 1980. Huizinga, by the way, would double this effort with the publication, in 1938, of *Homo Ludens*, the central thesis of which was to claim that the motor of history was to be found in cultural experimentation and cultural 'play'.

One of the central theses of *Herfsttij* was the one that both assumes as well as establishes a significant cultural difference, in the 14th and 15th centuries, between the Low Countries (and Burgundy) on the one hand, and Northern Italy on the other. Whereas, according to Huizinga, the Italian city states were the scene of a remarkable cultural renewal, cultural production in the Low Countries, in Huizinga's *reading*, seems to have expressed a continuation of a certain medieval 'spirit', or essence, that arrived at its highest peak. It may have been the last flare-up of this spiritual essence (a highly colourful and vivid one at that) but flare-up nevertheless it was; not so much a forebode to something new, as a last, bright and masterfully crafted performance of an age that was heading towards closure.[3] This thesis, and the enormous impact it had on many members of an academic community that would have tended to analyse and discuss Flemish masters and Italian painters in one breath (as Pirenne did, for example, when he situated both in similar social end economic conditions; Pirenne, 1900: 492), was another reason why Huizinga's book almost immediately turned into a classic. However, it is precisely this thesis that we wish to deal with here. In the essay at hand, we will focus particularly on how Huizinga's reluctance to analyse imagery when studying historical change has probably undermined his abilities to detect cultural change (concretely: the birth of early, *monadic* Modernity) at times and in places that, according to Huizinga, were largely breathing a quintessential medieval spirit.

[3] Indeed, Huizinga long played with the idea of entitling his work 'Autumn *Glow* of the Middle Ages' (information from Anton van der Lem's postface to the 22nd Dutch edition). The word 'autumn' includes both the notions of 'decline' and 'harvest'.

LOOKING AT CULTURAL CHANGE

The bulk of the book's 'empirical material' consists of all kinds of written texts, chronicles mostly. But the book does mention and sometimes even manages to briefly analyse a considerable number of drawings and paintings. The images themselves however were not included in the first editions of *Herfsttij*. This is somewhat strange for an author who was amongst the first (eg in a 1905 lecture on 'the aesthetic element in historical thought') and arguably the most influential to recognise the need for historians to study all kinds of cultural artefacts, including images, during historical work. Furthermore, Huizinga, an accomplished visual artist himself, on many occasions, stressed the fact that it had been images that had stirred him to write *Herfsttij*. In particular he often mentioned his visit, in 1902, to the international exhibition on old Flemish masters that was held in Bruges at the time. There, he claimed, the paintings by Jan Van Eyck in particular inspired him to write a book on Burgundian culture — a book, he often stated, that would situate Van Eyck's work in the broader context of Burgundian culture. The book whose subtitle included a phrase with a typically visual metaphor ('a study of the *forms* of life and thought') eventually only sparsely mentioned Van Eyck's and other paintings (see on this also Scheller, 1995).[4] We may safely assume that, to the author of *Herfsttij*, who started his academic career as a linguist (Huizinga's PhD dissertation was about Sanskrit drama), the specificities of visual materials will ultimately not have made a very significant difference and indeed, in later texts, Huizinga often showed himself very sceptical of the analysis of imagery (this was rather too subjective a method, he often claimed, with the danger of fantasy and speculation lurking) as a historian's tool (see on this eg Haskell, 1993: 493 ff; den Boer, 1995). Also in some of his early lectures he showed himself sceptical, as when he argued how for example Dante's literary work preceded the Van Eycks by almost a century (Krul, 1995: 86).

There are, however, reasons (Lacan's writings on psychoanalysis, culture and imagery may be amongst them, eg in Lacan, 1986) to take account of the specificities of imagery. Images, imagery, or visual material in general, we think, do have the capacity (at least as much as textual material) to radiate affect and emotion (e-*motion*), *move*ment and thus ... change. 'Visibilities' (Deleuze reading Foucault, 1988) allow culture to express its restlessness, its moves and its changes. It is in 'visibilities', in architecture, for example, or in the gaze that lurks in a *panopticon*, that a Foucault was able to detect historical *change* towards a disciplinary society. Looking at images can lead one to an early detection of the anxious aspirations, the social ambitions

[4] On Huizinga's interest in visuality and visual metaphor, see eg Tollebeek (1994), especially 193ff.

and *mobilisations*, the often restlessly rotating cogs of societies in motion. Cultural change often occurs in and through images, in and through imagery. Cultural change is where and when one is more likely to feel the emotions and the anxieties, to *watch* the moves and movements, to sense the restlessly rotating and spinning cogs and wheels of social and historical motion, movement, and change in the visibilities through which they *express* themselves or by which they aspire to *become*. Images and imagery may be able to harbour the anxieties and sensitivities that go hand in hand with cultural change and movement even before they are able to manifest themselves in consciously written, reasoned textual material. Cultural change, and, more specifically, the *e-motions* that go with them, that is, the e-motions in and through which this movement and this change themselves emerge and develop, can become manifest first in *un*reasoned (often *un*conscious) imagery, before they would find their way into written text. In the words of Ernst Bloch, archivist and analyst of the imagery of the *principle of hope* (1986), of 'forward-dawning' hope and social change, we could say that imagery is most likely to be able to capture the 'not-yet-conscious' of the principle of ever-moving, ever-aspiring hope. This, the 'not-yet-conscious' elements of 'forward-dawning' hope, simultaneously expressions as well as aspirations, are the materials the movements of which will tend to slip into imagery, even before any word is spoken or needs to be spoken.

However, we must do justice to Huizinga here. The author *was* aware of the importance of imagery for any project that is to assess Burgundy's 15th-century culture. Indeed, in *Herfsttij*, he *did* include two chapters that explicitly dealt with 'the word and the image' and with 'the image and the word'. In them, the author also clearly indicates that many aspects of Renaissance culture *were* already present in late medieval culture, and vice versa (*Herfsttij*, page 67). With this claim he criticised Burckhardt who earlier had established a clear divide between both cultures. But then Huizinga immediately seems to contradict himself by insisting on keeping both distinct, and by defining Burgundy's 15th-century as quintessentially late medieval.[5] He also addressed, to some extent, and with reference to Burgundy's 15th-century cultural production, the specificity of visual forms of representation, as compared to textual ones. According to Huizinga, literature seemed to have remained hopelessly stuck into 'desperate superficiality' whilst painting, including for example Van Eyck's, seemed to have expressed more depth. Both, however, according to Huizinga anyway, kept on losing themselves in that typically late medieval 'realism' that wants to show all and everything, that lumps together quantities of trivia, that never

[5] On the many contradictions in the book, see eg Ward (1954). For biographical notes on Huizinga's 'wavering' self-contradictions, see eg Locher (1945–46).

manages to achieve coherence, focus or symmetry, that struggles in vain to acquire some degree of composition. According to Huizinga, 15th-century Burgundian culture is largely the realm of flat and superficial symbolism and allegory. Van Eyck's realism for example, and his extremely developed sense for detail, was not so much a sign of a budding Renaissance (as Burckhardt claimed with reference to the Italian *Quattrocento*), but rather it was part and parcel of a medieval culture where imagination had perished (page 223). Every individual feature, in medieval culture, was attributed a single essence; all and everything was crammed into complex disorderly scenes that lacked focus or symmetry; this lack of focus and symmetry betrayed a 'puerile' inability to distinguish important aspects from unimportant ones ... this is the world Huizinga sees expressing itself on 15th-century Burgundian panels. Huizinga approvingly quotes Michelangelo (on page 293) who once heaped explicit scorn on the Flemish masters whom he accused of having no sense of 'symmetry and proportion' and of lacking an ability to 'choose', in short, of lacking 'greatness'.

On page 314 of *Herfsttij*, we read that 'the fundamental feature of the late medieval spirit is its abundantly visual character'. And, whilst literature, according to Huizinga, kept on rehearsing old themes and adopting old forms, painting, on the other hand, Huizinga suddenly admits (on page 324), during the 15th century, *did* adopt new forms, albeit to a moderate extent, gradually picturing 'static harmonies', but never 'dynamic' ones (not even Van Eyck managed to do that, says Huizinga, on page 345).[6] On the whole, however, Burgundian culture remained one where unleashed passion never gathered into focussed projects. Burgundian culture either displayed an extreme realism of hardship and death (Van Eyck's stylish *detailism* being only an impressive illustration of 'primitive' medieval realism; *Herfsttij*, page 303) or a flight from reality into divine sublime (at best) or mere fantasy (at worst). In Burgundian culture, there seems to be no place in the arts for social projects of symmetrical, harmonious, focussed cooperation, where the hardships of reality are dealt with, and where life is moving forward. There's either grime and death, pictured in abhorring realism, or imaginary escape, for example, to the *Land of Cockaigne*, that Herman Pleij recently (2001) has succeeded in bringing to life again. In-between there's only passion running wild and essences scattering on panels — something that, by the way, would persist on the canvasses of 16th-century Flemish masters such as Pieter Breughel whose bucolic mockeries (eg his *Land of Cockaigne*) consciously resisted Renaissance intellectualism and the tyranny of symmetrical order.

[6] Recent research however has shown how Huizinga predominantly made use of *elite* literatures (eg chronicles) that emerged from or were connected to the ducal court, and were therefore unlikely to reflect cultural change as texts produced by an already consolidated bourgeoisie or texts emerging from a slowly governmentalising bureaucracy would have. See on this eg Kempers (1995), Tilmans (1995) and Krul (1995).

Flemish masters, such as the Van Eycks, were also renowned for the amazing detail with which they managed to paint individual portraits. Although realism and individualism expressed itself (or *became*) on many Flemish panels, Burckhardt, who only looked at what was going on south of the Alps, defined both as fundamentally characteristic of Renaissance. Indeed, Burckhardt, who otherwise was not much interested in visual arts (*he* thought cultural newness presented itself first in literature), was struck (as well as abhorred) by the extreme realism that showed in sculptures such as Donatello's *Maria Magdalena,* in which he saw a budding Renaissance emerging (Haskell, 1993: 336). Huizinga disagreed. Realism and individualism, according to the Dutchman, were not so much signs of Renaissance announcing itself, as they were signs of a culture where imagination had perished.

RE-VISITING HUIZINGA

When referring to imagery, Huizinga did so mostly within the context of a reading of a textual fragment evoking an aspect of a highly peaking medieval 'spirit'. Below, we will have a closer look at some pictures and images which Huizinga himself referred to in his text. The word 'some' is important here. We will analyse only seven plates. This is only a fraction of the total number of plates referred to by Huizinga. It's a much smaller part still of all 15th-century imagery, most of which did not even reach the 20th century. Our main goal, however, is to show how at least Huizinga's *own* collection or selection of images already holds some clues as to 15th-century cultural change. True, much of the visual material in his collection does not. The point is, however, that some *do*, that is, that 'visibilities' in them, 'forward-dawning' visibilities, *do* start to slip through the meshes of medieval culture. The point, in short, is that some material bearing newness and change *does* start to emerge, and, in this age of transition and hybridity, *does* start to blend and merge and hybridize with other visual material, *before* any textual material (as Huizinga seemed to have found out) showed any sign of movement, motion, newness or change. The next three sections will outline these clues in three moves. We may therefore hopefully be able to at least add some nuance to Huizinga's thesis and to simultaneously argue and demonstrate the ongoing case for the need to pay much more attention to 'visibilities', to images and imageries when studying historical *change*. The illustrations which we will be using all depict scenes of justice (divine, sublime and social justice) and authority (divine, sublime, and social authority) as those are likely to comprise lines and shapes that simultaneously express social desire, social aspiration, in short: social change.

JUSTICE I: FROM IMMOBILE, ORIGINAL WHITENESS ...

What keeps societies apart/together? A sense of peace, perhaps? Fear and terror? Authority? Or submission? Or perhaps something that, elusively, hides and lurks somewhere under the sign of *Justice*. Let us have a closer look at *The Three Estates*, taken from the 1482 *Lichtenberger Prognosticatio* (Figure 1). This indeed is a familiar image of medieval life. Huizinga himself cites it in the context of the medieval assumptions of (the need for) 'hierarchical society'. Indeed, there you have aristocracy (those who protect) next to the clergy (those who pray) while both find themselves above those who labour. Nothing is very much in motion in this picture. Except for the labourers, that is, except for those who dwell at the bottom of society: they seem to be moving. Immobility seems to be the higher good in images like this. Whenever there is movement, whenever there is mobility, there is lowness, or potential trouble.

That which keeps all three estates apart/together is God, elusive and unnameable spirit, immobile mover, eternal origin. But let us look closer now. In many medieval drawings and paintings, scenes appear to be unconnected; at the most landscape features such as hills and trees may fill in the gaps. This 1482 picture, however, does not even manage to do that. What seems to be holding people, things and societies apart/together here, or, in other words, what seems to be lying at the heart of medieval society (its soul, its 'spirit', in Huizinga's words) is *whiteness*. An expression of a 'perished imagination' perhaps, or a sign of 'escapes' into a divine sublime, perhaps, it seems to be whiteness, an elusive force indeed, unnameable force, immobility perhaps, that we find here, at the centre of this picture. It is this whiteness that holds things and people apart/together. Unnameable, unspeakable, immobile whiteness. God, to medieval 'spirits'. Nothing earthly holds things and people apart/together, nothing earthy does. Neither do movement and mobility: these are earthly, earthy aspects of a labourer's world. Flowing from an immobile whiteness: this is how social life always has been, this is how it is, and this is how it should be. Unchanging. Unchangeable. There is no space for newness here. Immobile whiteness, immovable whiteness determines all, and this *all*, in turn, is nothing but immobility itself.

The 1482 picture rehearses a well-known theme, and much of the cultural production throughout the Middle Ages expresses and/or aspires (both, mostly) similar sentiments. *Lucifer's Fall* (Figure 2), for example, painted in the early years of the 15th-century, is another case in point. Huizinga refers to this painting when he discusses an allegedly typically medieval distrust of hubris. God and the good angels all are immobile. Only the fallen angels (Lucifer being the first amongst them) are on the move; and they're moving downwards indeed.

Figure 1 'The Three Estates', 1482, from: Lichtenberger Prognosticatio *(Mainz); taken from* Herfsttij, *1997, page 61*

Figure 2 'Lucifer's Fall', 1416, from: Les Tres Riches Heures du Duc de Berry, *by the Limbourg Brothers (cover sleeve of* Herfttij, *1997); Reprinted with kind permission of Musee Conde, Chantilly, THR, folio 64v*

Movement, here, seems to be a sign of something going terribly bad, and the movement is pointing downwards; and there (downwards) colour and movement seem to sketch what the evils of hell are about. The relatively empty skies take up the central space of this painting; overseeing a bluish white heaven, or a whitish blue one, God sits still on His throne. One could sense the same structure in Hieronymus Bosch's early 16th-century vision of hell, where a relatively small, immobile God, bathing in whiteness, floats above an enormously horrible mass of wriggling monsters, most of which looking like hybrid creatures. Hybridity (nothing is in its *proper place* in hybrid monsters, they're the evil result of unexpected moves and movement) and wriggling, crawling, moving mobility: this is, in short, Bosch's Hell.

Let us, finally, study *The Martyrdom of Saint Apollonia*, painted by Jean Fouquet, sometime between 1452 and 1460 (Figure 3). We will meet this painter, Fouquet, also in our next section. Huizinga used this image during a discussion of the 'individuality of saints', and their 'specialisation'. Saint Apollonia, for example, during her torture, got all her teeth extracted (as pictured in Fouquet's picture) and therefore later 'specialized' as a patron saint for all those suffering from tooth ache. The picture shows a shining white Apollonia who, completely immobile, occupies the centre of the image. Though strapped down completely by her torturers, it appears as if she still determines the scene. Somewhere in *Herfsttij* (pages 298–303), Huizinga writes on the symbolism of colour in medieval culture. White seems to generally have been a 'festive' colour, but it was also a colour that was associated with childhood and innocence. Taking account of medieval essentialism, then, whiteness *is* innocence, it *is* festive goodness (see also on page 213).

Power, justice, and authority seem to be radiating outwards from her shining whiteness, from her white immobility. Although she is suffering and strapped down, it seems to be Apollonia who is keeping the scene apart/together. Those who move — their movements, their mobility — once again, are (a sign of) evil. Movement, this time, comes from torture. It is torturers who move, and behind them, there is a dark mass of wriggling hybrid monsters (they prefigure Bosch's, who would appear half a century later). The monsters are in the background, however. It is Saint Apollonia who occupies the centre of the stage. Movement, evil movement and mobility, still are despicable signs of evil trouble (of evil *troubles*) and are therefore located in the marginal background. This background, it may be noted, in no way represents a horizon at the end of a perspective gaze. We'll witness an emerging pespectivism shortly, in another painting by Jean Fouquet by the way. Now let us recapitulate here. These are the dates: 1416, 1450s, 1482. Medieval images and imageries of justice as white, immobile power seem to be dominating. There is, however, much more to Burgundy's 15th-century visual culture than this. Let us now return to Fouquet.

Figure 3 'The Martyrdom of Saint Apollonia', 1452–60, from: Book of Hours of Etienne Chevalier, *by Jean Fouquet (taken from* Herfsttij, *1997, page 178); Reprinted with kind permission of Musee Conde, Chantilly*

JUSTICE II: ... VIA EARTHLY MOVEMENTS AND MELANCHOLY ...

At about the same time when Fouquet was illustrating the *Book of Hours of Etienne Chevalier*, which included the picture of Saint Apollonia's martyrdom, this high-ranking administrator (Etienne Chevalier) also ordered the painter, Fouquet, to paint his portrait (Figure 4). This portrait, *Portrait of Etienne Chevalier Commended by Saint Stephen*, formed a dyptic (the so-called Melun dyptic) with the painting of *The Virgin and Child*, also by Fouquet (Figure 5). Referring to this dyptic, Huizinga wanted to illustrate medieval 'religious sentiment'. He sees a Chevalier whose 'plainness' is in 'curious contrast' with the figure of the Madonna, suggesting 'decadent godlessness' and 'blasphemous frankness' (pages 167–68). But look at the marginality of the whiteness in Etienne Chevalier's portrait. Notice how

Figure 4 'Portrait of Etienne Chevalier Commended by St Stephen', 1450, by Jean Fouquet (taken from Herfsttij, *1997, page 166); Reprinted with kind permission of Staatliche Museen zu Berlin—Preussicher Kulturbesitz*

colours (very bright and vivid colours at that) take centre stage. Watch how the many finely painted folds of Etienne Chevalier's gown suggest movement. Then look at the extremely fine and very *earthly* detail (more true than life) with which the official's face has been painted. This, indeed, is the stubbled, pimpled and wrinkled face of Etienne Chevalier, make no mistake about it. It's not just *a* face, this really *is* Etienne Chevalier. This betrays an attitude that reminds of the one that is also to be sensed from Jan Van Eyck's portrait of *Canon George van der Paele commended by Saint George to the Madonna*, or his portrait of *Chancellor Rolin and the Madonna*, both of which finished some two decades earlier, that showed realistically painted individuals facing a Madonna who was losing *sublimed* features in symmetrical (as well as extremely detailed) settings. There is a difference though. Whereas both Van Eyck's earlier paintings showed individuals facing a Madonna in one scene, or, more concretely, in one and the same room, here, in Fouquet's painting, the individual Chevalier, the bureaucrat, the administrator, has managed to detach himself completely.

The face on the Melun dyptic is the individual Etienne Chevalier's, and this individual (dressed as he is in colourful movement) is not just anybody. He's not just a person of high rank. No, he's Etienne Chevalier; he's the one, individually one, person who is likely to have asked master Fouquet, self-consciously, not to make a mistake (about it). It is he who has convinced master Fouquet to acquire or to mobilise other skills than the ones he had just been applying in his *Book of Hours*. Etienne Chevalier is a self-conscious man, who is not prepared anymore to accept a vaguely resembling portrait. He's not just any high ranking administrator. Make no mistake about that.

Those amongst the viewers who still might have some doubts about the identity of the man in portrait may be able to read his name on the wall behind him. The wall betrays an emerging perspectivism. To our eyes, the lines of the wall that suggest perspective, may appear to be somewhat clumsily drawn. But they're there, unmistakably. Etienne Chevalier is positioned within a perspective. Etienne Chevalier (painted by and through Fouquet's eyes and hands) thus appears as a self-conscious individual; as an individual who looks at the world (instead of just living it); he's someone who occasionally may want to look forward, who may cherish life goals and a future, who will tend to put things, events and relations in perspective, albeit probably a *bureaucratic* perspective in his case. Etienne Chevalier may have been a bearer of a very early, fledgling Modernity. He may have been one of the early Modern monads, as authors like Burckhardt would have had it, who gradually discovered (as well as produced) individuality, and who, on this foundation of individuality, started to realistically scan the world, through a perspectivising gaze, for goals and means, with an eye on futures, and, possibly, progress. It may be important to note that Chevalier is not just a courtier, bearer of what Huizinga has called a medieval spirit. He's also a bureaucrat, a future planner of futures, a future composer of projects. 'The courtier civil servant', E F Jacob wrote, 'is the important man, and the growth of this class the key to the history of the later Middle ages' (1960: 150), especially in Burgundy and in France, less so in England (152–13). Chevalier is an emerging hybrid.

Fouquet's painting is not visualising a fully-fledged Modernity. Not yet. There is something hybrid, something transitional, going on in Fouquet's dyptic. Let us have another look at Etienne Chevalier, the monadic individual, the newly born gazer, who seems to have detached himself from the strictures of white immobility, the administrator who seems to just have found self-conscious individuality, yes, *that* Etienne Chevalier, the *one* who, after his move of detachment, has just begun looking at the world. He's not yet looking forward — at least not unambiguously he isn't. He's not yet peering towards a horizon of possibility. His gaze is not yet fixed towards future

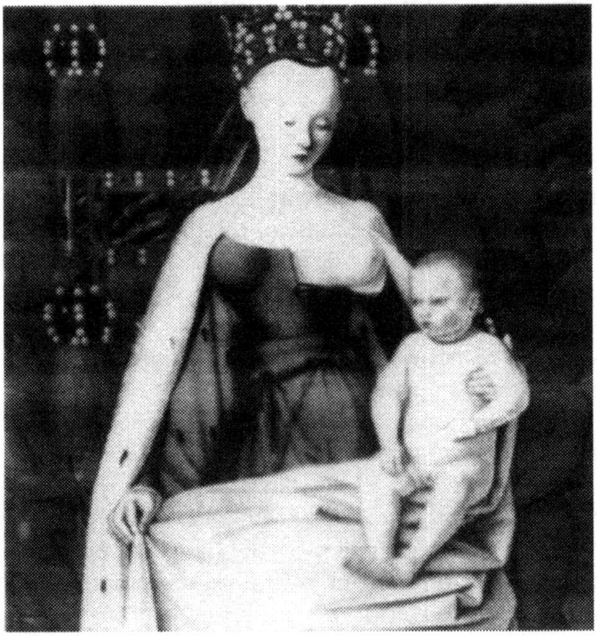

Figure 5 'The Virgin and Child', 1453–54, by Jean Fouquet (taken from Herfsttij, *1997, page 167); Reprinted with kind permission of Koninklijk Museum voor Schone Kunsten, Antwerpen*

goals. He's not yet in the business of constructing and organising projects and perspectives. Actually, the lines of perspective in the backdrop of Etienne Chevalier's portrait suggest that the administrator, commended by a bleeding Saint Stephen who carries the rock of Saint Peter and the book of Saint Paul, is looking backwards. He seems to be looking to the *Holy Virgin and Child*, who appear on the other half of Fouquet's dyptic. The Holy Virgin and Child are surrounded by cherubins who, although highly colourful, still seem to represent immobility. That which surrounds the Holy Virgin is thus already hybridising; it's already in transition. The Holy Virgin herself, who obviously is not an earthly individualising monad like Etienne Chevalier, still radiates whitish immobility. This Holy Virgin does not dwell at some perspectivised horizon. This Virgin still bears an original whiteness; hers is an immobility that springs from an eternal origin. Even her breasts do not seem to respond to the earthly, earthy laws of physics (what contrast with Etienne Chevalier's gown and wrinkles); they remain firm and immobile. This Virgin is the eternal mother, the eternal origin, this immovable force (elusive force though) that keeps societies apart/together. We may perhaps at this point want to return to Huizinga's aforementioned essay on the medieval symbolism of colours. The cherubins are all painted in either a vivid red or a vivid blue. Red, according to Huizinga, was predominantly the colour that symbolised solemnity, while blue was the colour of love, but also (and curiously so) of unfaithfulness in matters of the heart. Huizinga himself, when mentioning Fouquet's dyptic, does not refer to this symbolism of colours, although he mentions that the Virgin on the painting looks suspiciously like Agnes Sorel, one of the then mistresses of the French king, a woman whom, it is known, Fouquet himself was rather fond of. But, if Huizinga's reconstruction of medieval colour symbolism is correct, then the red/blue combination of colour may have suggested unfaithfulness; unfaithfulness of the heart, yes, but perhaps also the unfaithfulness emerging in a newly emerging cultural attitude.[7]

Fouquet's Virgin's immobile breasts (motherly breasts of origin; motherly, original breasts) may remind us of Christopher Columbus's religiously inspired notions of geography. In his diary of his voyages (later to be published as *The Four Voyages*) we read that Columbus (writing in the 1490s) assumed that the world was pear-shaped, the tip of the pear, 'like a women's nipple', being the source of the four rivers of Eden, that is, of that *original* place which all and everything (life, in short) comes from, that place of origin that keeps the world apart/together, this eternal, motherly place. Actually, Columbus himself firmly believed that he had discovered one of these four rivers when he sailed up the Orinoco estuary. Indeed, he thought he was about to discover this source that was supposed to be right on top of the world, 'like a woman's nipple'. The eternal motherly breast, immovably fixed in a place of origin: here's an image that both Fouquet as well as Columbus may have shared.

This scene, a white and immobile Virgin and Child amidst hybridising surroundings, is what the newly born, self-conscious Etienne Chevalier seems to be looking at. This is the world from which he has just detached himself. This is the world (a world of elusive, white immobility) that he has just left behind; a world that kept all and everything apart/together: wild passion, grime and death, sublime salvation. Now look at Etienne Chevalier's eyes again. Can we read melancholy in them? Is the administrator yearning for a world lost? Can we read regret in them, regret for

[7] Medieval colour symbolism was far from static or monolithic. On the importance of as well as the contradictions in colour symbolism in medieval culture, see especially Pleij (1994). The composition of red and blue cherubins in Fouquet's painting may express a typically medieval taste for contrasting colours. But, on the other hand, the conspicuous presence of blue cherubins could also express, whether consciously or unconsciously, the consolidation of a new, powerful elite of administrators and financial entrepreneurs. This elite, sometime near the end of the Middle Ages, started to develop a taste for blue and black — a taste that would be adopted, developed and modified during the 16th and 17th centuries in and by Calvinist-inspired circles.

the comforts and the security that he knows he will have to leave behind upon entering the world of newly born monads? Maybe we can. But perhaps there's also some distraction, or absent-mindedness, or indifference perhaps, to be read in Etienne Chevalier's eyes. Perhaps he just looks to this old world of origins for the last time, helped by Saint Stephen whose attributes (the rock and the book) seem to be holding back the newly born, for one last look. As Latour (1988) would have it, the lines of perspective that emerge timidly may suggest an already waning interest in divine and sublime spirituality. Look at Chevalier's eyes again. Can't we read distraction in them? Isn't Etienne Chevalier already contemplating the things that are to come? Isn't he pondering futures, strategies, plans, projects? Isn't he thinking about perspectives, about the lines of projects within which things have to have their ordered time and place? Is that where his mind is? Maybe it is. Maybe both e-*motions* are to be read in Etienne Chevalier's *movement* of the eye. His is an age of transition, of hybridity. Both worlds may have been his. Both may have been Jean Fouquet's, the painter who, at one and the same time, seems to have inhabited the old as well as the new. Both Chevalier and Fouquet may have been amongst those fledgling monads, newly born and somewhat stunned, or amazed perhaps, to find themselves stumbling in-between two worlds, where the old hasn't completely left yet, and when the new hasn't completely dawned yet. Early, budding Modernity, say, an age of earthly movement(s), melancholy, dazed bewilderment, a glimpse of bright futures and (says Bloch) a time of high *hopes*. It may also be worthwhile to note that neither of the gazes of this dyptic's personae do cross each other. Would that surprise us? Why would emerging monads, bewildered as they may have been, look for the gaze of others? The look for the other's gaze and the connection of gazes imply a further step of newness; they presuppose some further cultural *change*. Burgundian, late medieval culture may have been a 'puerile' culture, but, as Pirenne warns, 'les dehors sont trompeurs' (1900: 497; translation: *appearances are deceptive*): an individualist culture of 'homme politiques' and 'financiers' was emerging amidst hybridising surroundings.

JUSTICE III: ... TOWARDS MACHINIC JUSTICE

Such a step may be visible on another dyptic, Gerard David's *The Justice of Cambyses*. This painting tells the legend of a Persian king, Cambyses, who, long ago, had one of his high-ranking judges, Sisamnes, arrested and executed for corruption. Huizinga himself uses this painting in a discussion on medieval visions on duty and legal authority. The left hand panel shows Sisamnes being arrested, while the right hand one shows his execution. This dyptic was finished by 1498, at about the time when Columbus was still preoccupied with a trip to eternal Eden, way upstream the Orinoco,

Figure 6 'The Justice of Cambyses', panel 1, 1498, by Gerard David (taken from Herfsttij, *1997, page 260); Reprinted with kind permission of Groeninghemuseum, Brugge*

at a 'woman's nipple'. Huizinga does not often mention Gerard David, and when he does, he tends to accuse him of 'weak composition' or of displaying 'a certain stodgy composition' (page 345).

Look at the judge while he is being arrested (Figure 6). There he sits, immobile. His, however, is an immobility that has been produced. The judge is immobile because his movements have been frozen. His immobility is of a bad, corrupt kind. The movement that is going on here (courtiers' and soldiers' movements) are those that promise the goodness of real justice. The judge may be sitting immobile on his chair, and he may be taking central stage, he certainly is not the one who is keeping societies apart/together. His authority, his power, his justice is movable, it is of a freezable, as well as of a kneadable nature. It does not radiate an original, eternal force. It is a temporary glimpse of possibility, a short phase on a road towards horizons, a short blink of an eye. Time and movement are important here. The first panel shows us, somewhere in the background of the painting, the act of bribery. In the foreground we have the scene of the judge's arrest. The second painting, the judge's execution (Figure 7), shows a scene that takes place in future. The scene in the top right corner of this panel (we'll come back to this below) shows us what happens after the execution. The movement of time is what we are looking at here. This feels like watching a film, a coherent sequence of acts and moves.

Eternity, the Origin, Eden, the whiteness of immobility: they seem to have no place here. Movement and mobility (the promise of movement) is what seems to be dominating this picture. Let us focus on the execution first. The judge (his individualised reddish face in painful agony) lies on a bench. Although his body, whitish pale, fills the centre of the image, is does not determine the actions that go on in the scenery. On the contrary, his body (the body of Law, of authority, of power) is being flayed, like an ordinary piece of meat in the hands of a butcher. Its whiteness is being cut and slashed. Bloody red flows and drips, moves on the skin. The people who stand around (Cambyses amongst them) seem to be indifferent to what is happening. Some are talking to each other. Their gazes *do* cross. Some people in the background discuss matters. Maybe they are discussing tomorrow's business affairs. In the background, the son of the judge (*new* blood) takes over his executed father's office, and sits on a throne-like chair which is draped with the judge's skin. Notice the perspective in this image: look, for example, at the nearly perfect perspective that is woven with the tiles on the market square. Someone has been watching this scene. Someone has been projecting futures here. Someone has been studying and analysing actions and interactions, at a time, in an age, when eternal power and authority, when white, immobile, original justice was being exposed as only a skin-deep drape. This painting appeals to self-conscious gazers, moving planners of futures, users of possibility, makers of worlds. This is fully-fledged modernity at work, in interaction. We are witnessing here the birth of a modernity that has already moved beyond an earlier, bewildered, monadic stage. This here might possibly be seen as (paraphrasing Deleuze and Guattari, 1972) an emerging *machinic* modernity.

Machinic? Power, Authority, Justice, in David's painting, appear to be skin-deep. Draped around a throne (seat of government) however, this skin may be of some instrumental use, of course. This skin may be put to use in various projects of government. It can have its uses as part of an 'assemblage' (cf Deleuze and Guattari; have another look at the son's throne), as part of a machine, as part of a machine of governance, for sure, but also as part of any imaginable machine that is constructed in any project of hopeful desire. Such machines (assemblages that include instrumental power, authority and justice) are, in a way, what Machiavelli, a contemporary of Gerard David, tried to think. Machines of power and authority, or machines of justice, in David's vision, are instrumental assemblages that, instrumentally, are supposed to allow for and to support other machines of power and authority, other machines of justice, other assemblages, other projects. The second panel of *The Justice of Cambyses* has no fixed focal

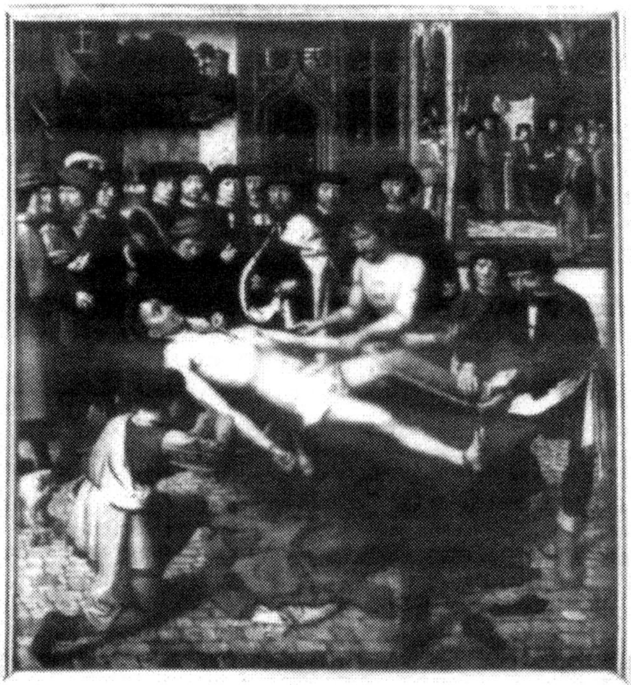

Figure 7 'The Justice of Cambyses', panel 2, 1498, by Gerard David (taken from Herfsttij, *1997, page 261); Reprinted with kind permission of Groeningemuseum, Brugge*

point at the horizon of its otherwise perfect perspective gaze. Indeed, as Huizinga would probably have claimed (although he did not when discussing David's dyptic), there still is that 'typically medieval' habit of 'putting everything in the picture', and there is no sign of one single focus of attention and effort. Straight lines and perfect perspectives, nicely traced order, absolute symmetry, ... all of this is still lacking. David's world is not (yet) the straight-lined world of absolute despots (Burckhardt for example situated the origins of Renaissance culture in Italian absolutism). Flemish and Burgundian architecture, for example, did not yet show the straight lines nor the austere symmetry of a Palazzo Pitti (which itself was probably a hybrid result of earlier medieval austerity and despotic symmetry). But it seems that David's was a culture of movement and machines. Individuals who, half a century before, managed to detach themselves from the immobilities of medieval culture, having scanned surroundings, were now on the verge of machinic exploration. It would take some time yet for new strictures, for straight lines, symmetrical order, clear focus, and absolutist harmony to set in. The force of absolutist rule was yet to transform an already individualising, realist, nomadic culture north of the Alps.

The son's authority, his *Justice*, is positioned in the top right corner of the painting. His court (it is actually a painting of the then Bruges correctional court, where it hung during the 16th century) looks as if it has been put there in a rather casual way. Nothing spectacular seems to radiate from that court. In small groups people are talking to each other, just like the people who, closer to the scene of the execution, seem to engage in conversations that are totally unconnected to the carving up of white skins and immovable authority. Are they forming and/or reproducing assemblages? Are they connecting into business networks? Are they making plans? Making projects? Are they putting power, authority, and justice to use, instrumentally? Will the son, will newness, help them realise their plans; will he help them achieve their goals? Will he allow their assemblages to proliferate across the market square? Will he use his machinic justice to these ends? This seems to be their hope (cf Bloch again). They couldn't care less about the execution. They do not seem to care about origins. Not even the past seems to be of any interest to them. They're probably indifferent to all that. They could be thinking about tomorrow. Their time is the future, the time of the promise of un-fixed, *nomadic* assemblages, of connecting and disconnecting machines, of power, authority and justice that know their place and their instrumental use — that is, of power, authority and justice that, *as machinic justice*, reproduce conditions for machinic justice.

Perhaps this machinic desire is what expresses itself on paintings like David's, who, machinically, seemed to have gathered — 'drawn together', in Bruno Latour's (1990) phrase — forms and sentiments from across the continent, from either side of the Alps, in a visual contraption, a machine in its own right, that in turn betrays machinic aspiration, machinic becoming. In a way, and referring to Deleuze and Guattari (1980) once more, visualisations of an emerging nomadic modernity seem to have appeared on David's dyptic. This is a modernity beyond *monads*. A nomadic age, just before centralised and absolutist state power (say, the 16th century) was able to get a grip on business networks and market squares. The Whiteness of sheer authority would be back, of course. On David's painting, it is being flayed painfully, and the face that goes with it — individual face, make no mistake — is reddishly winced with pain. But whiteness would re-emerge, albeit hybridised once again, as when — as Nick Lee (2001: 180) has aptly noted — it was applied in the form of bleach, applied that is by choosing hands that 'draw things together', on the faces of absolutist monarchs (Elisabeth, and later, Louis, come to mind) whose 'stylistically blanked face effaces' their 'private personhood', giving their words 'the status of non-negotiable', that is non-machinable, 'public declarations'. A particular whiteness, this, ... it would be back.

ENDNOTE

Burgundy's 15th century, one might argue, was much less a last flare-up of high and bright medievalism than Huizinga may have thought it was. A close examination of some of the imagery which he referred to in *Herfsttij* may lead us to look at this 15th century as an age of transition, as an age of movement and hybridity, where the old flourished next to the emerging new, with both sometimes merging into each other, hybridising in one and the same place, in one and the same painter and his work, for example. Huizinga may have been right in reading an abundantly superficial, static medievalism in literature as well as in other textual material (although this is open to critique as well). The visual material, however, leads us to another story. Indeed, before words, before the need perhaps to speak or write, change and newness gradually emerged and hybridised into 'visibilities' that may be detected in the imagery that flew out of painters' and artists' workshops. The emerging new cultural forms appeared there, sometimes in hybridisations, on these panels, in these miniatures. It is there, in these drawings and paintings, that the e-motions, ambitions, aspirations manifest themselves in lines and forms; it is there that an already emerging *newness* finds its first expression. It is there that hybrid in-betweens of *expressions* and *aspirations* are likely to visualise.

It should be stressed here that this chapter was not just about Huizinga's *The Waning of the Middle Ages*. Although we have explored 15th-century imagery, in order to criticise one of the main theses of Huizinga's, as well as to demonstrate the need for anyone who studies historical change (cultural change in particular) to focus on 'visibilities', we also hope to have been able to demonstrate here that cultural change may be *visible* before it is being spoken or written.

REFERENCES

Bloch, Ernst 1986. *The Principle of Hope*. Translated by N Plaice, S Plaice and P Knight. Cambridge: MIT Press. Original edition, 1959.

Burckhardt, Jacob 1990. *The Civilization of the Renaissance in Italy*. Translated by SGC Middlemore. Harmondsworth: Penguin. Original edition, 1860.

Columbus, Christopher 1969. *The Four Voyages*. Translated by JM Cohen. London: Penguin.

den Boer, Pim 1995. Huizinga's Oog. *Bulletin: Geschiedenis, Kunst, Cultuur* 3: 12–29.

Deleuze, Gilles 1988. *Foucault*. Translated by S Hand. London: Athlone. Original edition, 1986.

Deleuze, Gilles and Felix Guattari 1972. *Anti-Oedipe*. Paris: Editions de Minuit.

Deleuze, Gilles and Felix Guattari 1980. *Mille Plateaux*. Paris: Editions de Minuit.

Haskell, Francis 1993. *History and its Images. Art and the Interpretation of the Past.* New Haven: Yale University Press.
Huizinga, Johan 1999. *Herfsttij der Middeleeuwen.* Amsterdam: Contact. Original edition, 1919.
Huizinga, Johan 1997. *Homo Ludens.* Amsterdam: Contact. Original edition, 1938.
Jacob, EF 1968. Huizinga and the Autumn of the Middle Ages. In *Essays in Later Medieval History.* Manchester: Manchester University Press.
Kempers, Bram 1995. Huizinga en Rituelen. *Bulletin: Geschiedenis, Kunst, Cultuur* 3: 30–49.
Krul, Wessel 1995. Huizinga's *Herfsttij*: Achtergrond en Vooruitzicht. *Bulletin: Geschiedenis, Kunst, Cultuur 3*: 80–103.
Lacan, Jacques 1998. *The Four Fundamental Concepts of Psycho-Analysis.* London: Penguin.
Latour, Bruno 1988. Opening One Eye While Closing the Other. In *Picturing Power: Visual Depiction and Social Relations,* edited by Gordon Fyfe and John Law. London: Routledge.
Latour, Bruno 1990. Drawing Things Together. In *Representation in Scientific Practice,* edited by Michael Lynch and Steve Woolgar. Cambridge: MIT Press.
Lee, Nick 2001. Becoming. Mass: Glamour, Authority and Human Presence. In *The Consumption of Mass,* edited by Nick Lee and Rolland Munro. Oxford: Blackwell.
Locher, Th 1946. Johan Huizinga. *Jaarboek van de Maatschappij der Nederlandsche Letterkunde* 1945–1946; 88–109.
Pirenne, Henri 1900. *Histoire de Belgique.* Bruxelles: La Renaissance du Livre.
Pleij, Herman 1984. *Kleuren van de Middeleeuwen.* Bloemendaal: Aramith.
Pleij, Herman 2001. *Dreaming of Cockaigne.* Translated by Diane Webb. New York: Columbia University Press. Original edition, 1997.
Said, Edward 1995. *Orientalism. Western Conceptions of the Orient.* London: Penguin. Original edition 1978.
Scheller, Robert 1995. Huizinga en de Beeldende Kunst: Vorm en Inhoud. *Bulletin: Geschiedenis, Kunst, Cultuur* 3: 70–79.
Tilmans, Karin 1995. Chroniqueurs en Kroniekschrijvers. Over de Waardering van Nederlandse Geschiedschrijvers in Huizinga's *Herfsttij. Bulletin: Geschiedenis, Kunst, Cultuur* 3: 50–69.
Tollebeek, Jo 1994. De Middeleeuwen Dromen. Huizinga, Herfsttij en de Esthetiek van de Geschiedenis. In *De IJkmeesters.* Amsterdam: Wereldbibliotheek.
Ward, Paul 1954. Huizinga's Approach to the Middle Ages. In *Teachers of History. Essays in Honor of Laurence Bradford Packard,* edited by H Stuart Hughes. Ithaca: Cornell University Press.

9

Observing Victims: Global Insecurities and the Systemic Imagination of Justice in World Society

CLAUDIUS MESSNER

CAN JUSTICE BE imagined not to exist? For David Hume, in the early modern period, justice would not exist in a society in which there is no injustice.

> Let us suppose that nature has bestowed on the human race such profuse *abundance* of all *external* conveniences, that, without any care or industry on our part, every individual finds himself fully provided with whatever his most voracious appetites can want.

If we make this supposition, we will see that

> every other social virtue would flourish ... but the cautious, jealous virtue of justice would never once have been dreamed of. For what purpose make a partition of goods, where everyone has more than enough? Why give rise to property, where there cannot possibly be any injury? (Hume 1875, 179, 180)

If there were no injustice to worry us, we would have no reason to refer to justice. Justice is not an original notion, Hume argues, the sense of justice is derived from injustice and disorder. Justice, 'preserving order in society', is a function of 'the intercourse and social state of mankind' (Hume 1875, 181), its purpose depends, as today we would say, on the structures of the social system and its evolutionary situation. Given that 'the rules of equity or justice depend entirely on the particular state and condition, in which men are placed' (Hume 1875, 183), can we imagine the boundaries of justice without ignoring its contingency? If visions of justice indicate one part of a distinction the other part of which is injury and wrong-doing, then we can say that they owe their origin and existence to observations made by the 'law'.

At the high times of the ongoing *age of transition*, the former US Secretary of State Janet Reno explained in a public speech that, to her mind, 'victims embody America' (Simon 1997, 293). She did not refer to the 'United States' and its 'citizens'. For sure, when invoking 'America', she didn't mean the borderless space of possibilities which so many have dreamed. It could be that, in the context of a 'war on crime', she wanted to point out the difference between good and evil. Possibly, she was recalling the founding stories of the nation as a new haven for victims of old-world oppression (and as a business venture). In any case, she used not a genuine *e pluribus unum* narrative (as would be the nation-state as an 'imagined community' of modernity). To put victims into the centre of democratic citizenry is to give a very special version of these narratives in which part and whole are re-imagined. In a global world, the concept of the civil subject, the *citoyen* as bearer and model of democratic virtues, turns out to be too definite. The victim trope refers no more to citizens nor to the state. Whoever is included in modern victim categories turns into a representative of humanity. Humanity is what counts today. Victimhood, humanity and world are synchronised today by a kind of moral-legal discourse which would be, in its current form, unfeasible without the spreading, since the last three decades of the twentieth-century, of an ethnocentric and imperialist 'culture of human rights' (Rabossi).

However, these processes seem to have fully developed only now (after the 'end of history'), based on two premises: first, the unification of the planet commonly called 'global system', and second, the apparent shrinking of our world which could be explained as the unique social reality constituted by the mass media. 'Victim' indicates the individual's powerlessness and the vulnerability of the body, that is it signifies its uniqueness of an individual human being. As theme of social communications, however, personal experience is a social construct (Luhmann 1996, 135) and is of public interest only as far as it points to the possibility of all to become victims. Public attention is fascinated by the story of the injured individual who, at the 'ground zero' of a staggering experience that compels and makes possible a new worldview, is able to re-describe past experience and to anticipate future outcomes. 'Victimhood' (Messner 2001, 135–70) is a matter of the interpretation of injury affected by shifting frames of reference. Standing for the difference known/unknown, it acts as a symbol of time.

My approach here involves looking not at the concept of justice as such, but more broadly at the ways and the contexts where justice is invoked, that is in reactions against injustice as expressed, focused on and organised by victim narratives or, more precisely, by what I call the 'victimhood script'. What I propose now is to make this account plausible. From what we can call a cultural studies perspective, victim narratives could be described, taking some of Ulrich Beck's ideas (Beck 1986) as a point of departure, as a response to the end of a predictable kind of life and as an explanatory tool which a complex society is now using to account for a world out of control. In order to account for this, I will argue, a sociological theory is needed which allows us to clarify first, what we mean by society and what world we are talking about when we refer to the 'global system'. This question implies an epistemological problem. One of the answers to this problem can be found in Luhmann's 'postontological' theory of society (Luhmann 1996, Luhmann/De Giorgi 1992). From within this frame of reference, 'victimhood' can then be re-described as a matter of 'scripts' used in social communication. Scripts serve exactly to reproduce blueprints of expectation. Their role is to preserve the coupling between the social system and psychic systems (Luhmannn's terms for what ordinarily is called society and individuals) under changing conditions in which society has to balance the conflicting needs of necessary and tolerable complexity, stability and transformation, defence and creativity. A key problem of today's world society seems to be to mark differences and yet to absorb uncertainty.

ACCIDENT, UNCERTAINTY, SUDDENNESS AND THE END OF A PREDICTABLE KIND OF LIFE

Victim themes and narratives are flourishing in an ever changing context that is characterised essentially by 'double fragmentation', ie by cultural segregation and functional differentiation of modern society. Always modernising, modern society's evolution to the 'world system' has effected an enormous increase in complexity and instability. The economy was the first social system to be organised worldwide around dynamics of capital moving across borders and to show 'global' configurations (eg Hopkins/Wallerstein 1996). Today, all areas of society are comprised: information, religion, politics, education, knowledge, are plainly globalised structures. Globalisation, however, does not mean homogeneous and equal living conditions across the planet, but heterogeneity of people's life prospects as well as diversity and variety in their everyday life. The new world-space is becoming simultaneously, or so it seems, more fragmented. The dissolution of national spaces of political allegiance and economic regulation, the reshaping of 'imagined communities' of modernity, the fall of protective nets, the media show of an indefinite 'anything goes', the fragmentation of personal and cultural identities, the regressive models of political and social behaviour (Messner 2001) — all this is happening within an as yet unfigured horizon. The 'global/local assemblage ... enlivens and molests the textures of everyday life and spaces of subjectivity and reshapes ... contemporary structures of feeling' Wilson/Dissanayake 1996, 2). It is based essentially on dimensions of uncertainty and insecurity.

The ongoing debate on 'risk' reflects conditions of actual insecurity as well as of lack of orientation and the loss of socially binding rules. Risk, danger and security are the quintessence of what are seen to be the problems of today's society (Beck 1986; Luhmann 1992). According to Ulrich Beck (1986), what is creating new forms of social organisation and consciousness are the *inherent* risks of the continuous 'rationalisation' of society. Risks originate in the social organisation of knowledge and norms rather than in nature itself. Calculative practices which used to be oriented towards external, environmental 'dangers' are now reorienting reflexively around risk-production within society. Given that expert knowledge is implicated in the production of risk in the first place, the cultural authority of scientific experts is being undermined. Risks are not mere facts but artefacts of their observers. 'This means that the calculation of risk as it has been established so far by science and legal institutions collapses' (Beck 1986, 22). That's why, Beck believes, a paradigm shift in the understanding of risk is needed: a shift from the problem of knowing risk to the problem of the risks inherent in ways of knowing.

Where the main problem of the 'first modern' ie industrial society was the need to legitimise unequal distribution of social wealth, the problem of 'second modernity' is that of distributing and limiting risks. This changes the type of its 'distributive struggles' that now evolve into a matter of attribution leading to antagonisms of definition and imputation of responsibility which oscillate between revealing and concealing risk and can be described as processes of negotiation. These are definitional struggles not just about methods but also about who is affected. A complex victimology is emerging from these debates.

As risks are social constructions, in order to be considered something 'real' they must socially be 'recognised' (Beck 1986, 36). This implies that statements on risk have a normative dimension (Kaufmann 1970). Experienced risk points to a 'horizon of lost security'. They are tropes which reveal the loss of a clear vision of a decent life. So, 'risks' also transmit representations of such a life: 'Observations of risks reveal the new face of ethics in the 'centres of modernisation', Beck (1986, 77) argues without making very clear whether he refers to 'global cities' like Los Angeles, Vancouver or Seoul, or to the predominant centre of a capitalistic world economy, consisting of the 'triad' USA, EU, and Japan (Hirsch 2001, 111).

However, one thing seems to be certain: the promise of early modernity to create and to guarantee a rational social order has not been realised. Globalisation has not increased the freedom of the individual but has only redistributed it in a polarising way. 'Not only have incomes and fortunes, prospects and living conditions become more and more polarised, but also ... the right to individuality' (Bauman 1999, 65). The order of reason and the order of the world: excluded from it are those individuals whom are denied the symbolic materials of subjectivity, the markers of status and autonomy that prevent social death, and who are forced to live their subjectivity by experiencing the difference between individual and society, that is by feeling their own being to be 'other' (Messner 2001; 1998).

The correspondence between individual and social project, between our own life project and social order, is fundamental for the realisation of the project of modernity. Personal identity cannot exist outside the context of a common project, whose promise is to give steady and predictable conditions for individual spontaneity, freedom to choose, and power of decision. But individuals can only trust in the reliability of those conditions if they are lasting, constant and immune to problems caused by others or groups. This way people don't always have to check their lives and their environment conditions and they don't have to worry about an uncertain future. In modern society such *existential* security is given by the correspondence between the 'world' and the structure of individual needs and is basically the certainty of expectations. This certainty persists even in disappointment: we still know 'how to go forward'. The law is pre-eminently the structure in modern society that stabilises normative expectations. Setting the possibilities for action — without determining actions — the law ignores other possibilities, thereby reducing the open future to an 'If this, then that'. It produces and conditions links for the future and guarantees the certainty of expectations. Possibly globalisation is just an expression of our being surprised by the fact that we are losing our certainties. Victim narratives may reflect a sense that something has gone wrong in the modern world that we can neither assimilate nor put right.

According to Victor Turner, within complex societies and literate cultures, the dramatisation of social relations serves to structure spatial and temporal boundaries (see also Luhmann 1996, 55). Loosely following Turner (Turner 1969; 1974), we could say that the purpose of victim narratives is to convert, through symbolic actions and ceremonies, individual behaviours which are not left to procedural routines, into dictated behaviours that are predictable. Indeed, public discourse on victims (of increasing crime, traffic, smoke, discrimination and various other evils) communicates feelings of anonymity, helplessness, loss of control, threat of annihilation and traumatic stress, and rouses powerful emotions such as hate, fear, affection, and grief. As a result, it is characterised by the paradoxical presence of criticism of and fascination by the victim at the same time. But in he context of 'risk society', the mere acquisition of the victim status evidently means success: everyone who can present him/herself as a victim gains moral and interpretative superiority. However, this acquisition is highly ambivalent.

Victimhood being the result of the processes of interpretation and reconstruction of personal experiences of injury (*see*, for victimhood and crime,

Messner 2001, 162–70), it may be difficult to describe its dramatisation without implying a fictitious intrinsic unity, where what really exists are clusters of loosely interrelated, often competing narratives. Victim stories are developed to manage not only the changing sense of identity but acutely unstable expectations as well. They may serve different interests, and not always consciously so. At one extreme stories may signify a loss of heroic power and conviction; at the other they focus on themes of oppression and unfair treatment reinforcing the sense of injury.

In contemporary culture, both trauma and victimisation are medical and juridical syndromes and tropes: strategic fictions that a complex society is using to account for a world seemingly out of control (Farrell 1998; Solomon 1996; Ericson et al 1991). What holds for trauma, also holds for victimhood: as a social construct,

> it is glued together by the practices, technologies, and narratives with which it is diagnosed, studied, treated, and presented by the various interests, institutions, and moral arguments that mobilised these efforts and resources (Young 1995, 5).

So, victimhood is a process that depends obviously on social meanings. Injury entails interpretation of the injury; trauma afflicts the body, but it also demands to be communicated (or denied). Injury is always assessment of the injury, subject to all contingencies of communication. Stress is not self-evident. Injuries do not come in standard units. What common sense calls toothache is an interpretative construct. Like pain, risk entails communication — interpretative choices. In turn, interpretation is not self-contained, because a victim builds on past experience and anticipates future outcomes. As an interpretive process it is related to everyday life coping processes.

The problem, however, is not simply a victim's loss of trust in particular guarantees, but the recognition that the ground of experience, the taken for granted reality, has been compromised. So, when people feel traumatised, terror overwhelms not just the self, but that ground of the self which is the trust in the 'world'. With respect to this elementary certainty of expectations, the victim trope acts as an explanatory tool and enabling fiction.

The meaning of an injury and the nature of our involvement are essentially determined by the interplay between mass media and audiences. If ever, then here it is true that 'whatever we know about society, even about the world wherein we live, we know it by means of mass media' (Luhmann 1996, 9). Like obsessive headlines about illicit drugs and sex, images of tamed violence suggested by victim stories are an important means of regulating our needs for excitement and security. Desensitising us to shocks, disaster stories may function as a reality check — even as they frame and distance us from horror. Mundane accounts of a distant ferryboat catastrophe both are and are not real to us. We engage them in a spirit of *doublethink*, registering the data with safely mediated feeling. But because they frame and distance us from horror, they may suggest the unthinkable.

LUHMANNIAN INTERMEZZO: ON MEANING, COMPLEXITY, COMMUNICATION AND THE UNFEASIBILITY OF OBSERVING THE WORLD

Is the 'new world order' the global system of (regional) societies or is it the (one) world of the (unique) world society? Can we continue — maintaining the traditional meaning — to presuppose given societies in order to explain (as dependent variables) their different, but now converging worlds? Or should we describe how and why 'world society' preserves and increases regional particularities? What do we mean by society? Let's go back one step and clear some basic assumptions of the operative constructivism upon which Luhmanns 'postontological' theory of society is build before trying to answer these questions.

Luhmann's theory is about drawing boundaries. Spatial metaphors, however, are misleading here. Lines of separation are not fences or border markings on a map. Restrictions do not mark areas, they are distinctions which, by producing two parts, make possible differentiation. Protected spheres exist only as constituted by distinctions. For observing systems, such as psychic and social systems, boundaries are two-sided forms. The concern of 'systems theory' is to account for the emergence of such cuts in the world, of how they are preserved and reproduced (whereas the question of the theory of society might be seen in exploring how society induces itself to give actuality to certain cuts and not to others).

Luhmann's first cut was surely the introduction of his concept of meaning. Derived from Husserl's phenomenology (but without reference to a specific system type), this fundamental conception indicates the representation by a system of aspects of the current state of its environment that come to its span of attention, together with a simultaneous reference to other possible states that are not currently focused. Two types of systems operate over the medium of meaning: psychic systems and social systems. Since 'meaning is nothing but a way to experience and to handle enforced selectivity' it is according to Luhmann an anthropomorphic error to see any intrinsic connection between meaning and minds (Luhmann 1997, 55). Meaning is a result of operations which use meaning:

> 'In as far as recourses refer to what has gone (to established, known meaning), they refer to nothing but contingent operations', while referring 'to what will come, they indicate the infinitely many possibilities of observation, that is the

> world as a virtual reality … meaning, therefore, is a thoroughly historical form of operation' (Luhmann 1997, 47).

Meaning, then, is pointing to itself and is pointing 'beyond' to something other co-intended. Take, for instance, the meaning 'cube': a cube's concrete 'reality' consists exactly in having not yet experienced aspects. But the fact, that there is something which goes beyond one's actual experience, does not alter the sense of 'cube'. One experiences it as something with aspects which one does not and may never actually experience. It is one's expectations which reveal what one means by a cube. If one could not have these expectations, one would not experience a cube. At any rate, the sense of a cube is a determinate structure. All evident sense contains such a 'reference to the world' — excluding only *chaos*, even though it remains present, 'because the world of meaning is a complete world that can exclude, what it excludes, only within itself' (Luhmann 1997, 49). Meaning is a cut in the surface of what has been an 'unmarked space' until then: meaning can be reproduced only as this form. 'World', always carried on as the other part of the form, 'remains all the time unobservable' (Luhmann 1997, 54).

In other words, meaning is the specific form of reduction of complexity. Observing depends upon discerning. The use of distinctions is inevitable, observation of differences is not. We can identify something by confronting it with again and again new (factual, temporal, social) discriminations. The world, then, can be conceived with Husserl (Messner 1998, 57–58), as the horizon that allows for the substitution of the distinctions by means of which we are observing the same thing. But then, 'world' means 'the epitome of the unobservable which is reproduced with every change of distinctions' (Luhmann 1997, 152–53).

The second cut is the one between system and environment. Systems theory is dealing with systems that are self-referential (reflexive) and hence closed to direct contact with their environment. Systems cannot operate outside of their boundaries. Operationally closed systems cannot match their internal observations with their reality. For that reason, no system can 'adapt' to its environment. They are 'autonomous' in the sense that they do not pick up and process 'verbatim information' from their environment.

How is such a closure possible? Because systems produce their own operations and reproduce them by means of reflexive recourses and anticipations. It is by this operation that the system/environment distinction is constituted. It starts from a distinction of which one part re-enters into the other part (incidentally, in this way the conjecture of a common world is substituted by a theory of observation of observing systems, the 'second order cybernetics'). Processing meaning, systems operate at the level of a re-entry of their form into their form: they use their own output as input. This re-entry leads to an irresolvable indeterminacy. Since the system/environment distinction occurs twice within a system — as a self-produced distinction and as a difference within the system — systems become for themselves unpredictable: they surprise themselves by their own ongoing operations.

Meaning processing systems such as psychic and social systems, because of their medium 'meaning', are self-producing: 'autopoietic' systems. That is, they keep on producing their elements by means of a combination of the elements which they consist of. Elements are 'informations', ie distinctions which make a difference within the 'system' (Luhmann 1997, 152–53). Obviously, those elements have no 'independent existence', they are not produced until they are used. 'Autopoietic' closure has three important consequences for the interplay between systems: systems will produce effects to one another only if the 'passive' system is co-operating; systems are opaque for each other; systems cannot control each other, but only perturb, irritate.

Autopoietic systems cannot adapt to their environment. But they can operate *as if they were adapted.* Because they can observe, that is, communicate about whatever comes into their *span of attention.*

For Luhmann, observation means simply the (unique) operation of discerning and indicating. If, then, observation presupposes (and constitutes) boundaries, we can say, vice versa, that it consists of the attribution of meaning to selected irritations. All that is said, is said by an observer (Luhmann 1997, 35).

Cognition (or defining, analysing) is made up by observing and describing of observations (but this does not imply that all operations are observations nor that observations can be observed only as observations). So, with reference to cognition, operational closure of observing systems means that they cannot encounter distinctions within the environment, because environment does not contain boundary lines. Within it, there is no difference, there are no possibilities, no particularity.

Systems theory deals with psychic and social systems. While psychic systems produce themselves by producing thoughts, social systems do so by producing communications; both thoughts and communications have meaning in exactly the same way. Drawing this line, we can see that an autonomous domain of the social does open up before us, with human actors being situated, as Luhmann stresses, in the environment of society instead of composing it, as the sociological tradition tends to suppose.

Society constructs its environment around a basic distinction, that between individuals (bodies and minds) and other environmental facts. This distinction mirrors the requirements for the autopoietic reproduction of the social system, since only the consciousness of human beings is structurally coupled — through language — with the autopoiesis of the social system (Luhmann 1988). Conscious states in the environment of the system have to be presupposed at any moment in time, in every single communicative operation. They have to be presupposed, not only for the time being, but also in the form of a possibility of future communication on the one hand, and, on the other hand, in the form of a past that has already successfully reduced uncertainty and in which individuals have committed themselves to continue communication.

Since the production of a communication cannot be reduced to the activity of a single psychic system or to a simple aggregation of the activities of several ones, it is wrong to attribute the communication to human actors, as one does in the *theory of action*: a communication must be both sent and received, and the determining factors of what is communicated are largely contingencies of the immediate situation, such as communications that have previously been made, which are the result of the ongoing process of communication as it develops over time. Communication produces society.

Communication is irreducibly social. 'Autopoiesis' of communication, this is: it comes about on the basis of prior communications. We already know what we can say when we say something. We know the context and know what is and what is not acceptable. The extraordinary importance of individuals with respect to the ongoing reproduction of social communication is due to their external, not to their internal status; it is due to their own closure as 'conscious systems'. Therefore, the question of how a social system emerges is not about origins (first principles, last grounds), rather it is about what situations there are that make happen communication, it is about its consequences, and about how communication is self-reproducing. Communication is a self-referential operation. Communicating also the fact that it is communicating, communication 'carries along its own memory' (Luhmann 1997, 14). That means, all communications contain a reference to society, society is always co-intended as the unity of communications. Society is characterised only by the operation which (re-)produces society, ie communication. Communication, then, signifies historically concrete events. As 'meaningful praxis' (Luhmann 1997, 71), communication depends upon contexts. In this sense, society can be defined as: 'the comprehensive social system of all communications which refer one to another' (Luhmann 1990, 24).

Society's environment does not communicate, and one could not contact it by this kind of operation. If we look at concrete function systems, such as the law, we find specific juridical information which as such makes no sense for the economy or for education. Communication is a specific way to observe the world by means of the distinction information/utterance. By reproducing this distinction, a social system can observe itself (and second order observers can observe themes and functions of communications).

On such a view, the 'world' can't simply be presupposed as the same for all observers. According to our considerations, the 'objectivity' of the world is being constructed by its observers constantly in both the same *and* different ways. Whoever uses, at his point of observation, 'the world' as reference point of his cognitive operations ie for his selection of a distinction, cannot observe the world. As far as observation requires distinctions, the world cannot be for all observers the same, but surely it will be observable. Either the world is unobservable as the same, or it is observable as different (Luhmann 1997, 154–55).

The observer can execute only a social performance, an operation, that can be produced only within society and, consequently, produces only society. Objectivity is only a correlate of the operations, which produce society, a horizon formed through 'lived' experience. 'Lived' experience is the experience of the possibilities of the constitution of a horizon of further experiences. If the world therefore is this horizon and correlates with the constitution of 'lived' experiences, then, its constitution occurs concomitantly to the differentiation of society.

Thus we could define the boundaries of the world as boundaries of a societal system in which all internal boundaries depend upon the self-organisation of the self-producing system which always returns to itself. Its horizon, the world, expands with the differentiation of society. What is produced by the production of society is meaning, that is formation of sense, which, settling on one possibility of experience, points to alternative possibilities. World then is the horizon of possibilities, which are constantly reproduced every time when we 'make sense'. Society is *world society* because it is society (not individuals), that has 'world', because 'the world' is the horizon of the always open and probable possibilities; because this experience can be object of meaningful expectations and these expectations can be object of expectations. This experience of the world is the experience of its contingency, that is of the possibility of its being different.

OUT OF CONTROL: WORLD SOCIETY AND EXPECTATIONS

The traditional concept of society proclaims a specific combination of difference and identity, of differentiation and reconstructed unity, or, in traditional terms, of the parts and the whole. In traditional complex societies the principle of differentiation has been stratification (hierarchy), although the secularisation and de-cosmologisation of this concept changed the semantic context. This semantic change correlates, on the structural level, with an increasing importance of functional differentiation (Germani 1981). With the increasing de-naturalisation of the idea of human society, the principle of its unity has become a secular principle. The 'pursuit of reason' rather than reliance on tradition has been seen as the way to address difficult social problems and to provide for 'happiness' and the common good of all.

Within the frame of the possible, society needs a narrower frame of the tolerable. The social system produces then a variety of devices to enclose what can be regarded as meaningful expectations: a frame within the frame of the possible. This internal frame may be described in various terms, such as nature, morals, culture etc (1997, 1038). The most *grande histoire* uses a humanistic framework when referring to modern society as an 'incomplete project' (Habermas). Upon close inspection this project shows a paradoxical face: freedom and equality, self-realisation and solidarity. The paradox is called 'reason'. This reason is still the reason of an enlightenment that assured just living conditions would be made for mankind rationally, and that continues to insist that 'morality can be guided by critical reasoning' (Sen 2000, 33). The ambition of this tradition is to be able to define the unity of society; its project is to make appear, behind the nasty mask of the existing global system, the very face of society as community or civil society (Messner 1998).

We may well recognise the hardships and the injustice of stratification, but this appears no longer as the main problem in second modernity's society, because its codification scheme of difference and identity is no longer framed by differentiation. If we imagine stratification, we will tend to see injustice, exploitation and suppression; and we may wish to find corrective devices or at least to formulate normative schemes and moral or critical stands. Stratification would mean that we could know the addresses of influential people and, precisely, we would be able to change some structure or other. But there are no 'responsible' dominant individuals or groups who would have the power to suppress or to release other people. Since 'society' as such has no phone numbers, what we demand from it has to be addressed to organisations (Luhmann 2001, 70). There are of course individuals and groups who use their networks to their own advantage. But it is hard to impute repression to any one actor.

If we look at the 'victims' — the masses of starving people, deprived of all necessities for a decent human life, without access to any of the function systems — or if we consider all the human bodies, struggling to survive the next day, or those suffering or fearing social death, neither 'exploitation' nor 'suppression' nor 'victimisation' are adequate descriptions of society's actual state of affairs. On the contrary, such schemes seem to be misleading even if people are (or feel to be) suppressed and victimised. Certainly, they help account for a world in which power and authority may seem overwhelmingly unjust. But they cannot inform our actions. The character of a wrong, by its description, doesn't dictate the character of the appropriate response to it.

Therefore, we need to rephrase the problem and replace the humanistic approach by asking, what does it mean and how is it possible that a system can change its dominant form of internal differentiation (Luhmann 1997)?

We can conceive differentiation as the process of reproducing systems within systems, boundaries within boundaries and, for observing systems, frames within frames, and distinctions within the distinguished (such as being/not-being, true/false, inside/outside, good/bad, male/female, etc).

This presupposes the stability of boundaries as a result and as a condition of evolution. Only if protected by boundaries, and only inside its boundaries, a system can grow in complexity; only within its boundaries, a system can operate and build up, change or forget structures. A 'double closure' or 'double framing' by external and internal boundaries that separate the external environment from the internal environments of subsystems is a necessary condition for maintaining stability in view of an evolution toward an ever increasing improbability of structures. How, then, can society tolerate higher complexity, more structural contingencies and more risks — and continue to exist? How can society guarantee a balance between necessary and acceptable complexity? How can society live on despite the disappointments of its expectations? How can society control itself?

Modern society is differentiated into functional subsystems, each of which has its own specialised 'communications medium' that determines the way it interacts with its environment. Thus, the legal system is specialised for processing information in terms of the distinction legal/illegal, and the economy is specialised for doing so in terms of the distinction profitable/unprofitable. Functional differentiation means autonomy of the function systems and a high degree of indifference, coupled to high sensitivity and irritability, in very specific respects that differ from system to system. If function systems are operationally closed systems, their differentiation will produce more independencies and more dependencies at the same time — more independencies because of their operational closure and their highly selective structural couplings, and more dependencies because society can only maintain the present level of achievement if all the function systems operate and reproduce themselves appropriately. That is, society as the comprehensive system is without any top and without a centre; there is no centre, because there is no place for the representation of society within society.

Society evolves but *cannot control itself*. There are no longer cosmological, natural or rational guarantees that structural developments within function systems remain compatible with each other. On the contrary, functional differentiation leads us to expect very different solutions for the problem of rationality in different function systems. But any solution will depend upon complexity, that is on boundaries, on selection, and, consequently, on *neglect*. The very problem of world society seems to be the inevitable selectivity of its distinctions.

'Polycentric, polycontextural' world society (Luhmann 1996b) has reached a higher level of complexity with higher structural contingencies, more unexpected and unpredictable changes and, above all, more interlinked dependencies and interdependencies. If the question is how to construct (calculate, plan) meaningful expectations in view of an open future, a first solution could lie in the cognitive control of the legal control of counterfactual (normative) expectations. And in fact, normative structures are losing the leading role in the organisation of potential experiences in favour of cognitive structures. Once prevailing hierarchical and vertical structures become increasingly obsolete. This is not to say that they become superfluous or are replaced. Old structures still exist, but they undergo *heterarchical* 'modernisations' construction. Evolutionary advantage shifts to those social systems that are structured according to a cognitive design. It shifts to the system of science or to the economy for example, which already had this alignment at the beginning of the functional stabilisation of the differentiated social systems. But science does not add knowledge to power but rather uncertainty and risk to decisions. Law, as positive law, shows cognitive characteristics ever more distinctively. But legal control of risk leads to deformations of legal doctrine that undermine the predictability of legal decisions. Politics must strengthen its sensitivity for public opinion, to which it becomes ever more vulnerable. But the media represent politics as a never-ending soap opera and contributes to a decline of political trust. Public opinion strengthens its political function as a stock of themes, which can constantly be renewed, and is therefore strongly shaped by a cognitive attitude. And above all: since world society cannot uphold the old forms of the distribution of access to social communication, a differentiation occurs between inclusion and exclusion. But this increases risks and reduces interdependencies. As there is inclusion only because there is exclusion, the specialisation and the generalisation of forms of inclusion within world society leads to a continual increase of exclusion. If we can interpret inclusion as a mechanism which allows the treatment of the individual according to his significance as 'person', than we can say that in this society the number of non-persons increases in uncontrollable ways.

As the function systems of law, politics and science can no longer perform their orienting function without difficulty, the gaps of certainty of expectations left blank by traditional function systems are filled by the discourse of the mass media. The changing themes of these communications — prominently crime and justice — play their part here. In relieving the function systems, though not jeopardising them, mass media communications contribute to their (ie the function systems') further dedifferentiation and differentiation.

The discourse of the mass media does not serve the manufacture of social consensus (Ericson, Baranek and Chan 1991). Opinions about a topic may be unanimous or differing, individual or collective, but the reality of world society as produced by mass media does not depend on it (Luhmann 2001, 118). In view of the unfeasibility to guarantee certainty of expectations, the stability of today's society is based on the production of items, that can be presupposed in communications. It is a matter of the production of models of expectation. The mass media maintain the production of those patterns, of their different versions and their connectivity. And again, the problem of this discourse is not its (un-) truth, but its necessary selectivity.

The function of public opinion does not consist in social integration but in making possible the observing of observers. Public opinion can be seen as a nexus of schemes (frames) which serve the cognitive organisation of an opaque state of affairs and which control the succession of events. The structural function of such frames consists in the fact that communications can presuppose them as known and working. What is of crucial importance, then, are the themes themselves as reference points and links, as prerequisites of further communications. It is a question of operative conditions of social communication in fast changing contexts. Mass-media production guarantees that facts that are emerging from heterogeneous and contradictory points of view, find an orderly side by side in the reality of world society, after all. Differing points of view and experiences are not settled down by 'facts', it is rather that 'facts' find peace through differing communications.

SCRIPTS: THE PASSER-BY'S WAY OF SEEING

To sum up, we considered the constitution of world society as the consequence of the successful stabilisation of the principle of functional differentiation, and we said that the problem of modern society consists in the congruent generalisation of expectations. It therefore depends on the combination of normative closure and cognitive openness. The projection of an open contingent future is only possible, if there is certainty: the certainty to be able to persevere expectations despite disappointments, and the certainty to get consensus in doing so. Normative mechanisms serve the expansion of supportable uncertainties and the stabilisation of risky, unlikely possibilities. What is not probable, can be made probable by counterfactual affirmation and decision. The subsystems of politics and law in this sense are primary factors of the evolution of modern society. If normativity (as complexity reducing mechanism) is still necessary, however, the problem, in today's society, is how it can keep contact with other consequences of evolution.

From law's point of view, this leads to the question of how the law and the justice system change with this displacement of the primacy of control. Do they lose significance? Our answer, here, was yes and no. The question apparently has two aspects. The first, immanent aspect relates to the positivity of the law and involves its capacity to learn, ie the question, by means of which (new) forms and categories legal problems are experienced and processed; the second, external aspect refers to the social function of the law. This paper has taken into account only the latter aspect, ie the external boundaries of law.

From this angle, the most simple way of congruent expectation generalisation seems to be the Humean 'inductive' way, that is by taking the victim, individual feelings and experiences of injustice, as a point of departure. The only thing it presupposes is the capacity of self-observation, the capacity to observe oneself as observer and to identify with the own particular way of observing.

Considering the three dimensions of temporal, factual and social generalisation of expectations, social generalisation seems preferable under various aspects. Unlike mechanisms of factual generalisation, ie the fixing of behavioural models and their continuous alteration (by trial and error), its plus is not to create any additional acceptance problems. It can be used within the legal system or outside it. It can be used independently or in combination with 'conflicts' which can be seen as another instrument, that serves the same purpose: the incremental construction of a network of congruently generalised expectations (Luhmann 1987, 358). Victimhood provides the law with time, that law fails to have. The discourse about victims seems to be, then, a matter of 'holding open the law' (Luhmann 1987, 159) rather than to fix on or to enforce the law and, what is more, it is not at all about decisions. The 'victim' allows leaders, uninterested third parties, from time to time superiors and enemies, to appear; it organises opinions and pressures, it creates confidence, trustworthiness, tradition, in short it provides a *script* which normative regulation can always fall back upon. This form of normative expectation of normative expectations lies outside the established law and is, certainly, normative 'barbarism' in Kant's sense: 'law or not-law — humanity counts' (Luhmann 1993, 556).

Finally, the problem of legitimacy is solved elegantly. The problem consists in the fact that, because of individualisation and differentiation, ways of learning to accept disillusions as premises of individual behaviour cannot be programmed any longer for the whole of society. This problem is at first simply avoided: who presents himself to the public as a victim is presenting himself as a particular individual, insulated and depoliticised. Then, however, whoever receives recognition as victim is involved in social communication, and to this extent he is included and may have the outlook to find also institutional 'justice', that is to finish as a winner.

From society's point of view, however, the question is about what functional alternatives there are beyond the law. 'World society', according to our considerations, is constituted primarily through cognitive expectation attitudes. Put otherwise, the normative style of expecting normative expectation is on the wane. To the question of how congruent generalisation of expectations comes about within world society, we answered by pointing to the reality produced by the mass media. World society always generates new occasions for learning and predetermines a frame of possible solutions, but it does not determine any decision. Requests and limitations of learning vary and are not predictable. So, my proposal is to consider victimhood as a script in Luhmann's sense, that is as a particular scheme of social communication.

The 'evolutionary' advantage of scripts seems to be that scripts, like language, may freely flow in social communications rather than depend on devious routes across specific function systems. While the law settles on criteria (upon which it then depends, having to insist on them), schemes and scripts do nothing but reproduce sensibility by picking up irritations and constructing them as if they would produce good or bad results. Schemes and scripts are 'skilled' structures, able to learn. 'Scheme', however, does not mean pointless repetition; on the contrary, 'Only by means of the scheme one can observe deviations, only by the scheme one can be surprised, ... one can learn' (Luhmann 2001, 133). Schemes, we may say, have a somewhat heuristic function serving to find further qualifications. At any rate, their purpose is to increase operative complexity by reducing structural complexity. This way they may serve the continuous adaptation of the structural coupling between psychic and social systems to changing conditions (Luhmann 1997, 111).

Scripts are schemes that attribute things and events to intentions. Connecting causes and effects, they help to describe behaviours as actions and, eventually, to judge them by political or moral standards. The point, however, is that communication may take for granted the fact that meanings are known to all participating minds — but these meanings do not determine if and how the minds will track the narratives. Nobody will have to know 'the world or the truth. What one has to know, is his script' (Luhmann 1997, 111). So, scripts suggest to us what we may call, with Victor Turner, the passer-by's way of observing: like accidental witnesses, we may observe the observing of others — and nevertheless keep on observing and expecting in the particular way we do.

REFERENCES

Bauman, Zygmunt 1999. *Unbehagen in der Postmoderne*. Hamburg: Hamburger Edition.

Beck, Ulrich 1986. *Risikogesellschaft*. Frankfurt: Suhrkamp.

Ericson, Richard V, Patricia M Baranek, and Janet B Chan 1991 *Representing order: crime, law, and justice in the news media*, Toronto: University of Toronto Press.

Farrell, Kirby 1998. *Posttraumatic culture. Injury and interpretation in the nineties*, Baltimore London: The Johns Hopkins University Press.

Germani, Gino 1981. *The sociology of modernization. Studies on its historical and theoretical aspects with special regard to the Latin American case*, New Brunswick: Transaction.

Hirsch, Joachim 2001. Die Internationalisierung des Staates. Anmerkungen zu einigen aktuellen Fragen der Staatstheorie. In *Die Zukunft des Staates*, edited by Hirsch, Joachim, Bob Jessop and Nicos Poulantzas. Hamburg: VSA.

Hopkins, Terence K Immanuel Wallerstein, et al. 1996. *The age of transition: Trajectory of the world-system 1945–2025*. London: Zed Books.
Hume, David 1875. On Justice. In *Essays. Moral, political and literary*, 2 vol, edited by T H Green and T H Grose, London: Longmans.
Kaufmann, Franz-Xaver 1970. *Sicherheit als soziologisches und sozialpolitisches Problem*. Stuttgart: Enke.
Luhmann, Niklas 2001. *Short Cuts*. Frankfurt: Zweitausendeins.
Luhmann, Niklas 1997. *Die Gesellschaft der Gesellschaft* Frankfurt: Suhrkamp.
Luhmann, Niklas 1996. *Die Realität der Massenmedien*. Opladen: Westdeutscher Verlag.
Luhmann, Niklas 1993. *Das Recht der Gesellschaft*. Frankfurt: Suhrkamp.
Luhmann, Niklas 1992. *Beobachtungen der Moderne*. Opladen: Westdeutscher Verlag.
Luhmann, Niklas 1990. *Risiko und Gefahr*. St Gallen: Hochschule.
Luhmann, Niklas 1987. *Rechtssoziologie*. Opladen: Westdeutscher Verlag. Original edition 1971.
Luhmann, Niklas, Raffaele De Giorgi 1992. *Teoria della società*. Milano: Franco Angeli.
Messner, Claudius 2001. *Osservando il soggetto. Esercizi su individuo, diritto e società*. Lecce: Pensa Multimedia.
Messner, Claudius 1998. *Das Subjekt als Horizont. Zur Repräsentation von Individuum und Gesellschaft in philosophischen Diskurs*. Würzburg: Königshausen & Neumann.
Sen, Amartya 2000. East and West: the reach of reason. *The New York Review of Books*, July, 33–38.
Simon, Jonathan 1997. Gewalt, Rache und Risiko. Die Todesstrafe im neoliberalen Staat. In *Soziologie der Gewalt*, edited by Trutz von Trotha. Wiesbaden: Westdeutscher Verlag.
Solomon, Robert C 1995. *A passion for justice. Emotions and the origins of the social contract*. Boston: Rowman & Littlefield.
Turner, Victor W 1974. *Dramas, fields, and metaphors. Symbolic action in human society*. Ithaca : Cornell University Ensity Press.
Turner, Victor W 1969. *The ritual process. Structure and anti-structure*. London: Routledge & Kegan Paul.
Wilson, Rob Wimal Dissanayake 1996. Introduction: Tracking the global/local. In *Global/Local. Cultural production and the transnational imaginary*, edited by Rob Wilson and Wimal Dissanayake, Durham/London: Duke University Press.
Young, Allan 1995. *The harmony of illusions: Inventing post-traumatic stress disorder*. Princeton: Princeton University Press.